W9-DDO-710

Hunger 1996

Countries in Crisis

Sixth Annual Report on the State of World Hunger

BREAD FOR THE WORLD

INSTITUTE

1100 WAYNE AVENUE, STE. 1000
SILVER SPRING, MD 20910
USA

Bread for the World Institute

President
David Beckmann

President Emeritus
Arthur Simon

Director
Richard A. Hoehn

Editor
Marc J. Cohen

Co-Editor
Don Reeves

Design
Randi Pamela Busillo

Printer: Communications Graphics, Baltimore, MD

Cover photos: U.S. National Aeronautics and Space Administration,
AFL-CIO News, U.N. High Commissioner for Refugees, KNA.

Manufactured in the United States of America

First edition published October 1995

ISBN 1-884361-03-X

Table of Contents

Top Photo: Uprooted people: Ethnic violence
caused 250,000 Rwandans to flee to Tanzania
during a 24-hour period.

Below: Post-crisis reconstruction: Returning
Cambodian refugees build a new home.

Acknowledgments

We are deeply grateful for the valuable insights provided by sponsors, cosponsors and colleagues at a series of consultations related to this report and in response to earlier drafts. Those who provided comments include:

Peter Shiras, InterAction; Carol Capps, Church World Service/Lutheran World Relief; Alexander Rondos, International Orthodox Christian Charities; Michael Wiest, Geraldine Sicola and Margaret Horan, Catholic Relief Services; Col. Robert Norton, U.S. Department of Defense; Dawn Callabia, Office of the U.N. High Commissioner for Refugees; Shubh Kumar, David Nygaard, Annu Ratta and Peter Hazell, International Food Policy Research Institute; Hershey Leaman, Mennonite Central Committee; Ginena Dulley Wills, United Methodist Committee on Relief; Judit Katona-Apte and Antonio Donini, U.N. Department of Humanitarian Affairs; Sara Burns and Friedrich Von Mallinckrodt, U.N. Development Programme; Ellen Messer, Thomas Marchione, William Bender, Peter Uvin and Zerai Fesshaie, Alan Shawn Feinstein World Hunger Program, Brown University; Bruce Bennett, Len Rogers, Nancy Estes and Mary Knox, U.S. Agency for International Development; Charles Sykes, U.S. Department of State; Donald Brown and Vera Gathright, International Fund for Agricultural Development; Rob Buchanan, Michael Bedford and Laura Renshaw, Oxfam America; Douglas Coutts, Patrick Webb and Neville Edirisinghe, U.N. World Food Programme; Anne Griffin, U.S. Committee for UNICEF; Eva Jesperson and Joanne Csete, UNICEF; and Robert Seiple and Ben Hoskins, World Vision.

Also, Kathleen Newland, Carnegie Endowment for International Peace; Gareth Porter, Energy and Environment Study Institute; David Scotton, Benchmarks; Amos Tincani, Commission of the European Communities; Bernd Dreesman, EuronAid; Professors Kevin Clements and Hamdesa Tuso, George Mason University; Timothy Frankenberger and Marianne Leach, CARE; Professor Jane Guyer, Northwestern University; Tsegaye Hailu, Tigray Development Association; Professor Barbara Harrell-Bond, Oxford University; Professor Michael Horowitz, Institute for Development Anthropology; Akin Mabogunje, Development Policy Center, Nigeria; Professor Tom Reardon, Michigan State University; Peter Rosset, Food First; Professor Hans Singer, Institute of Development Studies, University of Sussex; Tom Burwell, National Peace Corps Association; John Coonrod, The Hunger Project; Gwen Crawley, Presbyterian Hunger Program; Gene Dewey and Derek Kayongo, Congressional Hunger Center; Jo Marie Griesgraber, Center of Concern; Jerry Leggett, Better World Artists and Activists Guild; Marisa Nightingale, Share Our Strength; Martha Pickett, Second Harvest; Mike Rock, Winrock International; Pat Bandy, Academy for Educational Development; Susan Swift, Appropriate Technology International; Professor Evan Vallianatos, George Washington University; Kathryn Wolford, Lutheran World Relief; Susan Van Lopik, Christian Reformed World Relief Committee; and Anwarul Hoque, U.S. Department of Agriculture.

Also, Michael Lipsey, Michigan State University; Professor Vidyamali Samrasinghe, The American University; Prasad Kariyawasam, Embassy of Sri Lanka, Washington, DC; Hiram A. Ruiz, U.S. Committee for Refugees; Irving Cramer, MAZON: A Jewish Response to Hunger; Peter Mann, World Hunger Year; Robin Shell, Food for the Hungry International; Art Gay and colleagues, World Relief; Edward Chesky; Nancy Wright, Coordination in Development; Larry Minear, Humanitarianism and War Project, Brown University; Gabriel Negatu, Forum for African Voluntary Development Organizations; Mary Lord, ACCESS; Alois Möller, BROT für die Welt; and Jean Camara, Food and Agriculture Organization of the United Nations.

We appreciate assistance from the following people in obtaining data and photographs: Larry Nowels, Congressional Research Service; Peter Thiel and Brian D'Silva, U.S. Agency for International Development; Lowell Ewart, Mercy Corps International; Pedro Alba and Kris Martin, The World Bank; Christian A. Chikhani, Food and Agriculture Organization of the United Nations; Sakiko Fukuda-Parr, U.N. Development Programme; Carl Haub, Population Reference Bureau; Simon Scott, Organisation for Economic Co-operation and Development; John Cook, Center on Hunger, Poverty and Nutrition Policy, Tufts University; Peter Cattan and David Smith, U.S. Department of Labor; J.W. Levedahl, U.S. Department of Agriculture; and Eve Weisberg, Office of the U.N. High Commissioner for Refugees.

The following Bread for the World/Bread for the World Institute board and staff members provided comments and assistance: Marie Bledsoe, Cathy Brechtelsbauer, Robert Cahill, Gary Cook, Beth Lepinski, Steve Nunn-Miller, Jim Shields, Arthur Simon, Sr. Christine Vladimiroff, Betty Voskuil, Fr. Clarence Williams, Nancy Alexander, Lynette Engelhardt, Sarita Wardlaw Henry, Donna Hodge, Leigh Ann Hurt, Elizabeth Keyes, Christine Matthews, Dorota Muñoz, Elisa Munthali, Susan Kay Park, Sharon Pauling, Kathy Pomroy, Phoebe de Reynier, Kathy Selvaggio, Katherine Simmons, Katherine Smith, David Suley and Mizanekristos Yohannes.

Jashinta D'Costa prepared the graphs and statistical tables. David Fouse was copy editor.

The quote from Amer Kuay on page 11 is from *The Oxfam Poverty Report*, and is reproduced with permission of Oxfam UK/I Publishing, 274 Banbury Road, Oxford, UK, OX2 7DZ.

We are grateful for financial support received from the 2020 Vision for Food, Agriculture and the Environment Initiative of the International Food Policy Research Institute.

Introduction

by Richard A. Hoehn

When the bricks of the Berlin Wall became souvenirs and doorstops; when Nelson Mandela, after 27 years under arrest, raised high the gavel of the presidency of South Africa; when Yasser Arafat shook hands with Yitzhak Rabin, signaling new possibilities in the Middle East, we breathed a collective sigh of relief and hoped for a more peaceful world.

Instead of melting away, however, the Cold War splintered into jagged fragments called Somalia, Bosnia, Tajikistan, Afghanistan – places that became more, rather than less, dangerous. We watched in horror, and with a sense of helplessness, as ruthless, power-hungry leaders rushed into political vacuums, exploiting age-old tensions and bringing misery to those who hungered simply for bread and water; for secure livelihoods and communities.

Superpower gamesmanship had pitted ethnic group against ethnic group in proxy wars. People were given machine guns to replace machetes as weapons of choice. Land mines were planted under crops and forest trails. Many people who should have been sowing seeds are now digging holes to bury their neighbors. The new world order looks old, tribal and disorderly.

Over time, the international community has developed effective systems to address famines caused by drought and floods. The green revolution, early warning systems, economic growth, grain reserves and the ability to move food fast have all made it possible to prevent mass starvation. And, we have learned strategies for long-term development.

Today, however, famine comes not so much from natural disaster as from human choices, in particular, complex emergencies – civil violence, uprooted people and failing states – which lead to murder, starvation, hidden hunger (vitamin and mineral deficiencies) and ensuing diseases

(Chapter 1). Warring factions steal and deliberately destroy crops, conscript or kill farmers. Drought may destroy the crop or even the following year's seeds, but violent conflict destroys people, the infrastructure and the environment. Getting food to people is manageable where there is a famine; much more difficult when hostile troops block the road.

Conflict situations are also dangerous for relief workers in ways that natural famines are not. Fred Cuny, who spent 25 years working in crisis areas, championing human rights and dignity against bureaucratic obstacles, is now missing and presumed dead in Chechnya.

> Nearly 100 million people worldwide are caught in a cycle of violent civil strife and hunger. We can respond more effectively to this suffering, but we have to care enough to mobilize the necessary political energy and funds. Specifically, we must also:
>
> - learn from experience with recent crises;
>
> - engage affected communities in every aspect of crisis response; and
>
> - complement and coordinate relief with peacemaking, reconstruction and development.

Lessons from responding to natural disasters and long-term development efforts are important, but not sufficient. Chapter 2 explores appropriate international interventions, including possible use of military forces for delivering emergency relief. Nations have a right to preserve and protect their sovereignty. But

Above photo: Violent civil strife worldwide has left 100 million people – including millions of children such as this refugee in Ethiopia – vulnerable to hunger.

Policy recommendations from *Hunger 1993: Uprooted People* (Bread for the World Institute, 1992):

Internationally:

1. The U.S. government must increase its financial support for refugee assistance programs.

2. Recent measures to strengthen the United Nations' capacity to respond to humanitarian crises are a step in the right direction, but the international community needs to agree upon rules and triggers for international intervention – including the use and financing of U.N. and other multilateral peacekeeping forces – to uphold the right to food and other humanitarian assistance.

3. The international legal definition of who is a refugee, and therefore entitled to U.N. protection and services, needs to change to fully encompass internally displaced people and victims of generalized political and economic chaos. At the same time, governments – including that of the United States – must improve their compliance with existing international laws prohibiting forced repatriation at borders and on the high seas.

4. Uprooted people themselves must participate in all phases of designing, implementing and monitoring programs.

5. Assistance must better address the needs of women and children, who account for 70 percent to 80 percent of uprooted people.

6. Durable solutions – repatriation or resettlement – must include opportunities to achieve self-reliance and must be integrated with national development plans.

7. Greater recognition must be accorded to the important role of groups with autonomy from the nation-state system, e.g., the International Committee of the Red Cross and nongovernmental organizations, in aiding uprooted people.

8. Development efforts must include indigenous people and their cultures; they often have vital insights on how to achieve sustainability.

In the United States:

9. Increase the funds available for refugee resettlement in the United States.

10. Make public assistance, including food programs, more accessible to undocumented and homeless people, and fully fund vital "safety net" programs for all poor people.

11. The public and private sectors must provide training and create jobs that allow people to meet their basic needs for food, housing and health care.

12. Drastic reforms are needed in the health insurance system to assure that everyone has access to care.

13. The federal government must provide amnesty and work permission to current undocumented residents while working for peace, human rights protection and equitable development in the countries from which undocumented people come.

---

their citizens have the right to food, which the international community has declared inviolable.

Chapter 2 also describes the public and private agencies involved in crisis prevention and response. Their efforts have saved millions of lives. It highlights the need for additional staff and budget for the U.N. Department of Humanitarian Affairs in order to assure timely coordination of relief and peacekeeping and their connection to long-term development.

Medium-term strategies that individuals and groups can undertake to alleviate complex emergencies include conflict prevention, mediation and management (Chapter 4). And, after the conflict come the tasks of repatriation of displaced people, physical reconstruction and reconciliation, and the critical problem of unexploded weapons before people can resume normal lives (Chapter 3).

> "If peace is to set down roots, it will need the nurturing of the international community. . . . We call upon the United States and the international community to join us in our historic task of making peace work not just for ourselves, but for a continent that is struggling hard to spread the blessings of peace and democracy to all its citizens."
>
> – Eduardo dos Santos, president of Angola

The best long-term strategy to prevent conflicts before they start is sustainable development – reducing hunger and poverty in environmentally sound ways:

- expanding economic opportunities;
- meeting basic human needs;
- protecting and enhancing the natural environment; and
- promoting pluralism and democratic participation.

As Chapter 5 points out, the political energy to raise funds for sustainable development and prevent crises is missing partly because "Media coverage of developing countries is 'MAD' – focused on misery, atrocities and disasters." An incoming rocket rates fuller coverage than a literacy program. Long-term causes and solutions do not sell cars and sneakers. And, good news is not news unless it is about local events. Recent military conflicts in Europe and Africa have received much more attention than the United Nations' successful role in negotiating peace in Mozambique (Chapter 3). Concerned citizens can influence the media to provide more realistic, in-depth coverage of crises and their causes, as well as more extensive reporting on developing countries generally.

There are reasons for hope: the famines that did not happen because of effective interventions, the conflicts that did not explode or that were mitigated by careful work, some thoughtful media coverage and the band of tirelessly compassionate and committed citizens who make a difference.

The Office of the U.N. High Commissioner for Refugees has kept millions of people alive in Bosnia. The agency also made it possible for millions of Cambodians who had fled during war to return home.

It is even possible for a government to provide a strong social service network and sustain high levels of human development when the country is enmeshed in ethnic and religious conflict, as in the case of Sri Lanka (Chapter 2).

Chapter 6 asks, "Who will foot the bill?" Rich industrial-country governments provide 97 percent of all official aid. Now that the Cold War is over, the United States and other industrial countries are slashing the aid programs that reduce poverty and

> "For every tragedy, there are half a dozen islands of hope. Progress is still tentative, often fragile. Which is precisely why we must not hesitate now."
>
> – J. Brian Atwood, administrator, U.S. Agency for International Development

protect the environment. At the same time, a proliferation of crises has required aid agencies to put more resources into emergency relief. They are giving short shrift to basic causes and long-term solutions. Yet the costs of responding to crises exceed the price of investing in prevention and mitigation; most certainly in terms of human lives, but often in monetary terms as well.

Most developed nations are not caught up in the same degree of civil conflict as Somalia, Bosnia or Rwanda. But in the United States, hunger and violence are both on the increase, and they are connected ("Creating Secure Livelihoods in the United States"). Means are available to deal with these problems – certainly to eliminate mass hunger in the United States – but the political will is lacking. Indeed, the mood of much of the U.S. public as reflected by its business and political leaders seems to have gone from "political will" to solve hunger and poverty to "political won't."

Short-term response strategies in the United States include strengthening emergency food programs, food stamp participation and the social service safety net. In the medium term, attention must be paid to government employment and training programs and making work pay so that people who work earn enough to rise above a marginal existence. In the long term, we need to address changes in employment patterns, job creation and the implications of the globalization of the world's economy. Bread for the World Institute envisions a multi-year program of study and education on "Hunger in a Global Economy" of which *Hunger 1997*, to be released in the fall of 1996, will be a part.

Hunger 1996 is about *Countries in Crisis*. Beneath the problems and solutions in individual crisis countries is a deeper worldwide crisis of

---

"The 358 billionaires on the planet listed by *Forbes* in 1994 had a combined net worth equal to the combined income of the bottom 45 percent of the world's population."[1]

In other words, 358 people's net worth = 2,350,000,000 people's income.

---

massive social change in which core issues – progressive values, voice for the victimized and a transcending spiritual commitment to one another – cut across nations, tribes and historical moments.

Our world is jammed with massive, complex events that rush by at dizzying speeds, carrying us with them. Events happen faster than ever before. We know about them sooner. We are bombarded with more knowledge, experiences and decisions than any previous generation. No wonder life can be so confusing, and knowing what to do, so difficult.

For tens of thousands of years we worked at home, walked to work or maybe rode a horse. We only talked with people we could see. Today, we can have breakfast in Los Angeles, lunch in Chicago, dinner in New York and the next day's breakfast in Brussels; or right on to Bangkok.

In 1860 one of the first internal combustion engines traveled six miles in two hours. Today, aircraft can reach 2,000 mph. The first cannons were bored in Spain in 1603. Dynamite was fashioned in 1867. Less than a hundred years later, we had nuclear weapons. It would have taken a line of soldiers 25 miles long, squeezed shoulder to shoulder and shooting their rifles with deadly accurate aim to kill as many people as died under one (now considered primitive) atom bomb at Hiroshima 50 years ago.

If there were starving children in China, Armenia or Africa a hundred years ago, by the time people in the United States knew, it was often too late to respond. No matter what our parents said about cleaning our dinner plates, we had a very low sense of responsibility toward events so remote from our experience; and little capacity to act. Today, we watch wars unfold, with only a four-second delay for the images to bounce off a satellite.

Where there is no ability-to-respond, there is little responsibility. But, we today have an enormously enhanced ability-to-respond. Thus, our response-ability, our opportunity to save lives, to help other neighbors in our global village, is huge. We have the means to prevent, mitigate and bring recovery to complex emergencies.

Countries in Crisis is about hunger and poverty, hatred and conflict. Tribal identities – racial, ethnic, geographic, linguistic, national, religious – persist. People allow themselves to be divided into Hutus or Tutsis, Serbs or Croats, rich or poor, powerful or weak – divisions that can make the difference between life and death.

But, *Countries in Crisis* is also about our shared ties to nature and one another – economic interdependence, common values, the arts, knowledge, empathy – the blessed ties that bind. No matter what distinctions people draw, we are one people and every "them" from their point of view is an "us." Because of our ever-closer connections, and the enormous capacities and wealth available to us, we can do more to end conflict and hunger than any previous generation.

Some people in all groups and nations seek answers in sureties – fundamentalisms and mysticisms beyond rational challenge, the solidity of material possessions, the buzz of ever-new experiences. But, as David Korten of the People-Centered Development Forum has written:

The answer lies . . . in a transformation of the values and institutions that define how we use the earth's bounty and distribute its benefits. . . . [T]rue movements . . . are characterized by values-driven, action-oriented flows of voluntary social energy given shape and direction by a broadly shared social vision.[2]

Our world needs, and many people have, economic values that affirm nature and people, especially those who are in greatest need; a cultural vision that lures us toward images of personal fulfillment in the context of community fulfillment, working and playing together; recognition that racial, ethnic and religious diversity enriches our common life; a politics that begins with the voices of the victimized, so that they become participants rather than mere objects of fate and other people's decisions.

We also need a new spirituality – vision and value-driven acts that embrace and enlarge peace, justice and the integrity of creation for all. This spirituality nurtures goodness wherever it appears, and contributes to creating it wherever it does not.

Each of us is invited to join with every other in the quest for peace with justice – and in so doing to help discover, create and celebrate the enlargement of the spirit of good in a troubled world. ∎

Dr. Richard A. Hoehn is director of Bread for the World Institute.

The Message of the Prophets

by David Beckmann

The prophets of the Bible taught that faithfulness and active concern for poor and vulnerable people would lead to prosperity and blessing for the nations of Israel and Judah.

The biblical books of Deuteronomy through Kings tell the story of how idolatry and hardheartedness toward people in need led to national destruction.

People in the privileged classes lost their sense of social purpose, devoted themselves to personal consumption and competed against each other for power. The nation was weakened through self-serving rulers and internal strife.

Today, too, right values and social justice are crucial to a nation's sustained peace and prosperity. When privileged people in a society neglect mass hunger or discriminate against a poorer ethnic group, they put their nation – and themselves – at the risk of a future crisis.

And now that the whole world is interconnected by trade and communication, people in the wealthy countries have similar obligations to people in need in far-off places.

If we can watch hungry children in Africa on television and yet slash the kinds of foreign aid that really help, something in us will die – something of our sense of social responsibility.

If we can also allow Congress to slash nutrition and other programs that help poor and hungry children in our own country, we may have become a nation in which most people look out for themselves and their own. That sort of nation is vulnerable to internal dissension, violence and decay.

The prophets taught that hardheartedness invites judgment – but also that God is patient and gives people lots of chances.

David Beckmann is president of Bread for the World and Bread for the World Institute.

"Rescue those who are being taken away to death; hold back those who are stumbling to the slaughter.
"If you say, 'Behold, we did not know this,' does not God who. . . keeps watch over your soul know it. . . .?"
– Proverbs 24:11-12

Countries in Crisis

Northern
Ireland

U.S.A.

Mexico

Guatemala — Honduras Haiti
              Nicaragua
El Salvador

Peru

Guinea
Sierra Leone
Liberia

Iv
Co

Czech Republic
Slovakia
Romania
Serbia
Croatia
Macedonia
Bosnia-Herzegovina
Turkey
Armenia
Georgia
Chechnya
Azerbaijan
Tajikistan
Syria
Israel
West Bank
Jordan
Iraq
Iran
Afghanistan
Pakistan
Kuwait
India
Burma
Laos
Viet Nam
Cambodia
Bangladesh
Thailand
Chad
Sudan
Eritrea
Djibouti
geria
Ethiopia
Somalia
Sri Lanka
Malaysia
Zaire
Uganda
Kenya
Rwanda
Burundi
Tanzania
East Timor
Angola
Mozambique
Malawi
Namibia
Zimbabwe
Botswana
South
Africa

Note: countries discussed in the chapters which follow
are indicated on this map

Chapter 1

An Explosion of Complex Humanitarian Emergencies

by Steven Hansch

Civil conflicts in such places as the former Yugoslavia are the major cause of today's food emergencies.

AP/Wide World Photos

Violent civil conflicts are engulfing many developing and former communist countries, putting 100 million people at risk of hunger. This proliferation of "complex humanitarian emergencies" stands in sharp contrast to the high hopes for a more peaceful and food-secure world expressed by many analysts as the Cold War came to a close.[1]

The character of emergencies is changing rapidly. Today, war and oppression are the principal, acute threats to large populations, not mere shortages of food. While grain from Asia, North America or Europe can be readily delivered to ports anywhere in the world, more people are forcibly uprooted than at any time in the past, as they flee in search of safe haven.

Complex emergencies combine internal conflicts with large-scale displacements of people, mass famine, and fragile or failing economic, political and social institutions.[2] These crises are slaughtering people and devastating their environment, from shattered urban neighborhoods in Afghanistan to refugee camps in Zaire, as well as in newly independent republics of the former Soviet Union and Yugoslav Federation.

Figure 1.1
Complex Humanitarian Emergencies, 1995

Country	Population at Risk[1]	Political Environment	Reference in *Countries in Crisis*
Afghanistan	4.2 million Includes over 3.2 million refugees, primarily in Iran and Pakistan	Escalated fighting 1994 Little government control Land mines	Chapters 1, 3
Algeria	N.A.	Insurgency Government consent to relief unlikely	None
Angola	3.7 million Includes 300,000 refugees in Congo, Zambia and Zaire	Civil war Intensified hostilities Limited government ability to support relief operations Corruption in security forces Land mines	Chapters 1, 3
Armenia	300,000 Includes 250,000 refugees in Azerbaijan and Russia	Government support for relief limited to ethnic Armenians	Chapters 1, 4
Azerbaijan	1 million Includes 300,000 refugees in Armenia and Russia	Limited government control in west Resistance to relief for Armenians	Chapters 1, 4
Bosnia and Herzegovina	2.5 million Includes 1.1 million refugees, primarily in Croatia, Germany and Serbia	Little government control All factions periodically oppose relief to other groups	Chapters 1, 2, 3, 4, 5
Burma (Myanmar)	N.A. Estimated 200,000 refugees in Bangladesh and Thailand	Civil war	None
Burundi	900,000 Includes 300,000 refugees in Rwanda, Tanzania and Zaire	Unstable Ethnic violence	Chapters 1, 2, 4
Cambodia	300,000	Factional strife Land mines Government supports relief Theft, corruption	Chapters 1, 2, 3, 5
Croatia[2]	500,000 Includes 300,000 refugees, primarily in Germany, Hungary and Serbia	Government permits relief Ethnic strife Land mines	Chapters 3, 4
Ethiopia	4.3 million Includes 200,000 refugees, primarily in Sudan	Anti-government activities in eastern, southern, western Ethiopia and Islamic Jihad anti-government activities in Eritrea not a threat to regimes Military could provide minimal support to relief operations Land mines	Chapters 2, 3, 5
Eritrea	1.6 million Includes 400,000 refugees in Sudan	"	Chapters 2, 3
Georgia	1 million Includes 150,000 refugees, primarily in Russia	Government supports relief Control of countryside doubtful	Chapters 1, 4
Haiti	1.3 million	Minimal government capability to support relief operations	Chapter 2
Iraq	1.3 million Includes 8,000 refugees in Iran	Government can deliver support throughout country Government hinders relief to Kurds and Shi'ites Land mines	Chapters 2, 3, 4

Figure 1.1
Complex Humanitarian Emergencies, 1995, continued

Country	Population at Risk[1]	Political Environment	Reference in *Countries in Crisis*
Liberia	2.1 million Includes over 800,000 refugees, primarily in Côte d'Ivoire, Ghana and Guinea	Civil war	Chapters 1, 2
Former Yugoslav Republic of Macedonia	10,000	N.A.	None
Mozambique	1 million Includes 200,000 refugees, primarily in Malawi, South Africa and Zimbabwe	Fragile security Bandits Returning refugees Demobilized military Devastated economy Government welcomes aid Land mines	Chapters 1, 2, 3, 4, 5
Russia (Chechnya)	N.A.	Government would support relief Some armed opposition	Chapter 1
Rwanda	4 million Includes 2 million refugees, primarily in Burundi, Tanzania and Zaire	Ethnic warfare	Chapters 1, 2, 4, 5
Sierra Leone	1.5 million Includes 300,000 refugees in Guinea and Liberia	Collapsed state Insurgents along Liberian border	Chapter 1
Somalia	1.1 million Includes over 200,000 refugees, primarily in Ethiopia and Zaire	No local authority can assist relief Opposition from clans, bandits, religious radicals Land mines	Chapters 1, 2, 3, 4, 5
Sri Lanka	700,000 Includes 100,000 refugees in India	Ongoing insurgency Government can provide limited support for relief operations	Chapters 1, 2, 4
Sudan [2]	3 million Includes 400,000 refugees, primarily in Ethiopia, Uganda and Zaire	Ongoing insurgency All sides use relief as weapon Government opposes relief to south and to non-Muslims in north Land mines	Chapters 1, 2, 3, 4, 5
Tajikistan	1 million Includes 300,000 refugees, primarily in Kazakhstan, Russia and Uzbekistan	Government cannot assist relief in south Armed opposition	Chapters 1, 4
Zaire	600,000 Includes 75,000 refugees, primarily in Burundi, Tanzania and Zambia	Government cannot assist relief Little or no civil authority Crime and extortion	Chapters 1, 4, 5

[1]The term "population at risk" indicates those people who are in need of or dependent on international aid to avoid large-scale malnutrition and deaths, including refugees, internally displaced persons and others in need.
[2]Does not reflect escalated violence of August 1995, which uprooted an estimated 150,000 additional people.
N.A. – Not available.

Source: U.S. Mission to the United Nations.

Figures 1.1 and 1.2 show the degree of vulnerability and key political factors in 26 countries currently experiencing complex emergencies or emerging from long-term civil conflict.

Complex emergencies disrupt economies, devastate physical and social infrastructure, and often lead to banditry and other breakdowns in social order. Governments sometimes collapse, or rulers coerce

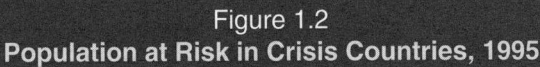

Figure 1.2
Population at Risk in Crisis Countries, 1995

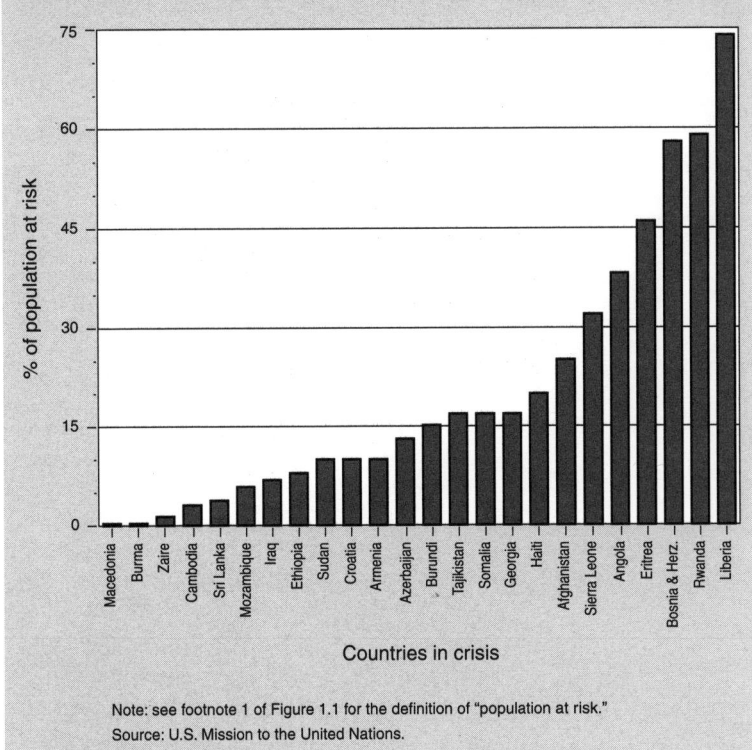

Countries in crisis

Note: see footnote 1 of Figure 1.1 for the definition of "population at risk."
Source: U.S. Mission to the United Nations.

fisherman. Some of the people in our group were dying of hunger even as we started to walk from our village. Young children and old people died. I lost my youngest girl. She was just two years old.[4]

The Roots of Crises

Civil strife stems from conflicts based on race, religion and ethnicity; competition over resources such as land, water and other assets and political power; ideological disputes, e.g., religious fundamentalism vs. political, social and economic modernization or, in most cases, a combination of these. Hunger and poverty often cause or contribute to the flare-up of violence.

Some analysts stress the environmental context of complex emergencies. Global fish harvests are decreasing. Topsoils are eroding at ever higher rates and large-scale population movements tax ecosystems beyond carrying capacity. In resource-poor areas, population growth rates are high and problems of food insecurity, poverty and environmental degradation are severe. These areas are prone to conflict, and conflict in turn is a cause of further environmental, social and economic stress. Hunger (such as food shortages in northern Ethiopia) leads to mass refugee flight, which causes yet more environmental damage.[5]

Other analysts emphasize the Cold War and its aftermath as causes of conflict. The Cold War contributed to civil strife in a number of countries, some of which are now at peace (e.g., El Salvador; see Chapter 3). Others such as Somalia are still coping with a legacy of conflict and arms. Superpower intervention suppressed factional and separatist conflicts in some countries such as Yugoslavia. The end of the Cold War has let those old demons loose.[6]

Most complex emergencies result from some combination of these social, environmental and political factors.

The Impact of Conflict

Violent conflict undermines economies. It kills and maims people, and forces them to flee from their communities. It destroys productive assets, and interrupts or demolishes marketing and

and attack civilians. Ensuring food security – access at all times by all people to adequate food for an active and healthy life – becomes extremely difficult. Conflict complicates the delivery of emergency relief supplies, and local food output declines.

In 1994, 164 armed conflicts raged around the world. Increasingly, this violence occurs not between nation-states, but within them. Twenty-two of these conflicts caused over 1,000 casualties and 82 others caused 100 to 1,000. Up to 80 percent of the casualties are civilians, mainly women and children, often deliberately targeted by the warring parties.[3]

All too typical is the case of Amer Kuay, a young southern Sudanese woman, as she reported to Oxfam:

We were attacked by cattle raiders working for the government. They took all of our cattle. They burned our houses. They took all our belongings. . . . We were left with no tools and hardly any seed, so we harvested very little. By February we started to starve. There were still attacks. . . . So we decided to cross the Nile to . . . where it was safer. We had to wait in the marshes for some time to get a fishing boat to take us across. We had no money to pay, so I had to give my daughter's clothes to the

In emergencies, as food supplies are restricted, people often subsist on dwindling supplies of a single food. Refugees who depend on internationally provided food aid may go for months eating just bulk grains and beans. So it is not surprising that severe micronutrient – vitamin and mineral – deficiencies ("hidden hunger") increase greatly during emergencies. In recent years, nutritionists working with uprooted people have documented epidemics of deficiencies of vitamins A, C and B-1, niacin, iron and iodine. Most foods provided in emergency situations are poor sources of these nutrients.

Hidden hunger has serious health consequences.[7]

- Lack of vitamin A causes eye damage and increased risk of death from infections. It is one of the major contributors to high death rates in emergencies;

- Insufficient vitamin C leads to hemorrhages, depression, frequent infections, bleeding gums, loosened teeth, muscle degeneration, bone fragility, joint pain and failure of wounds to heal. Vitamin C is essential for absorbing iron. Vitamin C deficiency occurs among populations displaced for long periods and forced to go for months without fresh fruits or vegetables such as boat people or refugees in closed camps with only dry food, as in Sudan, Ethiopia, Somalia and Kenya;

- Inadequate vitamin B-1 causes heart problems, muscle and nervous degeneration, mental confusion and paralysis. Outbreaks occurred in the 1980s among Southeast Asian refugees consuming diets high in white rice;

- Niacin deficiency causes diarrhea, irritability, loss of appetite, weakness, dizziness, mental disorders, skin and liver problems and low blood pressure. It is a constant risk among people who consume corn or sorghum and little else, including millions living in southern and eastern Africa and Central America;

- Iron deficiency – one among several causes of anemia – leads to reduced learning and work capacity and increased susceptibility to infections and lead poisoning. Refugees typically have high rates of anemia; and

- Iodine deficiency can cause serious mental and physical retardation in children. It is seen often among refugees from inland and highland areas or cut off from commercial food markets.

Micronutrient deficiency in crisis circumstances often goes unrecognized and undocumented, partly because refugee situations are seen as temporary. Yet refugees in Pakistan, Thailand, Malawi and Mexico have remained in camps for many years – well beyond the original disaster and anyone's expectations.

Long-term civil conflict can create hidden hunger among those who remain behind as well. These people may be lucky to receive any form of assistance. Conflict typically blocks access to fresh food markets. During famines, people will seek new sources of money and income, and even scavenge for wild foods or roots and tubers. Millions of people are at risk of micronutrient deficiencies in Mozambique, Angola, Rwanda, Burundi, Peru, Colombia, Sri Lanka, Liberia and Bosnia.

Micronutrients are so inexpensive that providing them to people at high risk of disease and death is extremely cost-effective. Ironically, this has received low priority in emergency relief efforts.

---

transportation networks. In a study of 16 developing countries at war between 1970 and 1990, Frances Stewart, of Oxford University, found that per capita incomes fell in every case. The worst performances were in Mozambique, Liberia, Nicaragua, Afghanistan (see "Afghanistan," p. 17), Guatemala and Uganda, all of which experienced civil wars. All 16 countries experienced heavy destruction of productive and social infrastructure. For example, Mozambique's civil war ruined transportation and energy systems, including 44 percent of the rail fleet, and 40 percent of the primary schools.

These conflicts also had enormous human costs. Civilian deaths accounted for over two-thirds of war-related deaths in 14 of the countries. Families disintegrated as adults were killed or migrated. Rape, pillage and witnessing the death of family members caused psychological shocks. Even when a civil war ends, peace means having to cooperate with the former enemy, whereas international war tends to unite a population against a common external foe.[8]

All these factors make the restoration of normal life – including secure communities and livelihoods, and food security – an enormous burden on poor societies.

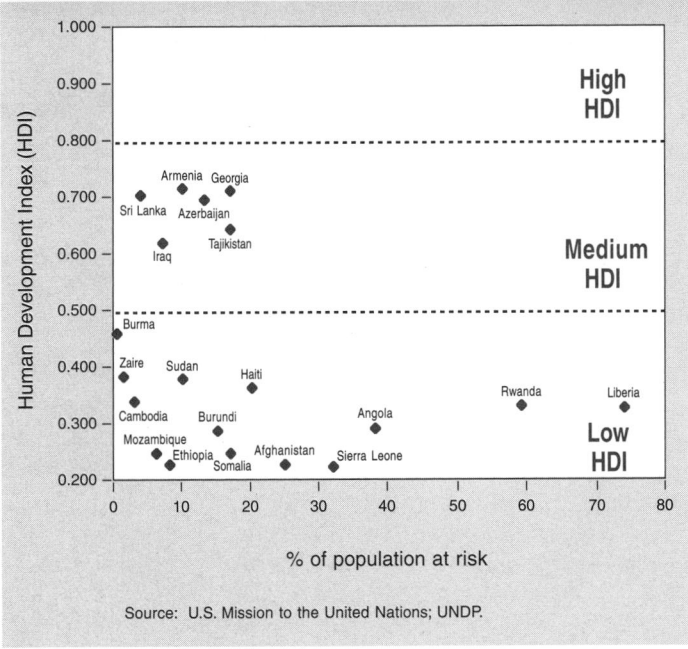

Figure 1.3
Conflict and Human Development, 1995

% of population at risk

Source: U.S. Mission to the United Nations; UNDP.

Conflict, Hunger and Health

Hunger contributes to conflict, and most armed conflicts lead to hunger. Figures 1.3 and 1.4 suggest a relationship between violent conflict and low levels of human well-being. Of 20 countries currently experiencing civil strife or just beginning to recover, 14 have low levels of human development (which measures economic growth, education and health). Among these countries, those with over 20 percent of the population at risk rank low in human development.

In complex emergencies, warring factions loot and deliberately destroy crops, draw labor resources out of food production (through conscription, market disruption and uprooting of farming communities) and use food as a weapon. Food production per capita dropped in 14 of the 16 countries Stewart studied. The decline was 15 percent or more in Cambodia, Nicaragua, Sudan, Angola and Mozambique. People had difficulty getting enough food because of reduced output, employment and earnings, as well as rising inflation. In the worst cases, drought and transportation problems further limited access to food, placing people at risk of famine. Afghanistan and Cambodia experienced massive destruction of farm animals. Land mines

and destruction of infrastructure took farm land out of use in Afghanistan, Cambodia, El Salvador and Nicaragua.

Violent civil strife in the Horn of Africa during the early 1990s resulted in mortality rates from malnutrition and disease more than 20 times greater than normal.[9] Countries in crisis often experience high rates of death among preschool children; this is a clear indicator of widespread hunger (Figure 1.4).

In the past, communities usually had coping strategies to respond to food shortages. But with the spread of modern weaponry, each tribal group, each village, each political faction can prey upon vulnerable people with lethal outcomes. Governments have greater ability to murder their opponents. Desperate people flee to cities, safe havens or other countries. Yet flight creates new problems. The risks of communicable diseases and poor sanitation usually increase when uprooted people congregate in refugee camps. In addition, uprooted people frequently forfeit their meager assets, including land and tools, so that return, recovery, long-term development and self-reliance – as well as productive

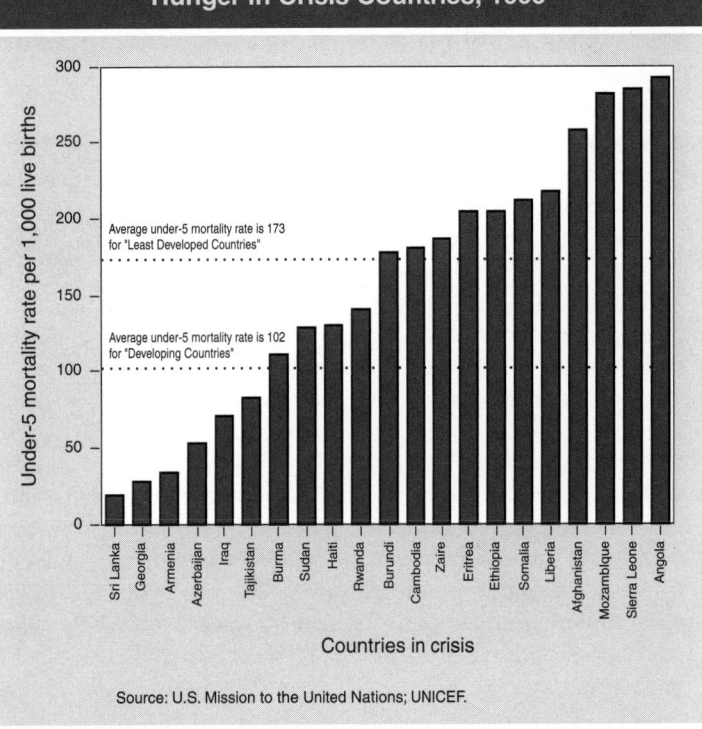

Figure 1.4
Hunger in Crisis Countries, 1995

Countries in crisis

Source: U.S. Mission to the United Nations; UNICEF.

"Among refugees and displaced populations, high rates of malnutrition and micronutrient deficiencies associated with high rates of mortality continue to occur. The magnitude of the problem has grown over the last decade. Increased political commitment to an accountability for the protection and promotion of the nutritional well-being of refugees, displaced populations, those under occupation, prisoners of war and other affected groups are urgently required in accordance with international humanitarian law. Governments, in collaboration with the international community, should:

"Provide sustainable assistance to refugees and displaced persons and work to monitor and ensure their nutritional well-being, giving high priority to the control of diseases and to the prevention of malnutrition and outbreaks of micronutrient deficiency diseases. Wherever feasible, such assistance should encourage their ability to support themselves rather than increase their dependence on external assistance. The food provided should be nutritionally adequate and safe. . . .

"Ensure and legislate for the fortification of foods or water with necessary micronutrients, where feasible, when existing food supplies fail to provide adequate levels in the diet. . . .

"Recognize that refugees and displaced persons, as well as being susceptible to iodine, vitamin A and iron deficiencies, are also susceptible to other deficiencies, particularly vitamin B-1 deficiency (beriberi), niacin deficiency (pellagra) and vitamin C deficiency (scurvy). Donor countries and involved organizations must therefore ensure that the nutrient content of food used for emergency food aid meets nutritional requirements, if necessary through fortification or ultimately through supplementation. To the extent possible, such foods should be culturally appropriate."[10]

Fighting in southern Sudan has created a "hunger triangle" for much of the population.

activities in the asylum country – become that much more expensive and difficult.

The rise in civil strife is a major reason why the number of people who have crossed international borders as refugees has grown tenfold, from 2.4 million people in 1974 to 23 million in 1995. In addition, there are an estimated 27 million "internally displaced" people – those who felt compelled to abandon their homes but remain within their country.

As many as 50 million more people are trapped within the conflict zones.[11] These vulnerable people are desperately poor, increasingly marginalized in a competitive world economy and subject to the threat of malnutrition, starvation and death. Micronutrient deficiencies ("hidden hunger") are a particularly serious problem (see "Hidden Hunger in Emergencies," p. 12).

The 100 million people severely affected by complex emergencies account for less than 13 percent of the 800 million people in the world who are chronically undernourished.[12] But most of the deaths that occur in complex humanitarian emergencies could readily be averted through known public health measures. In recognition of this, at the 1992 International Conference on Nutrition (ICN), 159 governments committed themselves to a Plan of Action that included provisions on ensuring the nutritional well-being of refugees and displaced populations (see "Excerpts," above).

Complex emergencies exacerbate – and are exacerbated by – disease epidemics. Increasingly, those attempting to control resurgent infectious diseases such as cholera, malaria, tuberculosis, AIDS and other maladies must contend with mass forced migration and regions rendered inaccessible by war and social breakdown. Health personnel migrate or are killed, and warring factions destroy clinics.[13]

Violent conflict also makes it harder for people to get clean water, which is essential to good health and nutrition. The problem is especially serious for those who depend on public water taps outside their homes. People carrying heavy water containers move slowly and make easy targets for snipers. The average person requires at least 15 liters of water daily for washing, cooking and drinking. People tend to put washing and personal hygiene aside if less water is available. This increases the likelihood of infection, infestation by parasites such as lice and possibly fatal diarrheal disease.

Starvation

Historically, starvation occurred primarily in famines that resulted from natural causes: drought, floods, pestilence and frost. The use of food as a weapon is as old as warfare itself, but during the 20th century, human-made famines have become the primary cause of starvation.

There are few comprehensive or reliable statistics on starvation deaths. During food emergencies, official records attribute most deaths to a primary illness: an infectious disease (pneumonia, measles or dysentery), dehydration or heart failure. The victims are predominantly infants, children, elderly people and those already anemic or carrying tuberculosis, parasites or other diseases. Most famine-prone countries already have sizeable malnourished populations prior to a famine. Malnutrition and illness interact in a vicious downward cycle: poor nutrition amplifies the consequences of illness, while chronic poor health drains the body of nutrients.

Very little is ever known about deaths in disaster-affected regions outside of major towns and cities or internationally-assisted refugee camps. Emergency aid is sent to locations where survivors are seen, not necessarily where the most deaths occur. Most information systems systematically miss the quiet victims who stay in the countryside.

At the ICN, the world's governments agreed:
to make all efforts to eliminate before the end of this decade: famine and famine-related deaths. . . . We also pledge to reduce substantially within this decade: starvation and widespread chronic hunger; undernutrition, especially among children, women and the aged. . . .[14]

The challenge is to turn this rhetoric into reality. We have learned some, but not all, of the necessary lessons.

Case Studies

The following case studies describe recent and ongoing complex emergencies. In each, civil war put large numbers of civilians at risk of food insecurity. In some instances such as Somalia malnutrition and diarrhea were the primary killers. In Rwanda, political killings were followed by fatal disease epidemics, in part caused by malnutrition, and then by malnutrition directly. Southern Sudan has some of the highest rates of malnutrition ever recorded. In Bosnia and the former Soviet Union, malnutrition appears to be less of a problem, although dependence on external food aid means that food security is fragile at best. The next three chapters will examine in greater detail responses to these and other crises, and draw lessons for the future.

Somalia

The 1991 to 1992 famine in Somalia received unprecedented international attention and, ultimately, assistance. A good deal of the aid arrived too late to prevent massive numbers of deaths. The relief effort focused disproportionately on a few areas and was poorly coordinated. Relief agencies disagreed among themselves whether to provide hot meals at feeding centers or bulk grain deliveries to villages. No single U.N. or other agency was available, particularly during the early stages, to provide leadership or coordination. By 1993, the U.S.-U.N. military intervention became embroiled in Somalia's conflicts and failed dramatically. Fighting still rages in parts of the country and Somalis continue to suffer since the withdrawal of foreign troops.

Tragically, more timely and effective humanitarian action early on could have prevented most of the deaths that resulted from malnutrition and disease.

During the 1980s, international assistance supported Somalia's corrupt government, which pitted clans against one another and provoked armed hostilities that remain resistant to reconciliation. After the fall of the government in 1991, rebel forces fragmented and factional warfare broke out. Drought and increasing banditry worsened the situation. Food security deteriorated. Much of the work force became unemployed. The crisis displaced 2 million of the 5 million to 7 million Somalis. Over 600,000 refugees fled to Kenya and Ethiopia.

Since no functional government was in place during this period, the fragile public health infrastructure collapsed. Violence and banditry made small-scale farmers fear for their lives whenever they grew or stored food. Because food made them a target, food production and marketing dropped precipitously.

Displaced-persons camps reported very high rates (over 20 percent) of severe, acute malnutrition. Half of all deaths occurred in rural villages among non-displaced people.

Waves of famine and death followed the movements of these uprooted Somalis (see Figure 1.5). The first wave began in April 1991, as the former government's troops retreated from Mogadishu. Fighting and insecurity led directly to 10,000 deaths and indirectly to economic collapse and dispossession of assets. Displaced people gravitated toward cities and relief centers, forming squatter settlements. Migrants from rural areas died in large numbers because they received little support. Those who escaped to Kenya faced health problems due to lack of potable water and overcrowding.

The second famine wave followed looting and slaughter of rural people by retreating troops loyal to the former government in late 1991 and early 1992. They pillaged and destroyed assets, leaving villages empty not only of food, but also of any means to produce, buy or barter for food.

The final wave occurred in mid-1992, after large displaced populations had settled around more than 1,000 feeding center sites. Another 100,000 people died from measles, pneumonia and diarrhea.

Surveys indicate that Somalis had numerous micronutrient deficiencies during this time. Severe anemia combined with dehydration and protein-energy malnutrition to increase the risk of death from infectious diseases. Measles caused 50,000 to 100,000 deaths between 1991 and 1993. These could have been prevented if Somali children had received low-cost vitamin A capsules.

Preventive public health and primary care measures – clean water, food safety nets and surveillance, immunizations, choosing appropriate sites for camps, vitamin A capsule distributions and recruitment of sanitation workers – could have saved over 150,000 lives, or 70 percent of the Somalis who died of malnutrition and infectious disease in 1992. Such measures could have averted:

- 95 percent of the severe malnutrition – and therefore almost all starvation deaths;
- At least 75 percent of deaths from measles; and
- 40 percent of other deaths related to infections and dehydration.

Nongovernmental organizations (NGOs) knew what was occurring and struggled desperately to meet growing emergency needs. Physical security could not be assured, so NGOs for the first time routinely hired armed militia for protection. Relief staff became hostages to militia demands for salaries and bribes. Ultimately, a higher proportion of NGO workers died than military peacekeepers. A recent analysis concluded:

> The heroism of many of the people working with [the International Committee of the Red Cross], NGOs and U.N. agencies, as well as with bilateral aid programs, is striking. Their ability to help people and save lives in the face of no end of difficulties and threats to their own well-being is praiseworthy indeed. Some had guns put to their heads for extortion; some, indeed, were killed in the course of service to the Somali people.[15]

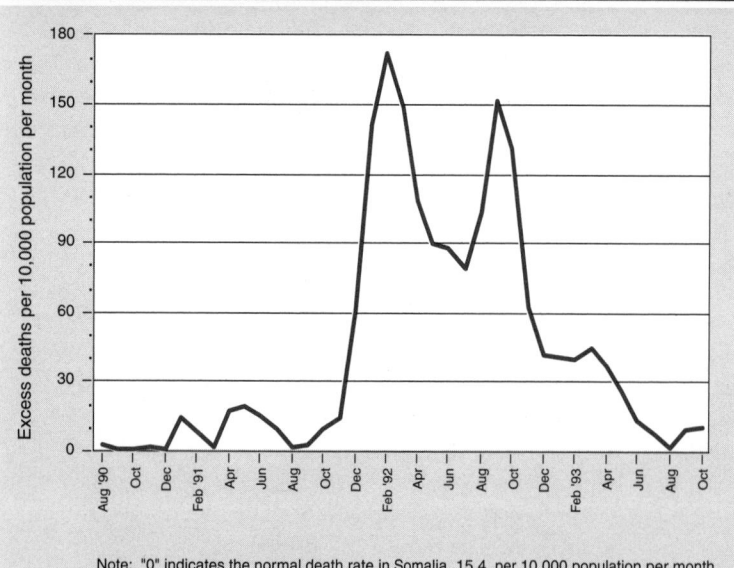

Figure 1.5
Excess Mortality in Bay and Bakool Regions, Somalia 1990-1993

Note: "0" indicates the normal death rate in Somalia, 15.4 per 10,000 population per month.
Source: Refugee Policy Group.

Afghanistan: Abandoned to Violence, Drugs, Hunger, Disease and Death

by Marc J. Cohen

Many analysts rate the estimated $2 billion to $3 billion in arms that the United States covertly provided to anti-communist guerrillas in Afghanistan as a foreign policy investment that paid handsome dividends. After failing for a decade to pacify the *mujahideen* ("soldiers of God"), Soviet troops withdrew in 1988. This Cold War triumph for the United States was a tragedy for the Afghan people, however.

The anti-Soviet struggle left a million Afghans dead, 2 million internally displaced and almost 7 million in refugee camps, mainly in Pakistan and Iran. The war destroyed much of the country's infrastructure, including irrigation works. Cultivated area declined by 40 percent. From 1990 to 1992, food production per capita was just 70 percent of the 1979 to 1981 level, and the average Afghan's daily calorie supply was 71 percent of minimum requirements.

Although the end of the Cold War raised hopes for peace, the *mujahideen* did not defeat the pro-Soviet regime until April 1992. Since then, fighting has continued as former rebels and Communists have vied for power, principalities, opium profits and position in a confusing game of rapidly shifting alliances. Adding to the complicated politics are conflicts across ethnic and Muslim sectarian lines and assistance to warring factions from neighboring countries. Powerful local warlords have gradually gained control over much of the country at the expense of the central government.

By late 1994, some semblance of normal life had returned in 80 percent of Afghanistan. More than 3 million refugees returned home. Agricultural activities – the prewar occupation of most Afghans – resumed on land cleared of mines.

But many problems remain. Service in a factional militia still pays double the average wage. The mortality rate of children under age five is 257 per 1,000 live births, the fifth highest in the world. Ten million land mines are still scattered around the country, more than anywhere on earth. Impoverished farmers find cultivating opium poppies the best way to earn some income. Their crops, refined in Pakistan, provide a major share of the heroin consumed in the United States.

The center of the war shifted to the capital, Kabul, which had survived the Soviet occupation in relative tranquillity. Indiscriminate shelling during 1994 and the first three months of 1995 killed 13,000 people, injured 50,000, and left the city without water and electricity. The battle displaced a million Kabulis within Afghanistan (including 400,000 within the city), and another 75,000 fled to Pakistan, despite that country's closure of its border.

Militia loyal to nominal Prime Minister Gulbuddin Hekmatyar blockaded northern Kabul between June and December of 1994, preventing deliveries of emergency food and medicine. This forced residents of the northern sector – 67 percent of them internally displaced people – to travel daily to Hekmatyar's southern zone to buy food. Food prices rose tenfold between February and June 1994 as the government ended subsidies and Pakistan's border closure made imports more costly. Surveys in December 1994 found acute undernutrition among 35 percent to 40 percent of city residents. Malnutrition is worse among girls because Afghan families tend to feed boys first and give girls leftovers. Kabuli children died of malnutrition-related disorders such as measles, dysentery and dehydration.

In March 1995, the government of President Burhannudin Rabbani gained control of the entire city for the first time in three years. This eased the food supply situation, although prices remained high.

Hekmatyar's base at Jalalabad, near the Pakistan border, is home to more than 500,000 internally displaced people, half of whom do not receive international assistance. Many live in camps without electricity or running water, exposed to harsh winter cold and blistering summer heat, depending on trucked-in water and food aid for survival. Mohammed Akbar, a 35-year-old camp dweller, remarked, "Here it's a desert and there is nothing to do, just to sit and wait for rations. This is not a life."[16] A January 1995 survey found inadequate and unclean food supplies in one of the largest camps, and no heating fuel. The United Nations reports that acute malnutrition had eased in the camps by April 1995. But in at least one camp, most children were not receiving measles immunizations.

The government still lacks control over much of the country and faces well-armed opponents. The United Nations and the Organization of the Islamic Conference have not succeeded in their efforts to broker a political solution. U.N. agencies and a few nongovernmental organizations, including the Afghan Red Crescent Society, provide some urgently needed assistance, despite the lack of physical security. A U.N. appeal for $62 million in humanitarian aid in 1994 netted just $20 million. With the Cold War over, the international community's interest in the country has waned.

Particularly disturbing is the U.S. policy response. The militias of Hekmatyar and Rabbani, which devastated Kabul in 1994, received most of the U.S. arms provided during the anti-Soviet war. Yet U.S. humanitarian aid, which could help contain the human costs, ended in July 1994. Assadullah, an Afghan Red Crescent worker, must have spoken for many of his compatriots when he asked, "Why America helping Afghanistan when Russians here, and not now? Where our American friends now?"[17]

Dr. Marc J. Cohen is senior research associate at Bread for the World Institute and editor of *Countries in Crisis*.

But for most of 1992, donor governments and institutions, which shared some blame for the deteriorating political situation, did not seem to know, or care, what was happening in Somalia. Hence, the resources and effort were not available when needed. Surveillance systems should have been in place to monitor malnutrition in the general population (not just camps) by August 1991. Immunization campaigns should have reached all large displaced populations beginning in 1991. Donors should have provided bulk food aid throughout the countryside instead of comparatively more expensive on-site feeding programs.[18]

The eventual U.S.-U.N. military intervention was dramatic and expensive, but far too late.

Violence and Starvation Among Southern Sudanese

Civil war has raged in the east African nation of Sudan for 29 of its 39 years of independence. The current fighting began in 1983 when the government, controlled by Arab Muslim northerners, attempted to impose Islamic law upon black southerners who are from a distinct culture, and practice traditional religions and Christianity. The south contains some of Sudan's best land, as well as oil reserves. Southerners have much experience coping with severe food shortages and the use of food as a weapon.

Both the government and the rebel Sudan People's Liberation Army use donated food aid in attempts to win the hearts and minds of the population. According to John Prendergast, of the Center of Concern:

Food becomes a powerful military instrument. Warring factions deny or disrupt access and distribution for relief; routinely divert food aid for their sustenance; use civilians as bait for internationally donated food; provide food aid to gain legitimacy; monetize, barter or otherwise manipulate food aid to obtain arms or fuel and differentially provide food aid to supporters at the expense of those most in need, who may be unsympathetic or of the wrong ethnicity, race or religion.[19]

Scorched-earth policies, theft of food supplies and the siege of cities have caused local famines in southern Sudan, killing up to 2 million people and uprooting millions more. Most displaced people remain in the south, where feeding camps operate. Those who have fled north to the environs of the capital, Khartoum, have faced further forced relocation and other government harassment.

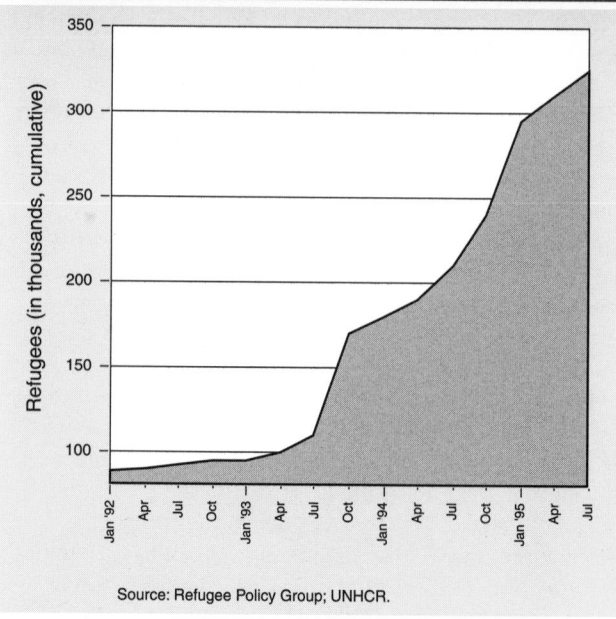

Figure 1.6
Sudanese Refugees Fleeing to Uganda
1992-1995

Source: Refugee Policy Group; UNHCR.

Since late 1993, stepped-up fighting has displaced still more people in southern Sudan. In February 1994, the government attacked relief camps with ground troops and aerial bombardment. Sixty thousand people fled to Uganda; others fled to Kenya.

Surveys in parts of southern Sudan in 1993 found mortality rates 10 times higher than normal. Seventy percent of all children were malnourished and millions of people were at risk of malnutrition.[20] Hunger worsened in 1994 because of a poor harvest. Traditionally, Sudanese have coped with crop shortfalls by consuming wild fruits and grasses, frequent and distant migration, and eating their livestock or even Nile hippopotamus and crocodile. The war has blocked some of these options.

Today, the U.N. World Food Programme (WFP) ships food into Sudan from Uganda and Kenya. But as the situation has become desperate, hundreds of thousands of Sudanese have fled to Uganda (see Figure 1.6). Others have sought refuge in Kenya and Zaire.

Rwanda and Burundi [21]

In both Rwanda and Burundi, ethnic conflict has erupted against a background of long-term food insecurity. Colonial rulers had favored a small minority of Tutsi people over the substantial Hutu majority in both places. Since independence, bloody clashes have occurred. The most recent confrontation in Burundi erupted after a failed coup

Tajikistan: Civil War and Food Dependence

by David Nassar

The fall of the Soviet Union in 1991 unleashed several conflicts within its former republics, but few as violent as the war in Tajikistan in central Asia. At its height in 1993, this bloody battle for political power among regional factions had killed more than 50,000 people, driven 100,000 refugees into neighboring countries and displaced 500,000 within Tajikistan.

Hunger resulted not just from the fighting, but also from a long history of dependence on the Soviet Union for food. The war created a short-term food emergency and ensured shortages for years to come.

In the early part of this century, Soviet dictator Joseph Stalin forcibly relocated thousands of Tajiks to the southwest corner of the country to work on huge cotton farms, which still occupy the majority of the arable land. Although the mountains, which cover 93 percent of the land, make agriculture difficult, farmers also produce grain, and the country could expand local food production. But Soviet Tajikistan shipped cotton to the rest of the U.S.S.R., receiving food in exchange.

The collapse of the Soviet Union cut off these supplies. The ensuing civil war crippled industry, and drained money and attention from needed agricultural reforms.

The United Nations and international nongovernmental organizations (NGOs) responded with staples such as flour, sugar and cooking oil, preventing starvation during the winter of 1993 to 1994. But malnutrition remained a concern. Experts recommended to the U.S. government and NGOs that they shift their food aid strategy from emergency feeding to promoting local food production.

There are a number of ways to link food aid to such development efforts. "Food-for-work" projects pay local development workers wholly or in part with food aid commodities. Another method is monetization, where food aid distributing agencies sell the commodities to indigenous merchants. This generates funds for development activities and, if done carefully, can strengthen local markets.

Mercy Corps International, a U.S.-based NGO, has used monetization in central Asia to generate funds for development programs that local communities themselves initiate. However, in Tajikistan, the agency believes that the situation is too insecure to implement such creative projects. Hence, it has continued to carry out more traditional emergency feeding efforts.

Other aid donors do not even seem to think about moving beyond emergency feeding to supporting Tajikistan in achieving food self-reliance. The international food aid system is driven by surplus availability rather than the needs of affected populations. Donors continued to distribute tons of food directly to Tajiks throughout 1994.

Food-for-work activities have expanded in Tajikistan more recently, with direct feeding efforts focusing on vulnerable groups. However, the local economy continues to deteriorate. If the country cannot meet its own basic needs, and the international community does not make a larger investment in its long-term development, hunger will fuel more violence. This could generate thousands more refugees needing fresh shipments of emergency aid from outside donors. The cycle will continue until the international community combines relief with assistance that helps Tajiks develop their own capacity to help themselves.

David Nassar has worked as a consultant on the refugee situation in Tajikistan and was a Bread for the World intern from 1992 to 1993.

d'etat against the first democratically elected government in 1993. Massive popular unrest followed, and then army suppression, resulting in at least 100,000 deaths. In 1994, the then Hutu-dominated government in Rwanda orchestrated genocidal slaughter of Tutsis and moderate Hutus. Violence continues in both countries.

Unscrupulous Rwandan leaders have repeatedly used perceptions of scarcity and injustice to mobilize violence. The 1994 genocide was the most extreme example. Its context included a decade of declining agricultural production, severe land degradation, falling incomes due to lower prices for coffee (the main cash crop) and high child malnutrition rates. Civil war in the 1990s led to increased food insecurity and reduced government services, both as a consequence of the fighting and because of diversion of resources to the military.

The most recent crisis in Rwanda left nearly a million people dead. Following the victory of the Tutsi-dominated rebels, over 2 million people, mostly Hutus, fled the country for Tanzania and Zaire. Another 1.5 million Rwandans are displaced within the country, and the new government violently evicted many of them from camps in mid-1995. Meanwhile, clashes in Burundi drove 45,000 Hutus from that country into Zaire and Tanzania. The situation remains extremely tense.

Liberia: Exporting Crisis

Since 1989, rival political factions have battled for power in Liberia. Large numbers of refugees and rebel soldiers have fled from the war to neighboring Guinea, Côte d'Ivoire and Sierra Leone. They have brought the violence with them to Sierra Leone. That country has become an arena in which armed gangs struggle for turf, displacing thousands of their fellow Sierra Leoneans. In Côte d'Ivoire, in contrast, Liberian refugees have settled with friends and families and become largely self-sufficient. However, local civilians were killed in June 1995 when Liberian armies entered the country in search of refugees.

Former Soviet Republics

Many of the Newly Independent States of the former Soviet Union (NIS) face difficult transitions from communism to a market economy, as well as violent power struggles, ethnic secessionist movements and serious food insecurity.

The most powerful republic, Russia, is ill-equipped to provide humanitarian assistance to people in need. Its own brutal efforts to suppress the independence movement in the Transcaucasus region of Chechnya have uprooted close to half a million people. Only a handful of agencies are providing relief.

Post-Soviet NIS governments have not had the capacity to manage serious problems of displaced people. Another separatist rebellion in Georgia has uprooted 300,000 people. A territorial dispute between Azerbaijan and Armenia has displaced 1.4 million people in the two countries. In Armenia, Azerbaijan, Georgia and Tajikistan (see "Tajikistan," p. 19), the Red Cross, U.N. agencies and international NGOs are working with local governments to assist large populations of refugees, internally displaced people and people suffering through conflict and economic transition.

Bosnia-Herzegovina

Fighting broke out in the spring of 1992 between Bosnian Serb rebels on one side and the Muslim-dominated government of Bosnia-Herzegovina and its Bosnian Croat allies on the other. Since then, the former Yugoslav republic's socioeconomic conditions have deteriorated from those of an industrial nation to the level found in many developing countries. The fighting has claimed almost 200,000 lives and forced more than 3 million people from their homes.

The largest number of deaths and cases of illness have come from the injuries inflicted by shooting and shelling during attacks upon civilian population centers, not from malnutrition or infectious disease. The international community's most important effort has been to provide protection through a U.N. military force. But even U.N.-protected "safe havens" such as Gorazde and Bihac have suffered from deadly Serb rebel attacks. Tragically, the United Nations was unable to keep safe areas in Zepa or Srebrenica from falling in July 1995. The ensuing exodus added to the ranks of displaced Bosnians.

Aside from injuries, conflict also causes health problems. Bosnia has very cold winters, and artillery shells have punched holes in many homes. U.N. agencies have distributed heating fuel and plastic to cover holes, but the cold remains a problem for vulnerable populations, particularly elderly and young people. Malnutrition exacerbates these difficulties, since cold weather increases calorie requirements. The cold also freezes roads, making transportation of food difficult, and pipes, damaging sanitation systems. Cold weather can also cause engineering problems for hospitals.

The conflict has disrupted water and sewer systems in cities. Much of the population lacks access to adequate water supplies even in urban settings like Sarajevo. Civilians have been killed by sniper fire while trying to get water from public taps. Waste systems have broken down, posing significant health hazards. ∎

Steven Hansch is senior program officer at the Refugee Policy Group in Washington, DC.

Chapter 2

From Crisis to Development: Transforming Relief

Even in refugee camps, people need opportunities to earn income, grow food and obtain education and training. These Somali refugees in Kenya are collecting firewood to cook their food.

UNHCR/21052/05.1991/B. Press

by Daniel U.B.P. Chelliah

n today's post-Cold War, interdependent world, preventing or mitigating civil strife is everyone's business. Major impacts of complex humanitarian emergencies – refugees, disease epidemics, environmental degradation, hunger and poverty – cannot be contained within national borders. What happens in southern Sudan, Kabul, Rio de Janeiro or Los Angeles has direct effects on economic, social and political developments throughout the world.

It makes sense to develop the wisdom to anticipate, and strengthen the capacity to manage, those disputes most likely to erupt into violent conflict (see Chapter 4). It also makes sense to reduce the social ills that create fertile ground for civil strife by investing in sustainable development. The costs of responding to complex emergencies far exceed the price of investing in better structures to prevent and mitigate crises. J. Brian Atwood, administrator of the U.S. Agency for International Development (USAID), has tallied some of those costs: "Disease, food shortages and poverty will cause more migration and instability."[1]

Concerned citizens and governments must also respond immediately to disputes that have erupted into warfare.

These situations are indeed complex, and efforts to help are fraught with problems. Yet the response to complex emergencies can be improved by:

- Learning from experience in responding to natural disasters and longer-term development efforts;

- Developing clearer guidelines for international humanitarian intervention, particularly for using military force;

- Strengthening negotiating capacity for dispute resolution and negotiating safe passage for relief supplies and cross-border relief operations;

- Improving coordination among relief agencies and among the policies of donor governments;

- Understanding the uses and limitations of emergency food aid;

- Engaging local communities and affected populations more fully in designing and implementing programs; and

- Linking relief efforts more directly to sustainable development.

Problems in Contemporary Crisis Response

Complex emergencies usually displace large numbers of people. They require multi-pronged approaches that combine food and health interventions with conflict mediation, negotiation for access to vulnerable populations, establishing safe havens, training in human rights reporting, tracking of dislocated populations and repatriation or resettlement efforts. All these need to be coordinated among regional governments and international organizations, and local and international nongovernmental organizations (NGOs; see "Dealing with Debacles: Who's Who in Contemporary Crisis Response," pp. 23-25).

Today, international humanitarian assistance is less hampered by the availability or timeliness of food aid than by the political complications of attempting to deliver it and the uses to which it is put. Food and other relief supplies may be diverted to support warring factions – inadvertently, or as a necessary bribe for permission to reach people in need. Serious ethical questions face relief organizations, since providing assistance may further fuel the conflict and suffering, and postpone helping affected people achieve food self-reliance or sustainable development. But failing to offer aid may lead to starvation.

Over the past five years, humanitarian assistance in the Persian Gulf, Sudan, Somalia, Cambodia, Central America, Afghanistan, western and southern Africa, the former Soviet Union and Yugoslavia, Rwanda and Burundi has a mixed record. In some instances, conflicting parties have welcomed external assistance (El Salvador and Mozambique), while in others, intervention has occurred without much local consultation (Bosnia). The extent to which peacemaking and long-term development accompanied relief has likewise varied (none in Somalia, but ongoing efforts in Cambodia), as has the success of the outcome. There are also instances in which a timely response prevented disaster (Iraqi Kurdistan), others in which the global community failed to intervene (East Timor) and yet others in which the response was primarily local or regional (Liberia).

The international community has yet to establish a global structure to coordinate prevention efforts, crisis response, conflict management and post-crisis development planning. The U.N. Department of Humanitarian Affairs (DHA) offers the framework to accomplish this. It is presently responsible for coordinating crisis aid, but interagency and intergovernmental cooperation remains inefficient and insufficient.

Lack of funds and inadequate numbers of staff limit the capacity of relief agencies to respond to needs and to do so in a timely manner. The total annual budget for U.N. peacekeeping and humanitarian operations is currently less than that of the New York City Fire Department.[2]

In addition, many agencies have limited mandates. For example, the major emphasis of the Office of the U.N. High Commissioner for Refugees (UNHCR) is on providing protection to refugees. But coping with complex humanitarian emergencies is a much broader task.

In the short run, food aid can be essential in helping repatriated refugees such as these Salvadorans to resume their lives and rebuild their communities.

In most crisis situations, the affected people themselves organize response systems and devise coping strategies, often in collaboration with local nongovernmental organizations (NGOs). Other major actors in crisis response include U.N. agencies, donor government agencies such as the U.S. Agency for International Development (USAID), national governments in the affected countries, local and international NGOs and the International Red Cross and Red Crescent Movement.

The U.N. System

Fifty years ago, governments established the United Nations to prevent future wars. Recently, the world body has devoted considerable attention to preventive diplomacy, peacemaking, peacekeeping and emergency assistance (see Chapter 6).

Department of Political Affairs

The Department of Political Affairs coordinates peacekeeping. Presently, it obtains troops from member governments on a case-by-case basis.

Department of Humanitarian Affairs (DHA)

The United Nations established DHA in 1992 to help coordinate response to natural and human-made disasters. It administers a central Emergency Relief Fund and is charged with coordinating various humanitarian agencies and linking humanitarian, political and peace-keeping activities.

Office of the U.N. High Commissioner for Refugees (UNHCR)

Established in 1921 by the League of Nations, UNHCR has since 1951 provided international protection to refugees as defined in the U.N. Convention: people who have crossed international boundaries because of a well-founded fear of persecution based on race, religion, national origin, political opinion or membership in a social group. In Africa and Latin America, UNHCR also assists people who flee to escape war, civil strife or political chaos. The agency coordinates assistance programs for other displaced persons in accordance with specific U.N. General Assembly resolutions.

In 1994, UNHCR provided aid and protection to 23 million people in 143 countries, including 16.4 million refugees, as well as some 3.6 million internally displaced people. More than 20 million additional internally displaced people do not receive assistance from UNHCR because they are not recognized as refugees, although they have fled their homes under similar circumstances.

As of 1994, the countries hosting the largest UNHCR assisted populations were Bosnia-Herzegovina (2.7 million), Iran (2.5 million), Pakistan (1.5 million) and Zaire (1.1 million). Governments and other donors contributed $1.19 billion to UNHCR in 1993 and $1.2 billion in 1994. An unprecedented number of new emergencies, notably in the Transcaucasus, Central Asia and parts of Africa, have stretched UNHCR's capacity.

UNHCR has sponsored major repatriations in recent years: to Afghanistan, Cambodia, Ethiopia, Burma, Mozambique and Somalia. Critics charge that some of these repatriations have not been completely voluntary and that UNHCR has not used the most effective approaches to rehabilitation. There is a need for greater coordination in these cases between UNHCR and other U.N. development agencies, particularly the U.N. Development Programme (UNDP) and the World Bank, and with NGOs.

U.N. Children's Fund (UNICEF)

Established in 1946 to assist children of war in Europe, UNICEF has since expanded its role under leaders like the late James Grant to meet the needs of poor children in the developing world. It supports programs during crises and post-crisis periods in nutrition, primary health care, water and sanitation, education and the environment.

World Food Programme (WFP)

The food aid organization of the United Nations, founded in 1963, coordinates food aid deliveries and assists bilateral donors in procuring and transporting food. It operates on the principle that food for humanitarian assistance must over time become food for development, and this must be followed by self-sustaining food production in times of peace. In 1994, WFP benefitted 57 million people, including 32 million affected by natural and human-made disasters. WFP works closely with UNHCR and NGOs.

United Nations Development Programme (UNDP)

UNDP provides technical assistance for development. Its country resident representative is usually coordinator of all U.N. activities, including emergency assistance and post-crisis reconstruction. Gus Speth, administrator of UNDP, wants to transform the agency into a U.N. Sustainable Human Development Program.

Nongovernmental Organizations (NGOs)

NGOs depend on contributions from private donors, and many also receive funds from governments and international organizations. The spectrum of NGOs includes grassroots people's organizations, broad social movements, faith-based service organizations, sector-based technical groups, and global, regional and national coordinating umbrella organizations. Sometimes governments create quasi-governmental NGOs.

Many people's organizations and local NGOs are active in emergency situations. In Bangladesh, for example, the Bangladesh Rural Advancement Committee, which works with local communities on development projects, began primarily as a disaster relief organization. The Grameen Bank, another Bangladeshi NGO, provides credit to groups of very poor people (mainly women) to begin small businesses, and also mobilizes its network for relief and rehabilitation activities.

National relief and development NGOs such as those associated with councils of churches in Tanzania, Sudan, India (through the Churches' Auxiliary for Social Action), Lebanon, Armenia and Serbia have shown considerable insight in managing crises. In Nicaragua and Guatemala, the evangelical Protestant churches have been active in conflict resolution efforts and reintegration of returning refugees. In east Africa, the All Africa Council of Churches, the Association of Member Episcopal Churches in East Africa and the Nairobi Peace Initiatives, with support from Lutheran World Relief, have urged African churches to become leaders in peacemaking, reconciliation and social change.

The American Council for Voluntary International Action (InterAction), the main association of U.S. relief and development NGOs, maintains a Disaster and Emergency Relief Committee (see list below), made up of member agencies active in service delivery and crisis-related policy analysis and advocacy. InterAction has encouraged its members to adopt ethical and professional standards, and has encouraged efforts to link relief and

development activities. A number of the members of the committee are U.S. affiliates of international NGO networks, e.g., Adventist Development and Relief Agency, CARE, Catholic Relief Services, Doctors of the World, International Action Against Hunger, Médecins sans Frontières, Oxfam, Save the Children and World Vision.

Several U.S. NGOs that do not belong to InterAction are active in crisis response, including the Mennonite Central Committee.

Well-established agencies such as those discussed here generally do effective work and use financial contributions carefully. An agency affiliated with a religious denomination generally has a board of directors comprised of trusted denominational leaders who oversee its work. Private donors need to be more cautious about new agencies that spring up and solicit charitable contributions.

Other well-known international NGOs active in crisis response include Christian Aid and ACTION AID in the United Kingdom; Trocaire and Concern in Ireland; a number of Japanese NGOs, which have increasingly focused on refugee issues since a Japanese national became U.N. High Commissioner for Refugees; Norwegian and Danish Church Aid; Dutch Inter-Church Aid; Norwegian People's Aid; Diakonische Werk of Germany and the Lutheran World Federation. EuronAid is a European NGO association that cooperates with the European Union's Commission in programming and procuring food aid for NGOs for both emergency and development purposes.

Red Cross and Red Crescent Movement

The International Committee of the Red Cross is an independent Swiss agency with the internationally recognized role of humanitarian intermediary between belligerents

during armed conflicts. It monitors governments' compliance with the 1949 Geneva Convention establishing the rules of war, including the treatment of civilian populations. It protects and assists the victims of international and civil wars, and provides medical aid, relief supplies, tracking and information services related to prisoners of war and missing persons. The International Federation of Red Cross and Red Crescent Societies, also based in Switzerland, coordinates relief operations of 163 national societies.

National Governments

Some developing country governments have established highly effective emergency response systems of their own. India has developed policies and institutions that have done away with famines within its borders. In the 1970s, Ethiopia established a Relief and Rehabilitation Commission to cope with periodic droughts. The current governing parties in Ethiopia and Eritrea created effective, grassroots-oriented relief agencies when they were engaged in armed struggle against the Mengistu dictatorship in Ethiopia. In the case of Eritrea, the agency has now become a formal government institution.

Neighbor and donor governments play crucial roles in facilitating aid to victims of conflict. India, during Bangladesh's 1971 war of independence; Jordan and Turkey, during the 1991 Gulf crisis, and Tanzania during the 1994 to 1995 Rwandan crisis; have all received and protected millions of refugees. Industrial country governments, along with the European Union (through its European Community Humanitarian Office), provide emergency and development aid to zones of conflict in the form of financial, food, material and technical assistance.

USAID's Bureau for Humanitarian Response provides food and other humanitarian aid. It assisted over 60 million people in fiscal year (FY) 1993, at a cost of $819 million. In addition to providing food and other relief supplies, programs focus on disaster prevention, mitigation and preparedness. In FY 1995, the bureau spent $20 million on its "Transition Initiative," helping countries emerging from disaster move into long-term development activities. The bureau implements most of its disaster assistance and emergency food aid programs through NGOs; it also provides commodities to WFP.

Other U.S. government agencies involved in crisis assistance include the Department of Defense, which has become increasingly involved in delivering, distributing and protecting relief supplies in the 1990s, and the State Department, which provides assistance to refugees.

InterAction Disaster and Emergency Relief Committee Members

Academy for Educational Development
Adventist Development and Relief Agency International
African-American Institute
African Medical and Research Foundation
Africare
AICF/USA International Action Against Hunger
Air Serv International
American Friends Service Committee
American Jewish Joint Distribution Committee
American Jewish World Service
American Near East Refugee Aid
American Red Cross International Services
American Refugee Committee
Ananda Marga Universal Relief Team
Baptist World Alliance (Baptist World Aid)
CARE
Catholic Medical Mission Board
Catholic Relief Services
Center for International Health and Cooperation
Child Health Foundation
Children's Survival Fund
Christian Children's Fund
Christian Reformed World Relief Committee
Church World Service
Council of Jewish Federations
Counterpart Foundation
Debt-for-Development Coalition
Direct Relief International
Doctors of the World USA
Episcopal Church of the USA, Presiding Bishop's Fund for World Relief
Eritrean Relief and Rehabilitation Agency USA
Food for the Hungry
Friends of Liberia
Fund for Democracy and Development
Grassroots International
Helen Keller International
International Aid
International Executive Service Corps
International Eye Foundation
International Medical Corps
International Medical Services for Health
International Orthodox Christian Charities
International Rescue Committee
Islamic African Relief Agency USA
Lutheran World Relief
MAP International
Médecins sans Frontières USA (Doctors Without Borders, USA)
Medical Care Development
Mercy Corps International
National Council of Negro Women
Operation USA
Oxfam America
Pan American Development Foundation
Partners of the Americas
Refugees International
Salvation Army World Service Office
Save the Children
Service and Development Agency
Southeast Asia Resource Action Center
United Methodist Committee on Relief
U.S. Catholic Conference, Migration and Refugee Services
U.S. Committee for UNICEF
Volunteers in Technical Assistance
World Concern
World Relief
World Vision
Young Men's Christian Association of the USA

Lessons from Experience

Lessons from responding to natural disasters and from several decades of development efforts can help inform attempts to respond to complex emergencies after civil strife has erupted, while also working toward longer-term goals of averting future crises.

Learning from Natural Disaster Relief

Famines that result primarily from natural causes require quick and appropriate provision of food, water, shelter and medical aid, usually with the cooperation of the local government.

The lessons of the famines in west Africa in the early 1970s and in east Africa from 1984 to 1986 led international relief agencies to bolster their early warning and response capacities. As a result, the enormous 1992 crop failure in east and southern Africa, from Namibia to Kenya, did not cost millions of lives. In fact, no starvation was reported, as local communities, aid donors and African governments effectively coordinated their response to warnings of famine.

Similarly, in 1994, the poor Ethiopian harvest led to predictions of record levels of starvation, absent external assistance. Again, a timely aid response and effective use of local capacities avoided preventable deaths. Surveillance systems established in Mozambique, Angola and west Africa continue to monitor disease, malnutrition and mortality rates and provide early warning of acute crises.

Parallel early warning systems to monitor social and political tensions that might escalate into violent conflict are in their infancy. For example, Save the Children Fund-UK is developing a computer program to analyze the impact of a variety of factors (including, at least potentially, conflict) on rural livelihoods. Relevant work is also underway at the Center for International Development and Conflict Management at the University of Maryland. In addition, both DHA and government relief agencies could benefit from the human rights monitoring being developed by several NGOs and the new Office of the U.N. High Commissioner for Human Rights.

Relief agencies have also learned from natural disasters that they can help in some instances even when they are unable to deliver food directly to people most in need – by selling food on the market during emergencies, they can bring the price down for everyone and use the local currency from these sales to pay for relief or development work. Led by the U.N. World Food Programme (WFP) and CARE, many agencies used food aid in this way during the latter stages of the Somalia crisis, making food more affordable for people who could not be reached directly.[3]

Learning from Development Efforts

Since the end of World War II, much international aid in support of development promoted economic growth, assuming that higher average incomes could solve many social ills. But decades of experience have led many to urge that the goal instead become "sustainable development." Bread for the World Institute defines sustainable development as reducing poverty and hunger in environmentally sound ways through four closely linked objectives:

- Expanding economic opportunities, especially for poor people, to increase productivity, earning capacity, and chances to earn income in ways that are environmentally, economically and socially viable over the long term;
- Meeting basic human needs for food, clean water, shelter, health care, education and opportunity to fulfill the human spirit;

- Protecting and enhancing the natural environment by managing natural resources in ways that take into account the needs of present and future generations; and
- Promoting pluralism and democratic participation, especially by poor people, in economic and political decisions that affect their lives, with full respect for internationally recognized human rights.

Each objective has direct relevance in responding to humanitarian emergencies. Relief efforts should not undercut, and will hopefully contribute to, sustainable development.

Two other relevant concepts emerging from development and natural disaster efforts are food security and livelihood security. Timothy Frankenberger of CARE defines livelihood security as the ability of a household to meet all of its basic needs – food, water, sanitation, shelter, health care, education – without making tradeoffs.[4] Food security – assured access for everyone to enough nutritious food to sustain productive human life – is a subset of livelihood security, and often of more immediate concern in crisis situations. But in the rush to feed hungry people, other basic needs should also be kept in mind and addressed, as possible.

Experience from responding to natural disasters or development efforts cannot always be transferred to complex humanitarian emergencies. Frequently, one or more parties to the conflict is not open to outside assistance, for example, and such emergencies are usually of uncertain duration, rather than only until the next harvest.

Coping with Complexity

Humanitarian Intervention: Evolving Law & Practice

People affected by civil strife have the right to protection, and material or financial assistance. They also have the right to be heard. Their needs and opinions, whether expressed directly or through advocates, should be carefully weighed.

At the same time, nation-states ardently defend their sovereignty. Sovereignty can help foster human rights and well-being, as when a state resists invasion, or prevents outside forces such as multinational companies from subjecting citizens to exploitative working conditions, unregulated pollution or hazardous products. But sovereignty can also be invoked to cover offenses of a government against its own citizens, or to stifle legitimate grievances against the government.

Getting assistance to people affected by crisis depends on the willingness of warring nations and parties to adhere to humanitarian principles. During civil wars, reaching an affected population with relief supplies often becomes an international legal issue when governments assert national sovereignty. Sudan's government, for example, has used its position as a nation-state and member of the United Nations to limit aid to southern Sudan. NGOs often work in rebel-controlled areas via neighboring countries, particularly in the Horn of Africa.

DHA is leading an effort to develop a code of conduct for international and indigenous relief practitioners. Progress is slow, mainly because many U.N. member-states see this as a challenge to their authority.

Because the United Nations is a voluntary association of states, its charter prohibits states from using force unilaterally against each other – even to further humanitarian purposes – and guarantees their territorial integrity. The U.N. Security Council may authorize the use of force only when there is a threat to international peace, an act of aggression or a human disaster that national and regional organizations cannot handle. But these are exceptions to a general right of national sovereignty. In addition, each of the five permanent council members – the United States, Russia, France, the United Kingdom and China – has veto power.

Nevertheless, consensus is emerging that the international community may intervene to provide humanitarian assistance and defend human rights, regardless of the objections of the affected state.

In recent years, humanitarian issues have often taken center stage at the United Nations (as well as in U.S. and other national foreign policy debates) – as, for example, in the cases of Iraq, Somalia, Bosnia and Haiti. In December 1988, the U.N. General Assembly adopted a resolution on "humanitarian assistance to victims of natural disasters and similar situations." Two years later, another resolution proposed consideration of relief corridors to facilitate access to victims. Then, in April 1991, the Security Council authorized protection of the Iraqi Kurds, allowing unprecedented "intervention in the internal affairs of a State." In January 1992, the council similarly authorized intervention in Somalia.

Unilateral intervention might, in some cases, be feasible. But even the most altruistic humanitarian intervention will be colored by the national, political and economic interests of the intervening country. Hence, a strong preference for international intervention, or at least multilateral action, appears to be emerging as a corollary to the right or duty of the international community to intervene on behalf of endangered communities.

Often, NGOs or even concerned individuals can complement the humanitarian actions of governments or international organizations. At other times, they can step in when governments can no longer cope, are frozen by political considerations or are a party in a conflict. NGOs are sometimes freer than governments to listen directly to people in distress and bring important counsel to public debates. But they must also remain aware of their own biases.

Use of Military Forces in Crisis Response

Some emergencies are of such scale or immediacy that only an already organized, disciplined structure such as a military force may be able to protect and assist people affected by crisis in a timely manner – as in the case of Operation Provide Comfort, when allied combat soldiers established a safe haven for Kurdish refugees in northern Iraq in 1991 (see "Providing Comfort?," p. 28).

In other situations, including Somalia and Bosnia, the intransigence of one or all warring parties, often coupled with the breakdown of government or deliberate policies of starving large populations, may make relief aid almost impossible without military protection. In other instances, a military force may actually deliver relief aid, as in Iraqi Kurdistan, for safety reasons, or Rwandan refugee camps in Zaire, for logistical reasons.

Military intervention for humanitarian purposes raises both practical and ethical issues. One set of practical questions centers around the strength of national and international commitment, the increasingly low tolerance for risk of casualties among donor nations' forces and the conditions that accompany withdrawal of the forces. In Somalia, Bosnia and Iraqi Kurdistan, getting in seems to have been much easier than getting out.

Many humanitarian emergencies cry out for diplomacy and mediation. Using the military to "force" delivery of relief assistance may complicate conciliation efforts. If military personnel take part in negotiations, additional skills and training are required. Such training is now being provided in Austria, the United States and elsewhere.

Military-backed intervention also raises ethical issues. The main mission of any military force is

The response to the Kurdish emergency was massive, due to high public attention, and relatively timely, given the massive resources already deployed in the region. Large numbers of displaced Kurds had congregated in camps that lacked fresh water and sanitation systems. Donors airlifted food, so most of the excess deaths resulted from diarrheal disease related to contaminated water. Because the relief agencies, including the Office of the U.N. High Commissioner for Refugees and nongovernmental organizations (NGOs), worked in concert with U.S. and European military forces, the root cause of the emergency – Iraqi aggression – was addressed forcefully at the same time that the Kurds returned home. Within a few weeks, over a million uprooted persons were assisted and resettled.

Iraqi Kurds still receive allied protection, but security and development issues remain. The Turkish government is fearful that Kurdish autonomy in Iraq will inspire Turkish Kurds to seek independence, and in March 1995 intervened with 35,000 troops.

U.N. sanctions, which prohibit items other than food and medicine from entering Iraq, are hindering the attempts of the 3.4 million Iraqi Kurds to reconstruct their villages. Baghdad's internal embargo worsens the situation. Revenue of the Iraqi Kurds' autonomous government, raised mainly by taxing trucks crossing the Turkish border, has dropped by one-third. The autonomous government has extreme difficulty paying its 200,000 employees and obtaining spare parts for factories and power plants. With kerosene too expensive for most people and international relief supplies too slow in arriving, most of the few trees that survived Iraq's scorched earth policy have been cut for firewood. Shortages of fertilizers, pesticides and diesel fuel frustrate Kurdish efforts to restore food self-sufficiency.

NGOs such as OXFAM (UK and Ireland), Caritas and Evangelical Shelter, as well as medical organizations, are providing people with minimal help to rebuild their homes, cultivate crops and start small poultry farms. The Kurds now need relief from the embargoes rather than emergency relief aid, so they can establish a viable economy and remain in their communities.

not to provide relief, but to prevail – killing or overrunning human rights if necessary. A military presence may also raise serious questions about the neutrality of humanitarian agencies that work with military forces.

Nevertheless, using military forces may be the only choice at times to contain hunger and disease, create and protect safe havens for affected civilians, provide logistical support, and protect relief workers and supplies. Military force can indeed facilitate the restoration of peace and social order, as in the case of U.S.-U.N. intervention in Haiti.

Military force for humanitarian assistance should always be authorized by the U.N. Security Council or another international body. To the extent possible, the force should be neutral with respect to the conflict at hand, multinational in make-up and utilized as part of a clear and comprehensive strategy of crisis response.

U.N. Secretary General Boutros Boutros-Ghali has pressed member states to place military forces permanently on call for U.N. duty and to create a permanent U.N. rapid deployment force. His suggestion is resisted by many government leaders, including many in the United States, who are unwilling to place national forces under international control. The creation of such forces, as well as further refinement of the circumstances under which they would engage and withdraw, and their modes of operation, should remain a high priority on the international agenda.

Safe Passage and Cross-Border Arrangements

Increasingly, U.N. agencies and NGOs responding to complex emergencies face a dilemma. Long-term credibility depends in part on being seen as remaining neutral. In reality, they may have to negotiate with, and make concessions to, one or more of the parties to gain access to populations in need of assistance. In the Horn of Africa, Bosnia and Central America, safe passage arrangements and cross-border operations into rebel-held territory have assured continued humanitarian aid, with varying degrees of success.

In El Salvador, the agreement of government and rebel forces to "Days of Tranquillity," during which they permitted children in the conflict zones to be immunized at the behest of UNICEF, may have also served as a confidence-building measure in the peace process. Operation Lifeline Sudan, also arranged with the leadership of UNICEF, helped provide some respite to war, but was ultimately overrun by renewed fighting.[5]

The parties in Bosnia – especially rebel Serbs – have repeatedly refused to abide by ceasefires, respect U.N. protected zones or refrain from attacking relief workers and supplies.

Coordinating Assistance

A study by the Humanitarianism and War Project at Brown University found that while many U.N. officials involved in relief efforts during the 1990 to 1991 Persian Gulf crisis worked tirelessly to meet urgent humanitarian needs, the U.N. system failed to coordinate the response effectively. In general, emergency aid programs suffer because of the difficulties in finding a coordinator. Agencies require field staff to refer decisions on the smallest matters to headquarters.

The report recommends changes in the United Nations, particularly DHA, and in the operations of governments and NGOs. It calls for the United Nations and its agencies to delegate greater authority and responsibility to the field, and engage the governments of a region in crisis in emergency response. Finally, the report sees as critical the designation of a single individual in a given country or region, for the duration of a major emergency, to assure effective coordination and accountability.[6]

NGO aid during the Gulf crisis also suffered from lack of coordination. This was particularly evident in Iran, where the government had assigned

Coordination in Evacuating Foreign Workers from the Persian Gulf

The evacuation of 850,000 African and Asian migrant workers from the Persian Gulf during the 1990 to 1991 war offers valuable lessons in coordination, although the major work took place in Jordan, outside the actual conflict zone. Non-governmental organizations (NGOs), led by the Middle East Council of Churches (MECC), established a coordinating committee to facilitate an effective response to conditions of serious overcrowding, and food and water shortages in transit camps in Jordan. Whereas international agencies depended on outside resources, local NGOs had the potential, autonomy and flexibility to act immediately.

The United Nations drafted a contingency plan to meet the evacuees' shelter, food, medical and travel needs. The Jordanian government established a committee drawing together key officials from various ministries and NGOs. The government provided tents, food and other emergency items, while embassies and local mosques, churches and NGOs also donated food and other supplies.

Local NGOs organized an information control center, providing daily press briefings. They devised a unified plan, so each agency knew exactly what it was supposed to do. Some agencies with individual agendas backed out. The NGO coordination committee purchased tents from the Jordanian army on credit through a guarantee given by the MECC.

Local volunteers and able-bodied refugees erected 750 tents within 48 hours. UNICEF put water tanks in place. The government provided food, water and security. Save the Children and the International Rescue Committee set up latrines. The U.N. Disaster Relief Office and International Organization for Migration assumed the lead transportation role, while the European Community helped finance the flights. The whole operation functioned in a flexible manner with close contacts among the Jordanian government, other governments, U.N. agencies, local and foreign NGOs and the press.

Even though there was a surplus of trained doctors and health workers in Jordan at the time of the crisis, many international agencies preferred to bring in expensive expatriate doctors, sanitation engineers and nurses. Some were first-time recruits to emergency response. Outside personnel in emergencies should be limited to coordinators who are skilled in human relations, diplomacy and leadership. Expatriates should include not just Westerners, but qualified people from other developing countries.

This case demonstrates the critical role that local and regional organizations can play, as well as the importance of involving affected people themselves in forging solutions to crises. The appropriate response is often not possible through existing international humanitarian structures.

coordinating responsibilities for NGO activities to the Red Crescent Society. Inundated with private relief agencies and material, however, the Society soon lost control of the situation. NGOs went their own ways, establishing access to regional and local government officials and proceeding directly to refugee camps.

Humanitarian aid agencies continue to struggle to better share information and work cooperatively. In some crises, few agencies respond at all. In others, they focus on high-visibility population centers to the detriment of remote, rural and pastoralist groups. And with all the experience in the world, most humanitarian agencies still have not adopted a policy of distributing can openers with canned food.

With each agency following its own interests, the collective humanitarian community is well-endowed with groups that specialize in flying physicians and journalists into crises, or in distributing food, water and medicine. Few organizations emphasize preventive health systems, environmental health, sanitation engineers, water systems, response to psychological trauma or protecting women from violence.

Coherence Among Policies

Donor country policies often work at cross purposes and undercut humanitarian responses.

Selection of food aid commodities, for example, may reflect the state of surpluses in the United States more than the food needs of Africa. The history of food aid is filled with examples of food commodities handled in ways that undercut local farmers. European countries and especially Japan are more inclined to support food aid programs that purchase commodities near the point of need. WFP purchases of Ugandan grain for Sudanese refugees gave a substantial boost to Ugandan agriculture (see below).

Over the longer term, asymmetrical trade policies in agricultural commodities may both contribute to crises, and delay recovery when emergencies subside. The industrial countries – particularly Europe and the United States – have subsidized their farmers. Part of the resulting surplus is "dumped" on world markets in ways that undercut food production in poor countries. At the same time, industrial countries have opposed price stabilization programs, which might have assisted growers of tropical crops – sugar, tropical oil crops, coffee and tea. Sharply lower coffee prices contributed to Rwanda's difficulties. Other agreements – the multi-fiber agreement, for example – have protected industrial country markets from imports of labor-intensive manufactured products.

The five permanent members of the U.N. Security Council – the nations that the U.N. Charter designates as guarantors of world peace – account for more than 80 percent of the world's arms exports. As Oxfam has pointed out:

These weapons have wrought human destruction on a massive scale. From time to time they have also been used against U.N. troops, or on soldiers from the supplying country, as they were during the Gulf War and in Somalia. Apart from destroying human lives, arms exports have reinforced the underlying causes of conflict by diverting resources from development. Developing countries now account for 15 percent of world military spending, or $188 billion annually.[7]

Developing countries currently account for two-thirds of global arms imports.

Uses and Limitations of Emergency Food Aid

In a number of recent emergencies, food aid has temporarily helped sustain the affected people. In Bosnia and Sri Lanka (see pp. 32-34), food aid has allowed large populations to maintain relative food security in the midst of crisis. In some instances, food aid has played a role in creative efforts to promote livelihood security. However, food aid alone is not a long-term solution to either crisis or the uprooting of civilian populations.

Food Aid Prevents Deaths in Bosnia

Large quantities of food aid from WFP and other donor agencies since 1992 have prevented starvation in Bosnia-Herzegovina. Almost half of all European humanitarian assistance in 1994 was directed to Bosnia. An international airlift has brought food, at great expense, to enclaves such as Sarajevo for over 1,000 days. In many places, such as Bihac, food aid is the only source of food, and many people would die quickly without it. In addition to food aid, urban Bosnians obtain food from such sources as gardens and hoarded food stocks. Civilian deaths have resulted from shelling and shooting rather than starvation.

Problems with food aid delivery stem primarily from the security situation. Serb forces often hold up U.N. convoys as part of their overall strategy. Warring parties have also occasionally hijacked food aid shipments, or demanded a substantial share for safe passage or protection.

Building on limited openings for food relief, U.N. agencies (led by UNHCR) and NGOs have also tried to provide water, sanitation, security, shelter, personal protection, health care (including immunizations) and child care. The International Rescue Committee has created women's groups to discuss the ravages of psychological trauma resulting from rape, murder and pillage. U.N. assistance has included peacekeeping protection and human rights monitoring, and the success of relief efforts has depended upon the political and security situation, which deteriorated drastically in 1995.

Engaging Refugees in Creating Food Security in Uganda

WFP's large refugee food aid program in northern Uganda is part of an even larger U.N. effort to respond to the crisis in Sudan. Over 300,000 Sudanese refugees in Uganda depend on food aid. WFP's Uganda program is unusual in that most of the food is produced and procured within Uganda.

Traveling mainly as intact families, Sudanese come to Uganda with very few possessions, little of their livestock and no cash. While recent incidents and conflicts have exacerbated their situation in Sudan, few decide to flee to Uganda abruptly. Most expect to remain for some time. The Ugandan government has welcomed the refugees, arranging timely assistance and generous asylum, largely out of reciprocity for earlier hospitality shown by Sudanese during Uganda's civil strife.

In the refugee camps in Uganda, many Sudanese grow enough food to sell vegetables, seeds and root crops to other Sudanese. By specializing, they have re-created economies where fish, tools, clothes and services are readily available and traded. The camps are open. The refugees can grow food where land suffices, can build permanent structures and can participate in local labor markets. Refugees can travel, inter-marry and take advantage of local markets relatively freely.

While lacking infrastructure, Uganda became relatively stable in 1987, after 15 years of conflict. At the time of the refugee influx, Uganda's agricultural sector was growing strongly. Since 1993, Ugandans have grown food provided to crisis-affected people in or from Somalia, Kenya, Ethiopia, Sudan, Rwanda, Burundi and Zaire. But food aid needs for the region are still great. Refugees must continue to be encouraged to help meet their own and the region's food needs.

Coping with Hidden Hunger

Micronutrient needs can be met through proper selection and fortification of food aid, as well as with supplements such as capsules and tablets. Field studies of emergency food aid find considerable variation among families' actual consumption, since swapping, barter, local purchases and local production take place. The implication is that planners cannot or should not depend on any single food to carry micronutrients to people at risk or suffering from malnutrition. Some donors regularly fortify their food aid commodities. A greater variety of foods need to be fortified and given as part of emergency operations (see "Hidden Hunger in Emergencies," p. 12).

Low nutrient quality is less of a problem where the recipients can engage in food production. Household gardens were common among refugees from Chad in Darfur Province, Sudan during the drought of 1985 to 1986. Community vegetable gardens in Salvadoran refugee camps in Honduras provided fresh vegetables to entire camp populations in the late 1980s.

Limitations of Food Security From Food Aid

Too often the norm is that refugees do not cultivate gardens. There are numerous obstacles to self-reliance such as laws in many countries that deny refugees access to employment or land. In conditions of armed conflict, access to local markets is often difficult or impossible. Another problem is male control of food aid supplies in many cases (see "Put Refugee Women in Charge of Food Distribution," p. 35).

In any event, emergency food aid is not a sustainable basis for achieving food security. It does not restore the conditions of normal life for uprooted people. Like treating an infection with aspirin, it temporarily relieves the pain without addressing its causes.

Furthermore, the future of global food aid is uncertain. The new General Agreement on Tariffs and Trade promises gradually to reduce industrial country agricultural surpluses and subsidized exports. Despite pledges of expanded food aid made during the 1992 election campaign, the Clinton administration has drastically reduced non-emergency U.S. food aid tonnage over the past few years. Recently it cut by half the U.S. pledge (the world's largest) to the global Food Aid Convention (an international agreement assuring adequate food aid supplies). Greater scarcity of food aid makes efforts to achieve sustainable food security all the more important in countries facing complex emergencies.

Sri Lanka: Food Security During Conflict

by Jashinta D'Costa

Sri Lanka stands out not only for its high level of human development, but also for its strategies to cope with a prolonged civil war. Years of violence have constrained the growth of the economy and threaten future social development. However, a strong public social service network and substantial foreign food aid have prevented serious hunger.

Long-standing conflict in Sri Lanka is rooted in ethnic and religious differences. The principal protagonists are the Sinhalese and "Sri Lankan" Tamils. The Sinhalese are mostly Buddhists and make up 74 percent of the population. The long-term resident Sri Lankan Tamils live mainly in the north and east, account for 12 percent of the population, and are mostly Hindu and Christian. "Estate" or "Indian" Tamils (6 percent) in the central region, whose families were imported by British colonialists to work on the tea and coffee plantations, and "Moors", i.e., Tamil-speaking Muslims, are not directly involved in the conflict. Nor is the small community of "Burghers," i.e., Sri Lankans of European descent.

Policies favoring the Sinhala language over Tamil form the fault line of ethnic tension. Language is also an instrument for gaining political power. Another key aspect of the ethnic conflict is control of territory. A separatist movement claims the north and east as a Tamil homeland.[8]

Legislation enacted in 1956 made Sinhala the only official language and left most Tamils ineligible for government employment. Between 1955 and 1963, the share of Sinhalese and Tamils in the civil service changed from 66 percent and 30 percent to 92 percent and 7 percent, respectively.[9] This led to gross inequities in political and economic power.

Throughout the 1970s, both leftist and conservative governments continued to pursue policies that favored Sinhalese in employment, education and land ownership. The state-sponsored colonization scheme moved many Sinhalese settlers into predominantly Tamil areas. This caused fear among Tamils, who saw the government's purpose as altering the ethnic balance and diluting what local political power they had.

In 1971, a Sinhalese Maoist movement made up of unemployed youth, called Janata Vimukti Peramuna (People's Liberation Front or JVP), engaged in a violent struggle with the government. Thousands died, and the government jailed thousands of dissidents. Although the violence occurred within the Sinhalese community, it led to further discrimination against Tamils.

In 1978, the parliament banned the Liberation Tigers of Tamil Eelam (LTTE), a militant separatist group. Using special police powers, the government often violated the human rights of Tamils and dissident Sinhalese.

Between 1979 and 1983, the global recession lowered prices for Sri Lanka's principal exports. Economic decline intensified ethnic tensions. In 1981, a series of presidential decrees further restricted civil liberties and provoked a riot between Sinhalese and Tamils.

In July 1983, LTTE guerrillas killed 13 government soldiers in the northern town of Jaffna. This led to large-scale ethnic violence across the island and threw the nation into civil war. India's efforts to intervene and make peace in the late 1980s did not succeed. Renewed fighting between government forces and the JVP meant additional violence, uprooted people and destruction. Over the past 12 years, the combination of the government's indiscriminate bombing and LTTE terror tactics have cost 50,000 lives, displaced over 600,000 people and left thousands missing.

Impact of Ethnic Conflict

In 1960, Sri Lanka's per capita gross national product (GNP) was $141, substantially higher than that of Thailand ($96) and Indonesia ($51), about the same as Korea's ($156), and 50 percent lower than Malaysia's ($273). By 1992, Sri Lanka's per capita GNP had risen to $540, but other Asian economies had grown much faster. Per capita GNP was $6,790 in Korea, $2,790 in Malaysia, $1,840 in Thailand and $670 in Indonesia. Sri Lanka's weak growth performance is partly due to civil conflict.[10]

Since the outbreak of ethnic warfare in 1983, Sri Lanka has increased its military expenditure. Military spending was 1.5 percent of gross domestic product (GDP) in 1983. It peaked at 5.7 percent in 1986 and remained at 4.7 percent in 1992 (Figure 2.1). Increased military expenditure diverted resources from high priority development activities. The estimated cost of conflict over five years, from 1983 to 1988, was $4.2 billion, equivalent to 68 percent of 1988 GDP. This was three times the budget of the country's largest development project, the Mahaweli hydroelectric irrigation project, which has been slowed down by

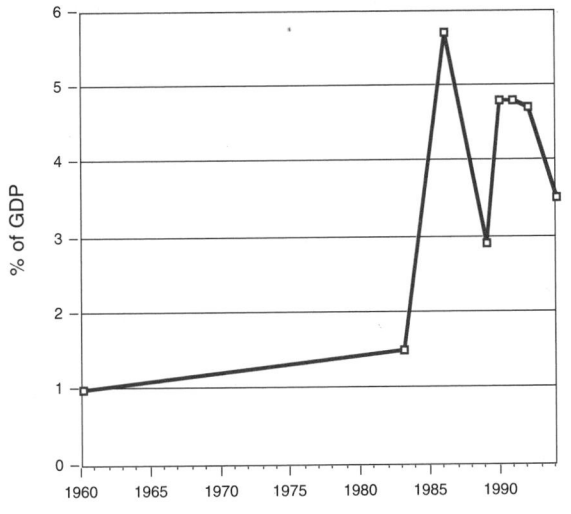

Figure 2.1
Military Expenditure As Share of GDP, Sri Lanka 1960-1994

Source: UNDP; U.S. Central Intelligience Agency.

resource constraints.[11] Increasing defense imports reduced non-military government spending and caused a trade deficit.

A dramatic decline in GDP growth, from 9.8 percent to 2.1 percent, occurred between 1985 and 1989, when the government was fighting both the LTTE and the JVP (Figure 2.2). The government was spending a million dollars a day on the military, according to its own estimates.[12]

Loss of human capital has also affected the economy. Between 1987 and 1994, more than 100,000 Sri Lankans, including an average of 750 per month during 1994, applied for asylum abroad, emigrated or went to live in other countries without documentation. Over 100,000 Sri Lankan refugees remain in India.

The Safety Net Threatened

Historically, the government has invested heavily in social welfare programs, including public health and education, and until 1977, substantial

food subsidies. As a result, the under-five mortality rate is lower and life expectancy is higher than in many wealthier countries. However, because of the conflict and austerity policies, social development expenditures increased just 0.6 percent from 1983 to 1992. The government depends on foreign aid for half of its revenues.

According to economist Amartya Sen, Sri Lanka's achievements in raising the quality of life are in danger of being overtaken by the violence and strife into which the country has plunged.[13] UNICEF has also warned that the impressive social service network is fast wearing thin.[14] Chandrika Kumaratunga, Sri Lanka's president, commented at the World Summit for Social Development in 1995, "High literacy coupled with high unemployment constitute a certain recipe for youth unrest and endemic insurgency, and this was the cross that Sri Lanka's human development strategy had to bear."[15]

A quarter of the population has fallen below the poverty line since the outbreak of the civil war.[16]

Conflict and Hunger

Despite growing economic hardship, no severe food crisis has occurred in Sri Lanka. In LTTE - controlled areas, hunger is reported mainly in the Jaffna Peninsula. The U.S. Committee for Refugees reports that in the Jaffna district, displaced pregnant mothers lack high protein food and many of their babies have low birthweights.[17] A government blockade of Jaffna has increased food prices threefold and

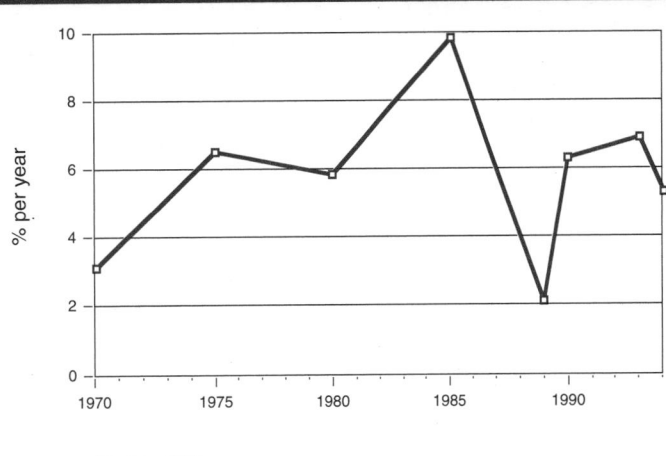

Figure 2.2
Sri Lankan GDP Growth, 1970-1994

Source: USDA.

raised the price of kerosene, the main cooking fuel. Also, displacement has left people dependent on food aid, which is not always nutritionally adequate. Finally, the LTTE leverages food to get political concessions, routinely confiscating about 30 percent of food shipments.

Inadequate water, sanitation and health facilities also contribute to malnutrition. In displaced persons camps, malaria has reappeared after decades. Health services in the Jaffna area have been completely ruined, and a recent polio and malaria epidemic affected at least 40,000 people.[18]

But at the national level, the Food and Agriculture Organization of the United Nations reports that food availability has not declined since the civil war began, despite falling domestic production.[19] In spite of 12 years of war, Sri Lanka has reported no cases of starvation. Public policies have made a difference for most Sri Lankans. The government's long-term emphasis on individual well-being has helped the country in general, and war-torn areas in particular, avoid widespread food insecurity. The government provides financial assistance and food aid to families and individuals displaced by the civil conflict in the north and east. There are many public welfare programs, and private nonprofit organizations also play a role in alleviating hunger.

According to the stated policy, the government is also supposed to provide necessary infrastructure (road repair and rebuilding of schools and other public buildings) and services (health care and education) to resettlement communities. But the government often cannot afford to provide all this.

Sri Lanka supports programs for displaced people mainly through foreign food aid, 84 percent of which comes from the United States. The country is one of the largest recipients of food aid in South Asia. Between 1989 and 1994, the government and donors signed agreements to fund $395.6 million worth of emergency relief projects.[20]

The Prospects for Peace

Peace in Sri Lanka seems elusive. While a series of political developments in 1994 and early 1995 raised hopes for a negotiated settlement, fighting flared up again in April 1995.

Kumaratunga won election as a peace candidate, and in January 1995, her government and the LTTE signed a cease-fire agreement, including an $800 million rehabilitation plan for the Jaffna area.[21] The government partially lifted the embargo. However, negotiators and government officials cautioned that the cease-fire could not end the war because "it does not address the most contentious issue of the conflict: the . . . Tamil demand for political autonomy in northern and eastern Sri Lanka."[22] Indeed, it was the Tigers who broke the fragile peace.

Following the renewal of hostilities, the government reimposed the embargo and launched an intense assault against the LTTE. By July 1995, the fighting had displaced another 300,000 people in the north.[23]

Conclusion

The Sri Lankan case shows how a stable social service framework can reduce the degree of human suffering even in the midst of civil war. Continuing failure to solve the conflict could well undermine that framework. Resolving the conflict depends on the government recognizing that the country is multi-ethnic and according the Tamils some measure of political, cultural and language autonomy. A solution also hinges on the LTTE renouncing violence. Aid donors need to encourage negotiations toward an equitable peace, rather than just continuing to provide food and money. Despite these problems, Sri Lanka's experience offers many positive lessons for reducing the hunger impact of crises elsewhere.

Jashinta D'Costa is a Bread for the World Institute intern.

Integrating Relief and Development

Emergencies cost human lives and resources. They disrupt development. They demand a long period of rehabilitation. They often spawn bureaucratic structures, lines of communication and organizational cultures that duplicate and sometimes cut across development institutions. By the same token,

development policy and administration have often focused on economic growth or technical improvements; they remain insensitive to the social or political inequities from which civil strife arises, and the variety of risks that vulnerable households face. Linking relief and development can overcome these deficiencies.

In complex emergencies, aid is often imperative to restore some semblance of secure livelihoods – assuring food, water, shelter and medical care. But emergency relief, if not linked fairly quickly to long-term development efforts, can lead to dependence for the affected communities. For aid donors, long-term relief demands can lead to "compassion fatigue."

The transition to development must include setting goals to rebuild damaged physical and social infrastructure, restore human capital, reconstruct institutions, and reinstate social and cultural ethics and values. People's hopes and dreams must be restored, as was done in Europe and Japan after World War II. Indeed, many contemporary development agencies began as emergency response organizations, including many NGOs, the assistance agencies of national governments, several of the U.N. agencies and the World Bank (formally named The International Bank for Reconstruction and Development).

The Institute of Development Studies (IDS) at the University of Sussex in the United Kingdom has recently published policy recommendations related

Put Refugee Women in Charge of Food Distribution
by Roberta Cohen[24]

International organizations and governments hosting refugees usually make decisions about food distribution without adequately consulting refugee women. Women and their dependent children represent 75 percent to 80 percent of the world's refugee population.

When agencies consult refugees, they usually talk with men. Men come forward during emergencies and assume leadership roles in the distribution of food and supplies. Refugee women are routinely ignored, even though they may represent the majority of the camp population and may have played a leading role in their home countries in the production and handling of food.

The consequences of distributing food and supplies through male committees or male elders can be serious for women. Sometimes, the food is sold on the black market or diverted to the military. Sexual favors may be expected from single women and women heads of households in exchange for food.

High malnutrition and death rates among refugee women have repeatedly been traced to distribution systems in which they have no say. Refugee women and children in Mexico in the late 1980s experienced high rates of malnutrition. In Pakistan, women refugees have high rates of anemia. Inequitable systems of food distribution in both places may have played a role.

In Kenya, in early 1992, food distribution policies were largely to blame for the high overall death rates reported in one of the camps. Food was distributed through clan elders, who diverted some of it for sale on the black market and to feed those fighting in Somalia.

Similar problems have arisen when male leaders have sole responsibility for distributing non-food supplies. In Ethiopia, in 1993, plastic sheeting to cover shelters during the rainy season hardly reached female heads of households in one of the large refugee camps. In Kenya, in 1991, a needs assessment of refugee women found that female-headed households were sometimes ignored altogether when supplies were distributed through men.

When refugee women have been given the lead role in food distribution, distribution is more equitable for the entire refugee community. In camps along the Thai-Cambodian border, the provision of rations to women and girls reduced the diversion of food to the military. In Malawi, when women became involved in distribution, complaints from refugee women about being forced to give sexual favors or money in exchange for food largely ended. In Kakuma camp in Kenya, Sudanese refugee women have managed food distribution so effectively that it now runs on an honor system. In southern Africa, women refugees have increasingly been used as food distributors because it was found that they are more aware of the need for distributing food fairly.

Recently, a report of a Working Group of UNHCR's Executive Committee recommended that the agency attempt "on an experimental basis" to place food distribution in the hands of women in one of its new operations and then evaluate the impact. But this does not go far enough or take into account the findings of earlier studies. UNHCR's own Guidelines on the Protection of Refugee Women, adopted in 1991, recommend that refugee women be the initial point of control for the distribution of food and basic supplies.

Limited concepts of women's abilities as well as cultural tendencies among the refugees regularly keep refugee women out of camp management. The participation of refugee women in decision-making and the administration of assistance programs should become a routine feature of refugee life.

Roberta Cohen, senior fellow at the Refugee Policy Group, was deputy assistant secretary of state for Human Rights and Humanitarian Affairs during the Carter administration.

to the relief-to-development continuum. These include the adoption of disaster preparedness plans, which will provide local governments with resources and skills that can keep problems from turning into crises. Relief operations should, when possible, move fairly quickly to an emphasis on recovery, through such activities as helping people restore assets and livelihoods, and food-for-work and other job creation projects that rebuild infrastructure, repair roads, plant trees, develop irrigation and conserve the soil.

In northern Ethiopia and in Eritrea, donors provided food aid through local NGOs. This helped build local capacity, and proved helpful for carrying out post-conflict rehabilitation. IDS notes that this is a two-way street: community development projects likewise create structures that can facilitate relief activities[25] (see "Guatemala," p. 37).

Interventions should focus on maintaining communities and the activities of everyday life, if the security situation allows – even at some risk. If people leave their homes for feeding camps, the process of rehabilitation and reconstruction becomes more difficult, especially if the conflict goes on a long time. But even in camp situations, people should have opportunities to grow food, earn income and obtain education and training. Above all, people should be encouraged to take control of their lives and communities (see "Put Refugee Women in Charge of Food Distribution," p. 35).

The relief community has come to recognize that education can contribute to peacemaking as well as provide skills for reconstruction. The U.N. Educational, Scientific and Cultural Organization (UNESCO), in collaboration with Rapid Ed, a coalition effort that includes the Academy for Educational Development, has sponsored a youth education program in Rwanda. UNESCO provided training and Teacher Emergency Packages to 11,000 teachers. These "schools in a box" contain basic school materials and teacher guides. They aided instruction of over half a million children in Rwanda and in refugee camps in neighboring countries.

Maintaining intact families is another aspect of linking relief and development. Food for the Hungry International, a U.S.-based NGO, has developed a program, Children Within Natural Social Systems, to keep families together during emergencies. It provides support to uprooted families so they do not have to abandon their children, and works with unaccompanied children so they do not have to go into orphanages.

Responding to Africa's Crises

Lately, relief and development agencies have focused on linking relief and development in Africa, especially the Horn. One key is expanding food production among small-scale farmers, who in Africa are mostly women. That makes food available to people affected by conflict and also reduces rural poverty. To expand food production among small-scale farmers, rural families displaced during complex emergencies need to be resettled on their land.

Declining soil fertility, water shortages and lack of fertilizer may present obstacles. Aid donors have pressed many African governments to abolish fertilizer subsidies in order to balance their budgets. Such policies must be reviewed. Terminating food aid before people have access to land, water, seeds and fertilizer will greatly increase food insecurity.

According to the findings of the U.S. presidential delegation that visited the Greater Horn of Africa in 1994, recurrent strife, drought and food shortages have the potential to create a human crisis of unthinkable proportions. Drought conditions threaten all the countries in the Greater Horn: Burundi, Djibouti, Eritrea, Ethiopia, Kenya, Rwanda, Somalia, Sudan, Tanzania and Uganda. While the bloodshed in Rwanda commands the headlines, civil conflict also continues in Somalia, Sudan, Kenya and Burundi. Approximately 320 million people are at risk.[26]

There is an urgent need for comprehensive strategies of relief and development in the Horn of Africa. Issues such as failed states; lack of trust among governments; tribal, clan and religious differences; and poor governance all need diplomatic attention. Long-term issues persist. These include chronic food insecurity due to inappropriate policies and production technologies, environmental degradation, recurring drought, pestilence and poor infrastructure. They also include population growth, high child mortality rates and high incidence of HIV/AIDS, measles and malaria.

Moving from relief to development in the Horn will require institutional changes – secure land systems; organizing small-farmer-oriented credit systems; policies that favor rural poor people; investments to provide fertilizer at affordable prices; the development of roads, markets and storage; extension services; schools and adult education.

Africa can only achieve food security with greater government support for agriculture. Without this, the efforts of the World Bank, other international donors, a strengthened NGO movement and rural people themselves will fail.

Guatemala faces the worst child malnutrition problem in Latin America, caused in part by 34 years of internal conflict. The areas most affected by conflict have the heaviest populations of indigenous people and the highest poverty and child mortality rates. Food security has been elusive, even given recent international intervention and mediation efforts that led to refugee repatriation and creation of a *Zona Paz* (Peace Zone).

According to the U.S. Agency for International Development, "The country is characterized by a very uneven distribution of both land and income; more than half of the population lives in extreme poverty at the margin of the 'money' economy." Food insecurity is especially severe in the highland areas of the Peace Zone.

Guatemalan women are the primary caretakers and often are required to work outside the home. Lacking opportunities to participate in economically productive activities, women have not been able to fully develop and use their talents. This contributes to food insecurity at the household level. This problem is intensified by traditional family feeding patterns that provide food to men and older male children before infants and mothers.

The vast majority of rural poor people is involved in agriculture. But productivity is limited by inadequate institutions and knowledge for marketing and credit. Violence and the uprooting of communities have also hurt agricultural production, communities' access to markets and distribution systems. Harvests have been lost when farmers were forced to abandon their fields or gave up planting due to insecurity.

The years of conflict severely affected children. Many were abandoned or left in the care of women without resources and whose husbands had "disappeared."

World SHARE began development work in Guatemala in 1987. Initially it operated with a few cooperating institutions in Guatemala City. SHARE was constrained from working in the rural areas where poverty and malnutrition were worst. These areas, then known as the "Conflict Zone," were dangerous. Migration and unstable communities precluded long-term development projects. Occasional relief efforts, in times of flooding, for example, were all that was possible.

A huge shift occurred in the late 1980s and early 1990s, as international intervention set in motion mediation, repatriation and a peace process. The United Nations, Lutheran World Federation and the Guatemalan Catholic hierarchy played key roles, as did many Guatemalan grassroots groups.

By 1993, SHARE had developed a network of small organizations to address food security in the most impoverished rural areas and involve local communities in program design and implementation. SHARE currently works with 40 local NGOs. Programs include maternal/child health, infrastructure development, agriculture, income generation, credit and community organizing. In the absence of violence, communities can again have the trust and confidence to work with the growing number of NGOs and build on their own self-organization and competence.

Elisa Sabatini is World SHARE's regional director for Latin America.

Above all, it is important to remember that there are grounds for hope in Africa. As USAID Administrator J. Brian Atwood has said, "For every tragedy, there are half a dozen islands of hope. Progress is still tentative, often fragile. Which is precisely why we must not hesitate now."[27]

For every Rwandan genocide, there are the efforts of such countries as Zimbabwe, Namibia and South Africa to peacefully overcome racial and ethnic differences. For every descent into armed anarchy in Somalia or Sierra Leone, there are multi-party elections taking place around the continent, from Benin to Zambia.

For every persistently hungry and violence-wracked Sudan, there is a Botswana pursuing a variety of strategies to achieve national and regional food security. And even in Sudan, local communities are eager to rebuild roads, plant crops, reopen local markets, and achieve the secure livelihoods they enjoyed when Sudan was a granary for the region and the world.

Conclusion

Just as people create violent conflicts, they can resolve them. People can instead create a world where food and livelihoods are secure, where

Advocacy for Countries in Crisis

NGOs should devote more effort to public information and public policy advocacy on behalf of countries in crisis and better coordinate advocacy efforts. In the United States, for example, Bread for the World helps mobilize political will on crisis-related structural issues and some specific country situations. In the mid-1980s, Bread for the World's campaign for aid to Africa generated tens of thousands of letters to the U.S. Congress, which approved $800 million in assistance, nearly 10 times the funds raised by high-profile events such as the "Live Aid" concert (see p. 59).

In 1991 and 1992, Bread for the World led a broad coalition that convinced Congress to adopt the Horn of Africa Recovery and Food Security Act. This helped shift U.S. policy toward the Horn from Cold War purposes toward support for democracy, peace and development.

In 1995, Bread for the World and its allies helped reduce cuts in development aid to Africa by $200 million.

Bread for the World might be able to help in more specific emergencies, within its current budget constraints, by relying systematically on coalition partners, particularly those with on-the-ground experience in the field, for country analysis.

everyone is accorded their full measure of human dignity and where diversity of ethnicity, religion, color, gender and age enrich our life together. It is a matter of collective choice.

In the face of complex humanitarian emergencies in a post-Cold War world, the accumulated experience from decades of response to natural disasters and development efforts provides many important lessons. But these lessons are not sufficient. International agencies, national governments, and both local and international NGOs are adapting proven approaches and trying new ones, often at considerable risk. New understandings are emerging, which already are contributing to long-term goals of food security and secure livelihoods for people who are deprived of both. It is a time of continuing challenge. It is also a time of hope. ■

Daniel U.B.P. Chelliah is coordinator of refugee affairs at Bread for the World Institute. Don Reeves, Bread for the World Institute economic policy analyst, and Steven Hansch, senior program officer at the Refugee Policy Group, contributed to this chapter.

Picking Up the Pieces:
Post-Crisis Reconstruction

Paul Smith/Panos Pictures

Since the peace accord, uprooted Mozambicans such as these refugees leaving South Africa have eagerly returned home to help reconstruct their communities.

by Marc Rempel

Several countries are emerging from years of civil war as a result of peace agreements, often brokered by the United Nations or other outside mediators. While war and crisis draw international media and political attention, the world tends to lose interest in a country's long, complicated struggle to reconstruct. But post-crisis countries face the burdens of physical reconstruction, social and political reconciliation and coping with the legacies of war. Local people will, of course, do most of the rebuilding, but international aid for rehabilitation and development is often necessary.

There are many issues to face. Buildings and roads are in desperate need of repair or replacement. Land mines, which combatants have often scattered haphazardly over the countryside, restrict access to crucial agricultural areas and pose a continued threat to innocent people. War-scourged economies are often extremely delicate. Uprooted people need help in returning and resettling, and ex-combatants have to find constructive civilian roles. A new political system is often in its infancy, trying to balance measures to establish its authority against a relapse into conflict. The people of opposing factions must learn to put aside old grudges and cooperate to carry out these tasks.

This chapter discusses the challenges of reconstruction and then reviews three current country experiences – Cambodia, Mozambique and El Salvador. All three are, on balance, success stories. The affected people themselves have made herculean efforts to recover normalcy. In each case, the United Nations has also been effective, but without the international attention devoted to failed U.N. efforts in Somalia, Bosnia and elsewhere.

Cambodia, Mozambique and El Salvador are all recovering from wars that were fueled by the Cold War. In each case, the United States and other industrial countries are investing much less money and attention in peace than they did in war.

This chapter also highlights the persistent bane of land mines in countries that have suffered civil war and urges a ban on the production and sale of land mines.

Physical Reconstruction

Warfare often destroys physical and social infrastructure such as schools, hospitals, transportation systems, irrigation networks, power facilities and factories. Meanwhile, governments at war often shift funds away from social services and infrastructure maintenance to help finance the fighting. Scarcity of funds can delay efforts to rebuild or repair the damage during and after the conflict.

Conflict frequently contributes to land degradation, too. This is partly due to the destructiveness of physical warfare and the inability of displaced people to take care of their fields. Therefore, environmental restoration and sustainable agriculture must sit high on the reconstruction agenda of post-crisis countries.

Land Mines and UXOs

Think of the horror of living day to day in a country where at any moment you could lose a leg, or your life, or your child's life, because of these hidden weapons. Where any open field, or patch of trees, or roadside ditch is a potential death trap. That is a way of life for tens of millions of people around the world.[1]
– Senator Patrick Leahy

The removal of anti-personnel land mines and unexploded ordinance (UXOs) is often a crucial reconstruction task. Land mines greatly strain a society's ability to function properly long after a war is over. Combatants most often sow mines in rural areas, and many of the countries most afflicted by mines depend predominantly on agriculture for income, employment and food security. Failure to carry out effective mine removal programs discourages and impedes refugees from returning home, leaves large areas of land inaccessible and seriously hinders reconstruction efforts (see "Coping with the Land Mine/UXO Crisis," p. 41).[2]

Economic Construction/Reconstruction

Economic revitalization is another key to rebuilding a post-crisis country. War frequently levels much of a country's industry, agriculture and commerce. In some countries, the emphasis is on restoring prewar economic life; elsewhere, the need is for first-time economic and social development.[3]

External aid is important. In some cases, industrial country governments have been generous in financing war – either Cold War conflicts such as El Salvador, or post-Cold War military operations such as Iraq or Somalia – but much less willing to help finance reconstruction. In other cases, reconstruction plans of fledgling governments are too much shaped by official donors, and implementation proves to be slow or unworkable. Official reconstruction programs work best when they are flexible and support initiatives to rebuild.

Local communities' efforts are essential to restoring the economy. Local and foreign nongovernmental organizations (NGOs) can assist communities in pursuing rehabilitation and sustainable development. NGOs usually are well suited to work in partnership with local people to achieve the participatory and equitable revitalization of the economy that must underlie successful reconstruction.

Another aspect of reconstruction that has economic implications is refugee repatriation. Post-crisis economies are often weak, with few income earning opportunities to offer people returning home, as well as those who never fled.[4]

The International Organization for Migration (IOM) seeks to assist skilled and professional workers to return to their home countries to help rebuild. IOM is an independent, non-political intergovernmental organization that plans and operates specialized technical programs to assist in refugee resettlement and migration for development. It has permanently resettled over 4.5 million people, including 20,000 assisted under its Return of Talent Program.[5]

Political Reconciliation

Perhaps the most important and critical aspect of successful reconstruction involves the government, often newly formed, taking effective, inclusive and democratic steps to foster a sustainable rehabilitative environment. The opposing factions must bring armed conflict to an end. This involves the signing of a peace agreement and the demobilization of armies. Once this tough challenge is met, formerly hostile groups must find a way to share power.

Frequently, this process takes the form of an election, where citizens vote on the balance of

Coping with the Land Mine/UXO Crisis

The statistics on the destructiveness of land mines are stark. The American Red Cross has estimated that mines cause more than 800 deaths and 450 injuries every month. Civilians account for 80 percent of the deaths and maimings due to land mines since 1975.

Thirteen countries have "extremely severe" mine problems (as judged by the U.S. State Department): Afghanistan, Angola, Iraq, Kuwait, Cambodia, Mozambique, Bosnia, Somalia, Croatia, Sudan, Serbia, Ethiopia and Eritrea. In these countries there is one buried mine for every three to five people.

Estimates of the number of mines scattered in 62 countries range from 65 million to more than 120 million. This works out to one mine for every 50 to 85 people on earth.

In 1993, de-mining efforts removed roughly 80,000 mines. However, in the same year, combatants in various countries planted another 2.5 million mines. More than 250 million land mines have been produced over the past 25 years and at least another 100 million lie in stockpiles around the world.[6]

Effective mine removal is dangerous, time consuming and very expensive. Only trained personnel can safely go about de-mining. Unfortunately, it is not the trained personnel who eliminate most mines. Rather, unlucky civilians stumble across mines, accidentally detonating them at the cost of their lives or limbs.

It takes roughly 100 times as long to detect, remove and disarm a mine as to plant it.[7] According to the United Nations, the cost of clearance (including training, support and logistics) is $300 to $1,000 per mine, compared to production costs of less than $25 – sometimes as little as $3.

According to U.N. Secretary-General Boutros Boutros-Ghali, "If the proliferation of land mines were stopped in 1996, at current rates of funding and clearance it would still take almost 1,100 years to rid the world of the land mines now in the ground."[8]

The United Nations provided Afghan refugees in Pakistan with mine-removal training.

Howard J. Davies/Panos Pictures

Land mines should be seen as an illegitimate weapon. Their production, stockpiling, transfer and use should be banned.

The United Nations has begun efforts to establish moratoria on production and sales of land mines. On December 15, 1994, the General Assembly passed a resolution introduced by the United States, one of the biggest producers of mines, urging member states to enact moratoria on anti-personnel land mine exports and to join in international collaboration to establish solutions to mine-related problems.[9]

Along with U.N. initiatives, some nongovernmental organizations (NGOs) are working to find ways to alleviate the crisis. For example, the Mennonite Central Committee (MCC) and the Mines Advisory Group (MAG), a British land mine clearance NGO with an emphasis on developing indigenous local capacity for unexploded ordinance (UXO) clearance, are working in Laos, where the problem of UXOs is severe. During the Indochina war, U.S. forces dropped the largest tonnage of bombs in history on Laos, leaving thousands of undetonated munitions that still have not exploded more than 20 years later. The MCC/MAG project staffs, trains and educates the indigenous communities to get a handle on the UXO problem. MCC also works with the governments of Laos and the United States to help get funding and support for this project. Similar projects in other countries must expand if the world is to solve the land mine/UXO crisis.[10]

power among competing parties. The United Nations regularly steps in to help ensure that elections are fair and free. Once a new government takes office, the final stage involves the strengthening of democratic institutions to assure a lasting government, future periodic elections and respect for minority rights. If the country can achieve genuine political reconciliation, this greatly boosts the chances of successful reconstruction.[11]

The following case studies examine how the various reconstruction issues played out in three recent instances.

Cambodia

In October 1991, opposing Cambodian forces – the Khmer Rouge, two pro-Western factions and the Vietnamese-installed government – signed a peace agreement to end the civil war that had plagued Cambodia for two decades. With the assistance of the United Nations, free elections in May 1993 swept Prince Norodom Ranariddh, the U.S.-supported royalist party leader, into office as first prime minister of the new National Provisional Government. Hun Sen, chief of the pro-Vietnamese Cambodian People's Party and head of the previous government, became second prime minister.[12]

El Salvador

by Kate Lawler, Refugee Policy Group

Peace has taken hold in El Salvador after 12 years of brutal civil war that claimed 80,000 lives and uprooted 1.5 million people. The 1992 peace accord between the government and the rebel Farabundo Martí National Liberation Front (FMLN) led to the disbanding of rebel armies and a two-thirds reduction in government forces. Mediated by the United Nations, the accord calls for demobilization; political, judicial, military and land tenure reform; the creation of a civilian police force; and the establishment of independent human rights agencies. In 1994, all factions peacefully participated in national elections.

Many obstacles threaten the peace: the challenges of rehabilitating infrastructure, an unprecedented level of crime and delays in establishing the police force, the need to reintegrate ex-combatants and uprooted people, the slow pace of land and credit transfers and a fragile economy.

U.S. aid, which averaged $250 million annually in the 1980s, has fallen to $48 million. During the Cold War, the U.S. government was willing to invest in the fight against communism, but the United States is not willing to invest as much in helping El Salvador rebuild now that the Cold War and El Salvador's war are over.

The true measure of peace and reconstruction will be improvements in the health, productivity, education and well-being of the third of the population that lives in extreme poverty. Rapid population growth complicates social and environmental problems, including deforestation, solid waste management and the depletion of natural resources. Nine in 10 rivers are contaminated.

Overall food consumption remained flat during the civil war years, but has improved noticeably during the post-war period (see Figure 3.1). Though food production has also increased, El Salvador remains dependent on food imports and has relied heavily on food aid for many years. The country has Central America's highest rate of vitamin A deficiency, related to lack of fruits and vegetables in the diet. Low birthweight and malnutrition rates remain high, reflecting limited access to preventive and primary health care.

El Salvador has made progress, however. Child malnutrition is half today what it was in 1976. Since the peak of the fighting, child malnutrition rates have decreased in both urban and rural areas. Child immunization levels are also high.

Nongovernmental organization (NGO) programs have moved away from crisis-related activities such as human rights work and emergency assistance. They are focusing instead on support for local reconstruction and development

Figure 3.1
Food Availability Per Person Per Day, El Salvador 1980-1994

Calories per person per day

Source: FAO.

This bright picture has a darker side. Cambodia is a struggling nation still haunted by the twin specters of Khmer Rouge guerrilla activity and the lingering effects of war.

The Khmer Rouge is a Maoist-inspired guerrilla movement led by the notorious Pol Pot, whose reign of terror over Cambodia began with the capture of Phnom Penh in April 1975. During the next three and-a-half years, the Khmer Rouge slaughtered a fifth of the Cambodian people. In 1978, a Vietnamese invasion forced the Khmer Rouge back into the jungles. A Vietnamese-installed Cambodian government took over, but the Khmer Rouge continued its guerrilla warfare, in loose alliance with pro-Western forces, until the signing of the 1991 peace accord. The Khmer Rouge boycotted the elections and violently seeks to regain power.[13]

The continuing instability has slowed vital international development aid, undermined long-term private investment, jeopardized essential revenue from tourism and hindered restoration of the country's infrastructure. The lack of a firm economic foundation dims prospects for building political stability.[14]

The new government has other problems, too. Many Cambodians and outsiders consider it corrupt. The Khmer Rouge threat has forced the government

efforts, notably fortifying local governments, providing credit and training to microentrepreneurs and rebuilding infrastructure. Recently, Salvadoran NGOs have created a network – Concertacion – to coordinate their development activities.

The Ministry of Health is receiving foreign aid to expand its community health worker programs, and assistance is also going directly to indigenous NGOs to train health promoters to address primary care needs in rural areas. Twenty percent of the 400 NGOs operating in El Salvador specialize in health.

Both the government and NGOs agree that the transfer of responsibilities and resources to regional and provincial levels is essential to consolidating peace and to achieving people-responsive, effective community development. The national government increasingly is channeling funds for road, school, water and electrification projects to local governments. These, in turn, often look to NGOs for the technical capacity to implement the projects. Because the majority of NGOs during the war were considered FMLN affiliates, this post-war NGO-government cooperation is an important point of national reconciliation.

Many refugees have returned from Honduras and Mexico with support from the Office of the U.N. High Commissioner for Refugees. Another 600,000 internally displaced people have returned to their homes or settled permanently elsewhere, often in urban areas. Land reform and policies to assure equitable access to clean water are essential to meet the needs of these returnees.

During the war, thousands of landowners abandoned their property. Landless peasants occupied these tracts. The peace accords provide that those occupying land will have an opportunity to own it if the landowner agrees. But the land transfer program has suffered delays, providing plots to only 32 percent of the potential beneficiaries by the end of 1994. Among the problems are government foot dragging, unwillingness on the part of potential beneficiaries to relocate, lack of interest in farming, unwillingness of landlords to sell and poor program outreach. Families who occupy land without a title are less likely to invest in it, because they remain at risk of eviction.

Speeding up the transfer of land will aid the reintegration of uprooted people and ex-combatants. To provide secure livelihoods, land reform needs to be accompanied by infrastructure improvements and income earning opportunities.

Although the violence of war has ended, Salvadorans now live in fear of new gang violence, car-jackings and armed robbery. Slow deployment of the new civilian police force contributes to lawlessness.

Other factors contributing to the crime epidemic include high unemployment, gang rivalries and the unresolved status of many ex-combatants who still own guns. Enraged by delays in the transfer of land and other compensation, they have carried out a major share of the violence. Salvadoran gang members deported from the United States have also contributed to the crime wave.

El Salvador's peace process serves as an encouraging example of the possibilities of negotiating a settlement even after years of brutal armed struggle. U.S. aid to El Salvador has plummeted since the end of the war, but Salvadorans themselves are rebuilding. Throughout the country, families are restoring their lives, and local governments and NGOs are playing an expanded role. The consolidation of peace depends on lasting resolution of economic, social and environmental problems – many of the same problems that drove Salvadorans to armed conflict in the first place.

to keep military spending high. Controversy over massive deforestation has also plagued the new regime. Both the government and the Khmer Rouge have stripped forest resources to finance the fighting, causing severe human and environmental problems. Deforestation contributes to drought and floods, leading to severely reduced fish catches and poor rice harvests, thereby increasing hunger and malnutrition. All these difficulties have increased the number of Cambodians who view the Khmer Rouge's brutal, but nationalistic and honest platform, with sympathy.[15]

Land mines pose a major obstacle to Cambodia's reconstruction. Opposing forces have used these low-cost devices, supplied mainly by China and Britain, to deny territory to one another. Until the mines are cleared, people cannot safely return to their homes, and Cambodia's mainly agricultural economy cannot recover. Since agriculture employs over 75 percent of the workforce, de-mining is imperative for development and food security.[16]

Estimates of the number of mines range from 4 million to 7 million, covering more than 40 percent of the land once farmed. Cambodia has the world's highest incidence of disabilities, with one of every 236 people affected. Each month, 300 to 700 amputations occur because of land mine injuries. Mine removal has proceeded very slowly and at high cost.[17]

The U.N. High Commissioner for Refugees (UNHCR) managed a large-scale effort to bring more than 350,000 refugees home.[18] But their reintegration has gone slowly because of the weak economy, lack of useable farmland due to mines and continued outbursts of fighting with the Khmer Rouge.

The United Nations' intervention in Cambodia – the world body's most expensive such operation ever – cost more than $2 billion. By many measures, it can be considered a success story. Internal and international cooperation have reduced violence, reestablished order and begun development. An elected government holds power and refugees have returned home. At the same time, Cambodia faces continued conflict, corruption, destruction of its natural environment, extreme poverty and serious food insecurity.

Mozambique

One of the most successful U.N.-sponsored transitions from conflict to peace is occurring in Mozambique. The 16-year civil war between government forces and the National Resistance Movement (RENAMO) ended with the October 1992 peace agreement. The U.N. Operation in Mozambique (ONUMOZ) facilitated demobilization and progress toward elections. The slow pace of demobilization delayed the elections, which did not occur until October 1994. Pronounced free and fair by the United Nations, the balloting returned incumbent President Joaquim Chissano to office with a comfortable 54 percent of the vote.[19]

A decade ago, the situation in Mozambique was horrendous. The war killed at least 1 million people, drove 1.8 million refugees into neighboring countries and displaced 3.8 million people within the country. According to the World Bank, Mozambique is the poorest country in the world, with a per capita income of $79 a year. Overall life expectancy is among the lowest in the world at 44 years.[20]

Now, with the establishment of a peaceful environment, Mozambicans have begun to rebuild their land, economy and government. These efforts include refugee repatriation and reintegration of demobilized ex-combatants and internally displaced people. The parties to the peace agreement seem strongly committed to supporting this process.

With peace, refugees have eagerly returned home to join in rebuilding their war-ravaged country. The number of people returning without official assistance is thought to be the largest such migration in history. While the world tends to view crises through the eyes of assistance agencies, this large-scale private migration provides another example of how people affected by crises are themselves prime actors in seeking solutions.

In addition, UNHCR's efforts to repatriate 1.5 million Mozambicans represent the agency's largest operation ever in Africa. UNHCR has assisted refugees in returning home from neighboring countries via boats, trains and buses. For thousands of Mozambicans, it has been an extraordinary experience. In October 1993, on a station platform at Goba, Mozambique, a former railway worker in his 60s greeted the first returnees from Swaziland. He noticed an older man leaning out of a coach window and realized that it was his 90-year-old father, whom he long ago had given up for dead. A refugee woman in her 30s tells of longing to show her children the place where their father was brutally murdered, to prove to them that she was a "normal" woman who had once owned a plantation, and that they too were "normal."[21]

The government, UNHCR and NGOs have implemented reintegration projects in returnee areas, focusing on water, education, health and road construction. The government has provided seeds and tool kits. The aim is to link these projects with long-term development activities that build local capacity.

Although it took a long time, more than 75,000 soldiers have demobilized (88 percent of those under arms at the time of the peace agreement), including hundreds of child soldiers. The country has established a new integrated army of 10,000 soldiers. Reintegration efforts have provided former soldiers with farm supplies, tools and job training, along with incentives to give up weapons.[22]

One example of a project that offers new economic opportunities is the OILS project, implemented by Appropriate Technology International, a U.S.-based NGO. It trains demobilized soldiers, small-scale farmers and entrepreneurs to grow oilseed crops and produce cooking oil.[23]

As in Cambodia, land mines clutter much of Mozambique. The United Nations estimates the total at 1 million. According to the Mozambican Association for the Handicapped, nearly 50 percent of all civilian war casualties resulted from land mines. In 1993, anti-personnel mines killed an estimated 600 people and maimed another 600. Uncleared land mines have rendered almost all major roads impassable and left 1 million acres of agricultural land uncultivated. This has interfered with repatriation efforts, economic reconstruction, expansion of food supplies and the creation of income earning opportunities.[24]

The United Nations, along with four private demining operations, has made some progress. Ronco – a U.S. Agency for International Development-funded contractor – has worked at clearing land mines and rehabilitating rural roads, opening areas previously inaccessible and enabling more than 80 percent of the internally displaced people and almost all refugees to return home. UNHCR has promoted mine awareness among returnees.[25]

While Mozambique has overcome a lot, it still has far to go. An urgent problem is the drought afflicting southern Africa. Successful repatriation has caused food reserves to dwindle. The threat of a poor harvest in 1995 for a third consecutive year puts many Mozambicans at risk of health and nutrition problems.

Donor countries are not providing the U.N. World Food Programme (WFP) enough food to meet emergency needs. In 1994, WFP fed a million Mozambican returnees. Because the country has been remarkably successful in recovering from crisis and is no longer seen as a checker in the Cold War game, it has not been prominent in world news. But precisely because of its successful, yet still vulnerable, recovery, it is imperative that adequate food aid be mobilized to help Mozambique continue the process of reconstruction.[26]

The newly elected government offers hope for the future, but a political struggle may lie ahead. True political reconciliation will not happen until RENAMO gets a more proportionate share of power. Economic problems are still immense, too.

Both the Mozambicans and those parties that helped arrange the October 1994 elections agree that no single factor has helped keep the peace. But Aldo Ajello, who headed the ONUMOZ mission, suggests that the flexibility of the United Nations and key regional and world powers helped the peacekeepers adjust to a complex situation. Ajello notes, "When you have a tall man and a short blanket, you either have to cut the man or change the blanket. Too often, we (at the United Nations) cut the man."[27] In Mozambique, the United Nations and interested nations adapted to unfolding events and what Mozambicans themselves were trying to do.

Conclusion

Assessments of global crises often overlook countries just emerging from vicious war cycles. But these countries are often in need of just as much attention as those still locked in conflict. Efforts to rebuild physical, economic and political structures are all needed.

Cambodia has made great gains, but is still quite unstable. El Salvador faces daunting problems, but has come a long way. Mozambique also faces political and economic problems, but the country offers a remarkably hopeful model of successful reconstruction.

All three countries' experiences show that local people's own efforts are the key to recovery. The United Nations and individual nations have provided effective help, but limited funding for aid will severely hamper reconstruction in Mozambique and especially in El Salvador. ■

Marc Rempel, a student at Eastern Mennonite University in Harrisonburg, VA, was a Bread for the World Institute intern during the 1994 to 1995 academic year. Heidi Whorley of the Refugee Policy Group contributed research on Mozambique.

Chapter 4

An Ounce of Prevention is Worth a Pound of Relief

The United Nations has an important role to play in preventing and managing conflicts. Secretary-General Boutros Boutros-Ghali visits a U.N.-supported orphanage in Somalia.

by Marina Ottaway

Conflict and Hunger

Humanitarian agencies aiding people affected by complex emergencies must deal with conflict. Ideally, this should mean developing an early warning system to identify potential crises and intervening promptly to prevent tensions from escalating into full-fledged, violent conflict. Realistically, emerging conflict cannot always be recognized early or nipped in the bud. Conflict management or mediation efforts thus must also be part of a strategy to prevent hunger.

The cause of contemporary hunger-producing crises is most often found in ethnic or religious conflict, or a combination of both. This problem affects developing countries and also industrialized societies with increasing frequency and virulence. Ethnic conflict has exploded in the former socialist bloc – in the former Soviet Union, Yugoslavia and Czechoslovakia. Bosnia provides the best-known, tragic example of the ravages that ethnic nationalism can inflict on people. Unfortunately there are many other examples in the former socialist world. Georgia, Armenia, Azerbaijan and Tajikistan have all been wracked by conflict between ethnic groups and rival clans.

In Africa, Rwanda and Burundi offer the most extreme, but not the only, examples. Ethnic cleansing has been perpetrated against minorities in the Shaba region of Zaire, in the Rift Valley of Kenya and in parts of Ethiopia. Ethnic relations have deteriorated in Nigeria, particularly in the oil producing areas in the east. In Sudan, ethnic and religious conflict are closely intertwined in the struggle that pits the north against the south. Ethnic conflict remains the major threat to the consolidation of a peaceful, democratic, post-apartheid system in South Africa.

In Asia, tensions between Tamil and Sinhalese populations continue to destabilize Sri Lanka; ethnic-religious conflict remains an ever-present threat in India, where relations among Hindus, Muslims and Sikhs erupt periodically into open violence.

In Latin America, ethnic tensions involving the indigenous "Indian" population – from the long-standing insurrection of the *Sendero Luminoso* ("Shining Path") in Peru to the more recent incidents in the Chiapas region of southern Mexico – fuel conflict and in turn human misery.

In the Middle East, the deep-rooted conflict between Arabs and Jews may be slowly moving toward accommodation. But other important tensions are worsening – between Sunni and Shi'a Muslims, between extremists seeking to use Islam as a political weapon and the rest of the Muslim population, between dominant ethnic groups and minorities. The minority Kurds, for example, are at the center of conflict in Turkey, Syria, Iraq and Iran.

Recently, the mobilization of religious identity for political purposes has been particularly frequent in Muslim countries. The potential for strife ostensibly based on religious motives is not limited to the Muslim world, however. Any religion can be used for political purposes by extremist groups. The conflict between Catholic Croats and Orthodox Christian Serbs in Croatia, and the release of poison gas in the Tokyo subway by a Buddhist sect in March 1995 are tragic reminders that it is not the character of a religion, but the political end for which it is manipulated, that creates conflict.

Ethnic nationalism has led to conflict and hunger in such former Soviet republics as Azerbaijan.

Developing country conflicts such as those in Somalia and Rwanda are of particular importance to organizations seeking to prevent hunger in the world. In wealthier industrial countries, conflict is less likely to create starvation on a large scale. But ethnic and religious conflict remain rife and cause much suffering even there. The United States provides a prime example not only of the persistence of ethnic tensions, but also of how continued racial bias contributes to poverty and food insecurity in a major way. In Western Europe, the long-standing strife between Catholics and Protestants in Northern Ireland is also a reminder that even democratic political structures cannot contain and solve all conflict. We can find no reason for complacency.

For every example of ethnic slaughter, there are scores of communities where people of different ethnic and religious backgrounds live peacefully side by side. Ethnic and religious differences do not inevitably lead to violence or hunger.

In March 1995, Christian and Muslim relief and development organizations established the Committee on Interreligious Development Action. In addition to cooperative development efforts, it seeks to promote reconciliation in conflicts, especially where religious differences are involved.

Open strife is usually triggered deliberately by groups trying to enhance their own power or by politicians building their careers on ethnic hatred and violence. In Rwanda and Burundi, Hutus and Tutsis do not periodically turn on each other with rocks and machetes without reason. They are incited by organized groups with political agendas. The 1994 slaughter in Rwanda was the result of a carefully orchestrated campaign to incite violence

In the long run, sustainable development is the most important factor contributing to conflict prevention: Ethiopian farmers work on reforestation.

conducted by duly licensed radio stations. Far from being a blind explosion of ancient tribal hatreds, the massacres were the result of deliberate decisions by identifiable individuals and organizations.

Conflicts are often made worse by poverty and hopelessness. Hunger is seldom the immediate cause of protracted, violent conflict, but it contributes to conflict by providing a large pool of discontented people who see no present and no future for themselves. Young men, even children, find in conflict an outlet for their energies and a source of sustenance. Conflict and hunger are thus tied to each other in a vicious circle of crisis.

Preventing and Managing Conflict

Conflict prevention and management are often important components of strategies to avert and alleviate hunger. Steps can be taken to reduce the likelihood of conflict and to shorten the duration of ongoing crises. We need to distinguish between measures that can make a difference only in the long term and those that can help in the medium and short term.

In the long run, the most important factor contributing to conflict prevention is sustainable development. It can help break the vicious circle of conflict and hunger. Sustainable development increases available resources. It creates better organized, more democratic communities, less open to manipulation by ruthless leaders and more capable of handling tensions before they explode into violence. Sustainable development also moves communities away from the brink of hunger, giving them greater capacity to withstand disruption without a serious humanitarian crisis.

But sustainable development is a long-term process that will not stop ongoing violence or suddenly overcome long-standing conflicts. Steps toward sustainable development for all may foster hope that peaceful resolution of old injustices is possible. Some of the changes needed to bring about sustainable development in the long run can increase tension in the short run, however.

The transition to more democratic government, for example, helps the great majority in the long run. But in the midst of the transition, many groups feel threatened by democratization. This has been amply demonstrated by the large number of countries that have experienced a democratic opening in recent years, but have also experienced a sharp escalation in the level of ethnic or religious conflict. Yugoslavia blew apart after multi-party elections were held in all its regions for the first time in half a century.

In the medium run, conflict prevention and management[1] efforts should focus on helping countries and communities understand better the concerns of all groups involved, and agree on a set of rules of the game that can address those concerns.

Those of us who live in democratic countries are used to defending and cherishing the rights of individuals, not of groups. We emphasize the equality of all human beings. We reject the idea that members of minority groups should be discriminated against. Unfortunately, even the most democratic countries do not fully live up to the principles they espouse. Discrimination against members of minority groups has not disappeared from the United States or European democracies. However, democratic countries offer individuals legal avenues to seek justice and redress discrimination.

But in the more numerous non-democratic countries, the situation is much more complex. Few individual rights are recognized. Persons cannot count on the protection of government institutions. Their only security is provided by membership in a group, most often defined in terms of ethnicity, region or religion. Recognition of the rights of the group becomes as important, or even more important, than recognition of individual rights.

In all cases of ethnic and religious conflict, the issue of the rights of the different groups is paramount. Hutus and Tutsis in Rwanda do not now seek salvation in a democratic government that will recognize equal rights for all individuals. They do not believe that such a government can exist. Thus, they seek protection in a government controlled by members of their own ethnic group. Since both groups want to control the government, conflict continues. In Bosnia, Muslims, Serbs and Croats also worry about the position of their groups. They are afraid that a government controlled by members of another ethnic group will violate their own rights and seek to destroy their own identity. Usually, all groups involved in ethnic conflict have legitimate demands and grievances, but they are unwilling to recognize the legitimate demands and grievances of others.

People in the United States, raised with the ideal of the melting pot – the amalgamation of citizens into a single national identity – sometimes find it difficult to understand the intensity of the separate identities of religious and ethnic groups in other countries. But for most people in the world, these separate ethnic or religious identities are more important than the citizenship they share with other groups.

Measures to prevent or mediate ethnic and religious conflict must start with the recognition of the depth of these communal sentiments. These feelings may be regrettable, even wrong to our way of thinking, but they cannot be wished out of existence. The problem thus becomes one of helping divided countries and communities devise rules that will allow all groups to coexist – without losing their identity, but without coming into violent conflict with each other.

Successful examples point the way. Many European countries have faced very serious ethnic conflict in the past. During the late 1970s and early 1980s, Spain was threatened by violence as Basque and Catalan separatist movements fought for independence with violence and acts of terrorism. The solution emerged only when the central government recognized that members of minority groups had legitimate grievances and demands, and that they should not be required to assimilate and renounce their language and culture. Recognition of cultural rights, together with the organization of a decentralized administrative system with strong regional autonomy, satisfied the demands of the minorities and greatly reduced the appeal of the extremist organizations.

Measures that enable minorities to maintain their language and culture, as well as preserve a measure of autonomy in their local governments, are helping in other countries. A possible serious conflict between the Slovak majority and the Hungarian minority of Slovakia will hopefully be avoided by the application of these principles.

Successful instances of avoiding ethnic and religious conflict are more frequent in Europe than in other parts of the world at present. Institutions such as the Council of Europe, the European Union and the Organization for Security and Cooperation in Europe have been very active in discussing the issues and preparing model charters of minority rights, language rights and local autonomy. These charters provide governments and minorities alike with guidelines for solving these problems.

But there are examples in other parts of the world as well. In Malaysia, a complex constitution, electoral law and equal opportunity policy have helped ease tense relations between Malays and Chinese. Nigeria suffered a disastrous civil war in the late 1960s, triggered by the attempt of the Ibos to form their own state of Biafra. But Nigeria then established a redesigned federal system that maintained a degree of ethnic peace for 20 years. In South Africa, a combination of power-sharing at the center and regional decentralization opened the way to successful elections in April 1994, preventing the large-scale ethnic violence that appeared very likely only a few weeks earlier.

In none of these cases was the problem entirely solved. Ethnic tensions remain in all these countries and so does the potential for a new explosion. Nigeria appears to be moving in that direction now. Nevertheless, these cases show that it is possible to devise rules to control and manage the level of tension in the medium run, preventing the development of humanitarian crises.

In the short run, measures such as those just described will probably not help much in defusing ongoing conflicts that have already become violent. The rules that offer hope of reconciliation in Slovakia, where moderates on both sides may still prevail, cannot provide a solution in Bosnia, where power is in the hands of extremists. Where conflict is already acute, different measures are needed to restore peace.

U.N. interventions, with the deployment of large peacekeeping forces, as in Somalia, Bosnia or Cambodia, is only one of many different ways to help resolve ongoing conflicts. At the other end of the spectrum are modest interventions at the local levels by small organizations or even individuals.

In the Natal region of South Africa during the late 1980s and early 1990s, violence often flared between members of the African National Congress (ANC) and those of the rival Inkatha Freedom Party. Thousands of people were killed, mostly in night-time raids on the homes of sleeping families. Communities became deeply divided. Individuals were forced to take sides.

One of the communities most deeply affected by this slaughter was the hill-top town of Mpumulanga.

Racial and ethnic conflicts persist even in democratic, industrial countries such as the United States.

Yet in 1992, Mpumulanga became peaceful, despite continued slaughter in the region. No U.N. blue helmets occupied the town, no foreign countries sent in troops. The South African government did nothing different there than in the rest of the region.

The secret was simple. Local leaders of Inkatha and the ANC decided that the villagers had suffered enough and that no one benefitted from the violence. They set out together to calm the community. They spoke to the young people in their respective organizations. They toured the trouble spots jointly, trying to defuse tensions, suggesting solutions and compromise. Mpumulanga settled down.

Intervention to make and maintain peace can thus take many different forms. Each has its limitations and poses dilemmas. The United Nations has the means to deploy large numbers of soldiers in situations where nothing else has worked. But U.N. interventions are costly, and the United States and other nations are now reluctant to fund them. U.N.-led military interventions also depend on difficult-to-achieve international consensus; they are hampered by narrowly defined, rigid rules and, often, continuing disagreement among the major powers. The United Nations must also respect the sovereignty of any country where it intervenes, no matter how much its government violates human rights. These factors have rendered U.N. intervention in Bosnia and Croatia ineffective.

In contrast, the successful transition to independence and democracy in Namibia in 1990 showed the impact of the United Nations at its best. The world body monitored the transition from South African occupation, and supervised free and fair elections under one of Africa's most democratic constitutions. Unfortunately, the United States and other world powers are cutting funding for high-impact U.N. work along these lines.

Most U.N. peacekeeping activities initiated by or through the U.N. Security Council have been carried out under the U.N. Charter's "enforcement" procedures, and have relied heavily on armed forces contributed by member states. Relatively less resources and attention have been directed toward "pacific settlement of disputes" – also provided for in the U.N. Charter:

The parties to any dispute, the continuance of which is likely to endanger the maintenance of international peace and security, shall, first of all, seek a solution by negotiation, enquiry, mediation, conciliation, arbitration, judicial settlement, resort to regional agencies or arrangements or other peaceful means of their own choice.

The Security Council shall, when it deems necessary, call upon the parties to settle their disputes by such means.

– Chapter VI, Article 33, *Charter of the United Nations*

Modest additional investment by the international community in mechanisms to monitor, investigate and facilitate peaceful resolution of disputes might avert some conflicts that would otherwise develop.

Interventions by regional organizations have been advocated recently as an alternative to U.N. action, particularly in the case of African countries. Regional bodies such as the Organization of African Unity do have an important role to play, but they cannot be expected to solve all problems on their own, providing the United Nations and the industrial countries with an excuse for doing nothing. Regional organizations have severe limitations. They have even more difficulty than the United Nations raising money to pay for peacemaking interventions, so regional organizations depend on the often poorly equipped and disciplined armies of member countries. They bring to their peacemaking efforts a better understanding of the region and its people, but they can also become embroiled in the politics of the conflict more easily. Nigerian troops in Liberia are more likely to become part of the conflict they are attempting to solve than troops from Bangladesh, for example.

International peacemaking does not always entail military intervention. Foreign governments and private individuals can play very important roles as mediators. American, Soviet, Cuban and South African diplomats together helped bring about peace and independence in Namibia, opening the way for the successful U.N. deployment. An Italian lay Catholic organization, the S. Egidio community, played a crucial role alongside diplomats from several countries in brokering the agreement between the Mozambican government and the guerrilla movement RENAMO that put an end to the long war in that country. Former U.S. President Jimmy Carter made major contributions to defusing a looming conflict between the United States and North Korea in 1994 and to restoring the elected government in Haiti. Many types of organizations and individuals can serve as mediators and help solve conflict.

The Role of NGOs

Nongovernmental organizations (NGOs) can contribute in important ways to conflict prevention and management. Their activities to strengthen civil society and promote sustainable development make a long-term contribution to conflict prevention. But NGOs can also participate directly in conflict resolution.

Southern NGOs are particularly well placed to work for conflict prevention and management in their own countries. Indeed, their role can be expected to become even more central in the future as their numbers and strength increase. Traditional institutions such as councils of elders are also reasserting their importance as instruments of conflict management in some countries.

Northern NGOs can have a significant impact, often in partner roles with Southern NGOs. Northern NGOs find it easiest to raise money for relief during crises, but they could do much more peacemaking as they carry out their relief, reconstruction and development activities.

NGOs can be particularly active in addressing conflict at the community level, but do not operate exclusively there. Cases like that of the S. Egidio community, which played a central part in the peace process in Mozambique, are rare. But NGOs have at times been able to open "back channels" (informal communications) in situations where politicians and diplomats were unable to initiate a dialogue. It was a group of Scandinavian academics that opened the back channel that eventually led to successful negotiations between Israel and the Palestine Liberation Organization. In many African countries, church organizations are actively seeking to initiate a dialogue between government and opposition.

Most frequently, however, NGOs are able to work at the community level. This is very promising, particularly since a community may remain peaceful even if conflict continues in the rest of the country.

There are many examples of these community-based activities.

In Transylvania, Romania, a U.S. organization, the Project on Ethnic Relations, has been working for several years to defuse tensions between Hungarians and Romanians in a number of towns and villages. Dialogue among the parties and discussion of grievances has reduced tensions in some communities even in the absence of an agreement at the national level.

In the Czech Republic, the German Marshall Fund contributed to improving relations between the Czech population and Roma (Gypsy) minorities in several towns, in part by sensitizing authorities to the grievances of the minority and suggesting simple steps that could be taken to address these grievances.

South Africa offers many examples of organizations trying to mediate local conflicts. Practical Ministries, a South African Christian organization that works in Port Shepstone, Natal, addresses the same cycle of violence and revenge between ANC and Inkatha supporters that wracked Mpumulanga. Practical Ministries convenes individuals and groups to work toward reconciliation. It counsels families of people killed in the violence, hoping to break the pattern of revenge killings. Signs of hope have emerged as many family members have been willing to enter peace negotiations with those allegedly responsible for the murders. The organization also hosts community peace rallies.

In southern Sudan, the Presbyterian Church (USA) helped settle a conflict over grazing rights and access to water between two communities. Because of the civil war that rages in the country, weapons are everywhere. This local conflict had become violent, costing 1,300 lives and destroying 75,000 cattle and large stores of grain. Violence and hunger were directly associated. In July 1994, funding from the church made it possible to bring together representatives of all affected groups. The meeting continued for 45 days. All grievances were heard, and a compromise was reached on the basis of customary law and local mediation practices.

In the Middle East, numerous NGOs have long tried to bring about better understanding among all groups. They work quietly on people-to-people initiatives to complement the formal negotiations undertaken by the politicians. One example is provided by the Palestinian Centre for Rapprochement Between People. It is supported by Lutheran World Relief (LWR) through the Mennonite Central Committee. This organization is located on the West Bank and seeks to open a dialogue between Palestinians and Jews.

In Central America, the efforts of international agencies are also supplemented by peace-supporting initiatives taken by NGOs. In Nicaragua, LWR has supported the efforts of a local NGO to train agricultural extension agents and groups of peasants in conflict resolution, because the official end of the war did not put an end to local conflicts. In another project supported by LWR in Nicaragua, the Evangelical Committee for Development (CEPAD) trains lay people and clergy to address local, small-scale conflict over property or between neighbors. Such modest projects can be crucial in re-establishing normal life in communities.

Conclusion

Ethnic and religious diversity can enrich human communities, from the local to global levels. But differences are also a source of tension, subject to manipulation by leaders pursuing personal or ideological agendas. When tension escalates to open conflict, the more vulnerable members of society are the first to suffer hunger and privation. Food itself often becomes a weapon.

Managing tensions and resolving conflicts require a broad range of activities by a wide spectrum of actors. National governments can adopt long-range goals of sustainable development, while protecting the rights of minority groups. In the intermediate term, regional and international agencies, including the United Nations, should strengthen their capacity to monitor and mediate potential conflicts. This will require funding at a time when governments are reducing their contributions and demands for urgent humanitarian relief are increasing.

In the short run, NGOs can often model peacemaking and peacekeeping in innovative ways not open to governments and formal institutions. They can support what affected people themselves do to establish harmonious relationships.

Individuals – in crisis countries and elsewhere – must actively demonstrate tolerance, good will and reconciliation in ways that are as infectious as fear, intolerance and conflict. ■

Dr. Marina Ottaway is visiting professor of African Studies in the School of Foreign Service, Georgetown University.

Chapter 5

Shifting Focus:
The Role of the Media

by Carole Zimmerman

Media coverage of hunger in developing countries is "MAD" – focused on misery, atrocities and disasters.[1]

Sometimes this coverage has played an essential role in galvanizing an international response to a hunger crisis. For example, BBC and NBC broadcasts of famine footage from Ethiopia in October 1984 caused a public outcry, prompting stepped-up relief efforts. Foreign aid institutions had known of the deteriorating food situation in much of Africa for at least a year, but had not responded adequately.

In general, however, modern media present the Western public with a distorted view of the developing world, from Angola to Guatemala, Cambodia to Zaire. Peter Adamson, founding author of UNICEF's annual *State of the World's Children*, writes of "an impression that the developing world is exclusively a theater of tragedy in which poverty and human misery figure prominently in almost every scene."[2]

Pictures and action are television's lifeblood. "For Western news media," comments critic John Fiske, "the Third World is a place of natural and political disasters and not much else."[3] Television news as generally practiced is not well suited to exploring the social and economic disruption that leads to and follows disasters and that affects far more people than immediate victims.

Television news is even worse at covering the tenaciously achieved triumphs in millions of individual communities. In both developing and industrial countries, the vast majority of people daily pour out their lives to improve the lot of their families, communities and nations; and most governments attempt to provide quality education, health care and safe, sustainable food systems.

Good news is too often considered not newsworthy. Bad news is not "news" until it offers good visual images. Murder in a small town and its big-time equivalent, war within or between nations, makes better news than a nutrition program that improves a million lives.

News from developing countries is usually reduced to a formula or squeezed out all together, because that is the way most contemporary journalism treats serious, complex issues, especially those that focus on low-income people. Glamour and glitz – or their opposites, misery and depravity – are increasingly the norm as news becomes another form of entertainment rather than education.

There are exceptions. Large national newspapers still have overseas bureaus. They continue to cover international news, and sometimes present thoughtful analyses of fast-breaking events. Even such medium-sized newspapers as the *San Jose Mercury News* and the *St. Petersburg Times* manage to provide readers with in-depth coverage of global affairs; the *Times* has also focused extensively on domestic hunger. Public broadcasting – both television and radio – generally offers more detail and deeper examination of events and issues than its commercial counterpart.

The news media's general short-term focus is at odds with the long-term view that an informed citizenry requires. The U.S. public gets too little information from the media about the economic, social and political background of the developing world – whether or not it is in a crisis situation. Most crises form slowly from causes that are well known. But they do not become "news" until there is a dramatic social eruption.

Countries in Crisis argues that the public and politicians in industrial countries have not learned the lessons of recent crises, underestimate what

people in crisis situations are doing for themselves and focus too much on relief as the response. These misunderstandings have roots in the nature of the news business.

The News Business

Our idealized picture of the news media is one of newspaper editors and network anchors presiding over great switchboards of daily knowledge, gathering news from around the world, sifting, evaluating, challenging everything to separate wheat from chaff, to eliminate bias and deceit. But journalists do not hold the commanding position they once did in the ever-expanding information universe.

"News" is selected to attract maximum audience rating, because that is what pays the bills. That news is a business is not news.[4] But in recent years, the practice of selecting and packaging news in order to increase advertising revenue has achieved scientific precision.

By the 1980s, almost all U.S. news organizations came under the control of national and multinational corporations, creating new pressures for maximizing profits. In 1986, Wall Street acquisition expert Christopher Shaw urged investment in media firms because of "profitability" and "influence." The latter means getting the company's point of view to become everyone's point of view.[5]

> ## "The main purpose of television is to sell television news."
>
> – Howard Rosenberg, *Los Angeles Times* television critic[6]

Corporate ownership increasingly turns "news" papers to "advertising" papers. In 1992, when the circulation of *The New York Times* was 1,181,500 daily copies, its columns were "60 percent advertising, 40 percent news," according to its corporate relations department.[7] Financial pressures – such as anticipated price increases of 30 percent for newsprint in 1995 – have forced publishers, editors and producers to alter news to fit merchandising goals. This tends to reduce coverage of important issues in the developing world.[8]

Short-term profits are now imperative in the major media almost without regard to the future of media institutions themselves. Circulation has declined as a significant source of revenue for newspapers. They must satisfy advertisers, investors and parent corporations. Investors look for dividends and quarterly, if not daily, stock price increases. Advertisers demand immediate sales based on the appearance of their ads. Parent corporations can always sell or liquidate media subsidiaries that do not perform well enough financially.

One editor described the current newspaper format as "a device to deliver consumers to producers"[9] – advertising drives layout and editorial decisions. The medium of money not only shapes the news media's message, but dilutes print media's superior ability to analyze events and discuss their root causes. The profit maximization drive also negatively affects the media's responsibility to keep the public informed: as Tom Goldstein puts it, "Public service – the reason newspapers and broadcasters have been granted constitutional protection in the first place – requires sacrifice, and a slavish preoccupation with profits makes sacrifice unfashionable."[10]

Bias in Coverage

Most advertisers seek to reach affluent readers between the ages of 18 and 49. The "wrong age" people – younger than 18 and older than 49 – constitute 54 percent of the U.S. population. Many magazines primarily send subscription solicitations to mailing lists of affluent 18- to 49-year-olds, and

sometimes do not send renewal notices to low-income ZIP codes. Broadcasters design their programs to attract younger, affluent viewers. Newspapers promote circulation in affluent neighborhoods and limit reporting on neighborhoods of low-income and elderly populations. Major series on domestic poverty and hunger in 1994 in *The Washington Post* and *Los Angeles Times* were exceptional.

The "unwanted population" that is systematically discouraged by advertising-supported media, and under-reported in its coverage, is huge. In 1984, "undesirable" families with less than median household income constituted 70 percent of African-American families and 64 percent of Hispanic families. Even this understates the exclusion of people of color from coverage, because many families with incomes higher than the median are forced by informally segregated housing patterns to remain in neighborhoods generally shunned by the media.[11] Specialized newspapers and broadcasting outlets that serve minority communities generally have limited resources for news gathering and outreach.

Mainstream U.S. newspapers and broadcasters would deny that they have a class, age, racial or ethnic bias. But their policies on reporting events in developing nations are indistinguishable from policies that deliberately exclude minorities at home.

Who Owns the Media?

Control of media outlets has narrowed rapidly. In 1981, 46 corporations controlled most daily newspapers, magazines, television, book publishing and motion pictures. In 1992 these media generated even larger amounts of money, but the number that get the lion's share of it shrunk to 23 companies.

Media giant Gannett's acquisition of Multimedia, announced in July 1995, will put 93 daily newspapers, 15 television stations, 13 radio outlets, a news wire, a major polling firm, cable franchises with half a million subscribers, the largest billboard company in North America and a syndicate producing major television talk shows in the hands of a single firm. Recent acquisitions of ABC by Disney and of CBS by Westinghouse will accelerate concentration even further.

Most of the 14 corporations that dominate the daily newspaper industry have acquired additional dailies (and other media) in the last decade. The number of daily papers in the country fell from 1,763 in 1960 to 1,643 in 1989 to 1,556 in 1994. Total national daily circulation has risen slightly from 62 million to 62.9 million readers.

The three largest television networks – Capital Cities/ABC, CBS and NBC – despite mergers, attempted takeovers and declining prime-time viewing, still dominate the field. They command more than two-thirds of the audience.

Concentration is most dramatic in magazine publishing, which from 1981 to 1988 went from 20 dominant corporations to three.

Book publishing, less driven by the force of mass advertising, is still highly concentrated. The 2,500 companies that regularly issue one or more books a year are dominated by six corporations that grossed more than half of book revenues. Five of these companies are active in other media.[12]

Crispin Hughes/Panos Pictures

Television covers confrontation between Somali militia and Pakistani U.N. troops.

Fairness and Accuracy in Reporting (FAIR) published an analysis of 40 months of programming on ABC's "Nightline." Of the 1,530 guests featured, 92 percent were white, 89 percent male and 80 percent professionals, government officials or corporate representatives.

To compare diversity and inclusiveness, FAIR conducted a comparative analysis of the guests on PBS's "MacNeil/Lehrer News Hour." That show is known for its in-depth coverage, including award-winning reports on the roots of the Somalia crisis. Nevertheless, FAIR found that, in most respects, "its guest list represented an even narrower segment of the political spectrum than 'Nightline's.'"[13]

In the future, widespread access to cable television and computer information networks may offer news alternatives. But this potential so far is largely unrealized, and appears to be coming under the same profit-driven influences.

News As Entertainment

Television is the quintessential short-term medium. For the U.S. public, it is the principal source of news and information. Like a juggler, television lives for the split second.

Relationships to viewers are measured in tiny fractions. One percentage point in ratings can mean a difference of $30 million in a year's profit. The content of the news media is not designed primarily to serve the consumer – the reader, viewer, listener, citizen seeking to become informed. It is designed to please a third party – the advertiser. As Anne Winter has put it,

The world of television and particularly of television news, is what has been called a "peeka-boo" world where an event pops into view for a moment and then vanishes. It is a world of fragments, discontinuities, where the worth of information lies in its novelty and entertainment value rather than in its relevance to social and political decision making and debate. Give us 22 minutes and we'll give you the world.[14]

Television news is widely watched because it is attached to prime-time entertainment, and has thus evolved to meet entertainment standards. By the end of the 1970s, network news had become a major factor in overall network budgeting, both in costs and revenues.[15] While many journalists want to be involved with news that solves problems and makes a difference, the gatekeepers (owners, producers, publishers and editors) must focus on audience share and profit.[16] As a result, according to a *TV Guide* article:

Television reporters frequently complain that once they begin researching a story, they discover information contradicting what they had expected to find. But because advertisements have already been placed and viewers expect to see the story that was advertised, compromises must be made.[17]

Criticism from Within

Journalists and editors have criticized these trends. Dan Rather, anchor and managing editor of the "CBS Evening News," has addressed the thin line between news and drama – the theatrical atmosphere where reality is rearranged to suit the needs of producers: "They've got us putting more and more fuzz and wuzz on the air, copshop stuff so as to compete not with other news programs but with entertainment programs, including those posing as news programs, for dead bodies, mayhem and lurid tales."[18]

Similarly, Michael J. O'Neill, former editor of *The New York Daily News* and former president of the American Society of Newspaper Editors, says that the central ethical problem facing the media is:

the corruption of journalism by the culture of entertainment . . . the casual replacement of fact with fantasy and fiction, in the blurring of the lines between what is real and unreal. . . . The greatest challenge to a free press is the progressive corruption of news and information by entertainment, fiction and moral indifference.[19]

The thought that news should "make a profit" was unthinkable to journalists and executives for decades. CBS journalist Eric Sevareid argued that "the trouble began when the news organizations began to turn a profit. People forget . . . that television news started out (30 years ago) as a loss leader."[20]

> "[T]he greatest challenge of all, the most serious threat to a free press, is the progressive corruption of news and information by entertainment, fiction and moral indifference."
>
> – Michael J. O'Neill, former president of the American Society of Newspaper Editors

> "Journalists are supposed to gather, weigh, organize and evaluate information – not just put on pictures."
>
> – Bill Moyers[21]

Mainstream journalists' consciousness of problems and limitations offers hope for change.

The Closure of Foreign Bureaus

"These days," says "Nightline" anchor Ted Koppel, "news divisions make . . . and are expected to make money. That has meant, among other things, a cutback in the number and size of foreign bureaus. Foreign correspondents, as a category, are simply shrinking." This has led to intense, but relatively short-lived, coverage of international crises, as in the recent cases of Haiti, Rwanda, Somalia and, to a lesser degree, Bosnia. According to Koppel:

In decades past, news organizations stationed reporters full time around the world. Their ongoing presence allowed them to develop expertise in a country and make reliable contacts with key players that proved invaluable when important stories surfaced. Today, stationing reporters abroad is too expensive. Instead, news organizations wait for a story to break, then "parachute in" a complete news crew to cover the event – at considerable expense.

The media are only willing to marshal and dispatch enormous resources for "the kind of event that engages the interest of a huge American audience. . . To satisfy its advertisers by attracting a large audience, 'Nightline' has to balance a program on Bosnia – which draws few viewers – with one on the O.J. Simpson murder trial," says Koppel. Slow fuses like southern Sudan that burn over years are not going to capture attention in the same way as the Rwanda explosion did in 1994.[22] The magnificent story of national and international efforts to restore peace and begin development in Mozambique (see

Chapter 3) received virtually no attention, while the image of a dead U.S. soldier being dragged by jubilant Somalis is branded into all of our minds.

McNews

Deadlines have always driven journalism. Thirty years ago broadcast journalists had one deadline a day – the evening news. An occasional bulletin of a major event might interrupt regular programming, but time, a natural ally of reporters and editors, was available to research and prepare reports.

Today, journalists may have an evening news program, news segments for morning shows, news magazines and occasional late night news shows. Cable News Network (CNN) runs around the clock. For a single reporter covering a breaking story, especially one overseas, there is less time available to gather material for each of the two, three or more stories a day.

Reporters who are sent to cover crisis-driven developments are expected, Koppel says,

to feed information to news programs scheduled throughout the day. The newly arrived reporter – usually relatively ignorant of the background of an area or conflict and without many local contacts – has to file several stories a day, leaving little time for research or reflection and resulting in shallow reportage. Moreover, when a crew is stationed in, for example, Somalia, the news organization is likely to focus on live coverage of the story even when there is not much to report.[23]

No wonder the media tend to see events through the eyes of diplomats, soldiers and relief agencies from North America and Europe, while many local efforts to resolve problems are overlooked.

One important form of public affairs programming – the documentary – often offers greater volume, depth, continuity and sophistication. The documentary unit "CBS Reports," established in the early 1960s when the networks were moving to head off regulatory pressures, stood apart from commercial constraints. For example, works such as "Harvest of

> "We process information as we eat – 'McThought' – on the run. Fast food and fast thought are harmful to the body and to foreign policy."
>
> – Ted Koppel[24]

Shame" and "The Selling of the Pentagon" were hour-long statements about serious issues. Featuring a clear point of view, they provided a unique perspective on many problems, policies and controversial issues. Thanks to greater profit consciousness, such programs appear much less frequently on commercial network television.[25] Public broadcasting continues to air documentaries regularly, but reduced government support will weaken public broadcasting's relative independence from commercial pressure.

Technology has given the news media the ability to transmit events as they occur. This "real time" broadcasting has both connected and distorted the world. Television gives the illusion of shrinking the world. It makes us feel that we have, in a few minutes, understood and mastered problems of enormous complexity. But in fact, we cannot solve the real world's problems with the flick of a button.

Strategies for Change in Media Coverage

People can encourage socially responsible journalism by writing letters-to-the editor and opinion articles or by providing information to reporters and editors. Grassroots anti-hunger organizations such as Bread for the World and RESULTS[26] offer tips on writing letters-to-the editor and opinion pieces, as well as on arranging editorial meetings (which can result in printed editorials), getting interviewed by radio and television call-in programs and making effective calls to those shows. Hundreds of Bread for the World and RESULTS activists have been successful in explaining root causes of hunger – and pressing Congress for changes in legislation – through the media.

Concerned citizens can also:

- Urge editors, publishers, journalists and advertisers to upgrade the quality of their product;

- Request extended coverage of developing countries, both to unreported crises and beyond the short, sharp peaks of most crisis reporting;

- Protest the simplistic formulas used by the news media to portray crises in developing countries;

- Ask the news media to delve more deeply into the meaning of crises;

- Encourage the news media to create departments that regularly cover the developing world and permanent international correspondents;

- Demand more analytical, less frenetic evening newscasts. They may ultimately be cheaper to produce. And they would provide what has been sorely lacking – an attempt not simply to cover the world, but to explain it;

- Urge a redefinition of news that emphasizes thought as well as action, harmony as well as conflict and explanation as well as scandal;

- Ask that independent journalists or "stringers" be used more widely;

- Press for creation of a new advocacy organization for journalists dedicated to re-imagining the purposes of the profession; and

- Praise good coverage.

It is important that like-minded groups and individuals work together to convince the media and advertisers that a constituency exists for news about the developing world that goes beyond simple but dramatic images.

World Hunger Year's Harry Chapin Media Awards, which recognize in-depth hunger reporting, have helped encourage mainstream, as well as alternative, media to move in this direction. Over the last few years, awards have gone to ABC for coverage of domestic hunger, CNN for analysis of population growth, and the *Houston Chronicle* and *Dallas Morning News* for coverage of conflict and hunger in the Horn of Africa.

Nongovernmental organizations (NGOs) involved in relief and development can help by developing relationships with journalists and encouraging them to look at causes of crises and successful or promising responses. Some groups are already doing this (e.g., Food for the Hungry International), and correspondents usually value the information which NGOs provide. NGOs need to coordinate their media messages better, and this can help lessen public misperceptions of foreign aid (e.g., that it accounts for 20 percent of the federal budget, when in reality the figure is less than 1 percent). Inter-Action's Alliance for a Global Community, a broad coalition of organizations interested in international development, is seeking to serve as a vehicle for such media outreach. It is also important for NGOs to deepen their relationships with the academic institutions and "think tanks" whose experts the media generally seek out. ∎

Carole Zimmerman is director of communications at the Committee for the National Institute for the Environment and former director of communications at Bread for the World.

by Jim Stipe

Rock Music and Hunger

Anti-hunger advocates have used rock 'n' roll music to draw attention to the realities of hunger, as well as raise money for programs.

Earlier social movements similarly used music to move people to action. In the United States, for example, music played a key role in union organizing in the 1920s and 1930s, the World War II mobilization, and the civil rights, feminist and Vietnam protest movements of the 1960s and 1970s.

Rock music has helped spur people to donate money to address global hunger. During the African hunger crisis of the mid-1980s, a number of concerts and organizations combined music with social consciousness.

The largest of these was Live Aid/Band Aid, a joint British-U.S. effort that raised $140 million. It began in December 1984 with release of a single, *Do They Know It's Christmas?*, performed by a group of well-known rock stars and dedicated to people caught in the Ethiopian famine. Following the song's success, Band Aid, led by Irish rock star Bob Geldof, staged simultaneous concerts in London and Philadelphia to raise money for Africa. The proceeds went mainly to relief efforts in Ethiopia and Sudan.

Perhaps the best known effort in the United States was the *We Are The World* campaign, centered around a pop song, which raised $61 million. Proceeds from the song – written by Michael Jackson and Lionel Ritchie, with the recording participation of 45 other well-known performers – were funneled through an organization called United Support of Artists for Africa, or USA for Africa. From 1985 through 1989, USA for Africa took in $96.8 million.

After a large fundraising event such as *We Are The World*, one always asks, "What did they do with the money?" USA for Africa sent 90 percent of the funds to Africa, while 10 percent went to U.S. programs.

USA for Africa spent money for immediate relief programs such as the delivery of medicine, chemicals to purify water and fuel for truck fleets to deliver food; and for long-term recovery and development projects such as rural primary health care training and water supply facilities and strengthening of African nongovernmental organizations (NGOs).

As USA for Africa gained experience in determining where to distribute aid money, the organization worked through many channels. It distributed the $49 million disbursed for Africa between 1985 and 1989 as follows:

Industrial-country NGOs	50 percent
African NGOs	20 percent
United Nations	18 percent
African Development Bank	10 percent
African governments	2 percent

In all, agencies in 19 African countries and the United States received grants.

Although rock concerts raise large sums of money for ending hunger, the total amount is much smaller than the resources NGOs raise each year through their own efforts. And, in 1993, governments and international organizations provided over $18 billion in aid to Africa. Therefore, the concerts' greater value is raising awareness of hunger, both nationally and globally. At the same time, they give concert-goers a sense that they can actually do something about hunger, as small as their contribution may seem. Raising awareness is the first important step in the struggle to end hunger.

Figure 5.1
A brief listing of music events staged to raise money for anti-hunger organizations:

August 1971	Concerts for Bangladesh	Organized by former Beatle George Harrison, the two concerts included well-known stars Bob Dylan, Eric Clapton and Ringo Starr. During intermission, the concert organizers showed a film about Bengali refugees.
1975	World Hunger Year (WHY)	Singer Harry Chapin and radio host Bill Ayers started World Hunger Year, an organization that educates the general public, media and policy-makers about hunger and poverty problems in the United States and abroad. Chapin performed many benefit concerts against hunger, sometimes as many as 100 per year.
1979	Concerts for Cambodia	Former Beatle Paul McCartney staged a series of London concerts to raise money for Cambodian refugees.
April 1984	Have a Heart	Pat and Debby Boone, Glen Campbell and other Christian artists recorded the single *Song for the Poor*, and also staged a concert in February 1985.
April 1984	Together We Will Stand	College-aged students from around the world went on singing tours to raise money for hunger relief and development. The album *Together We Will Stand* was released by the Continental Singers and Amy Grant, Steve Taylor and Sandi Patti in July 1984.
1985 to present	Farm Aid	A series of concerts has raised money for U.S. American farmers. Many well-known artists have been involved, including Willie Nelson, Neil Young, Elton John, Arlo Guthrie, Bonnie Raitt and Guns 'N' Roses.
January 1985	Christian Artists United to Save the Earth (CAUSE)	Following the Dove Awards (the Christian music industry's equivalent of the Grammy Awards), singers joined together to record the single *Do Something Now*.
January 1985	USA for Africa	Forty-five American rock stars joined together to record *We Are The World*. As a follow-up, an album was produced featuring songs by members of the original group.
February 1985	Hear 'N' Aid	Forty heavy-metal bands – such as Quiet Riot, Dio and Mötley Crüe – recorded the single *Stars*.
February 1985	Northern Lights for Africa Society	Fifty-three musicians from Canada – including Anne Murray, Joni Mitchell, Gordon Lightfoot and Neil Young – came together to record *Tears Are Not Enough*. The group also held a telethon during the Live Aid concert.
February 1985	West Coast Musicians' Aid for Africa	Another collection of Canadian musicians released the album *Open Your Heart*, and staged two benefit concerts in June 1985.
March 1985	Chanteurs sans Frontières (Singers Without Borders)	Six French musicians recorded *Ethiopie*, which sold 2 million copies. The groups also held a benefit concert in Paris in October 1985.

March 1985	Hermanos (Brothers and Sisters)	Members of the Los Angeles Latino recording industry – including Placido Domingo, Jose Feliciano and Julio Iglesias – released a single, *Cantare, Cantares*. The single sold 100,000 copies in the United States and 200,000 in Mexico.
March 1985	San Diego Aid for Africa/91-X Radiothon	San Diego musicians and employees of radio station 91-X held a 53-hour radiothon in April 1985. The station also released an album featuring San Diego musicians under the name *SANDAID*.
May 1985	Calypsos for Africa	Percussionist Ralph MacDonald assembled 70 Calypso musicians from Trinidad and Tobago to record the single *Now Is the Time*.
July 1985	Live Aid	Irish and British pop stars, who previously recorded the single *Do They Know It's Christmas?*, joined with U.S. musicians and staged simultaneous benefit concerts in Philadelphia and London.
September 1985	Rock for Africa	The Danish Red Cross and three Danish band workers organized a 10-hour concert that included 25 bands.
1986	Hands Across America	Established as an off-shoot of USA for Africa, Hands Across America raised funds for anti-poverty efforts solely in the United States. Some Hands Across America money went to create Handsnet, a hunger bulletin board on the Internet.
1995	Tom Petty/USA Harvest	Rock star Tom Petty, in collaboration with USA Harvest, asks people to bring cans of food to his concerts to be distributed to food banks.

Jim Stipe was a Mickey Leland Fellow at Bread for the World Institute from 1994 to 1995. He has a degree in music from Wheaton College.

Chapter 6

But the Cupboard is Bare:
The Crisis of Aid

Bread for the World members support aid for sustainable development and humanitarian relief at a meeting with House International Relations Committee Chair Benjamin Gilman (left).

Timothy Achor-Hoch

by Marc J. Cohen

An international consensus is emerging on how to improve crisis response. Key elements include strengthening and engaging local communities' capacity to cope with emergencies; coordinating assistance efforts, including those of nongovernmental organizations (NGOs); and linking emergency relief with support for sustainable development. Institutional reforms are also needed to improve crisis response and prevention activities. Some analysts and policy-makers have even proposed the creation of a permanent U.N. military force, available when needed to deliver or protect relief supplies and engage in peacemaking and peacekeeping.[1]

All of this begs the question, "Who will foot the bill?" Money is a real problem. At present, donors do not seem to be operating along the "relief to development continuum" so much as dishing out slices of a shrinking development aid pie for short-term emergency purposes.

Official development assistance (ODA) from the industrial countries declined 6 percent in real dollar terms in 1993 (the last year for which complete data are available) to $56 billion. Preliminary data indicate a further 2 percent decline in ODA in 1994.[2]

In recent years, industrial countries have provided 97 percent of all aid resources. The average donor nation's share of gross national product (GNP) devoted to aid declined to 0.30 percent in 1993 from 0.33 percent the year before, well below the U.N. target of 0.7 percent. The United States provided 0.15 percent of its GNP in 1993, the lowest figure among industrial countries.

Most donors are not planning aid increases over the next several years. In many cases, the planned level of resources will decline when inflation is taken into account.[3] This fall in ODA contrasts with steady growth of 2 percent to 3 percent annually during the 1980s (see Figure 6.1).

The end of the Cold War deprived aid of its most powerful political motive. Fiscal austerity in most donor countries contributes to the drop in aid. The "peace dividend" for assistance to sustainable development, which development advocates urged in the early 1990s, has not materialized. Meanwhile, the need for aid in former communist states, which received $6.9 billion in 1993, drains funds from poorer countries.

At the same time, only a modest proportion of aid supports sustainable development and poverty reduction. Aid to agriculture has declined since 1988 (see Figure 6.2), even though the majority of poor people in the developing world get their income and food supplies from local agricultural activities. Less than one-sixth of aid resources presently support agriculture, and even less – about a tenth – go into such "social development" sectors as education, primary health care and reproductive health.

In the case of the United States, Bread for the World Institute's study, "At the Crossroads: the Future of Foreign Aid," found that in fiscal year (FY) 1994, just 17 percent of the $15.2 billion U.S. foreign aid budget (including military and security aid, bilateral economic aid and U.S. contributions to multilateral institutions) focused on supporting sustainable development.

The share of the industrial countries' aid going to poor countries fell below 50 percent of the total in 1993, after averaging 55 percent for a decade. But the World Bank warns that the number of people worldwide living on the equivalent of less than a dollar a day will increase from 1.3 billion in 1995 to

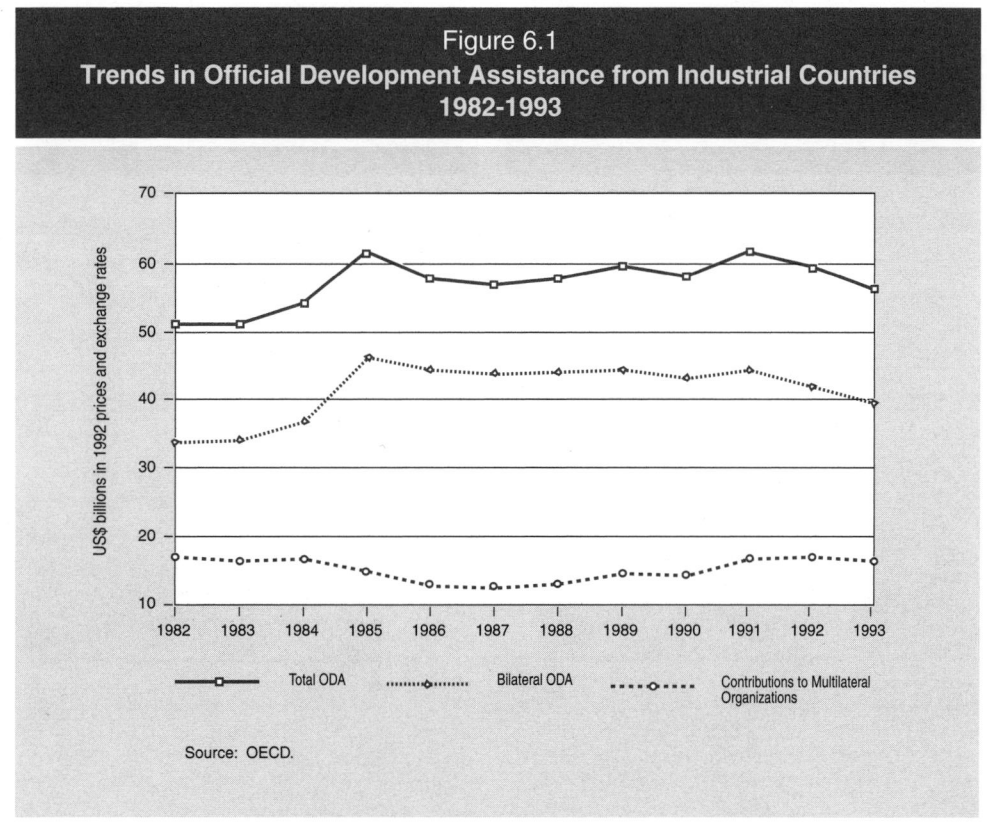

Figure 6.1
Trends in Official Development Assistance from Industrial Countries
1982-1993

Source: OECD.

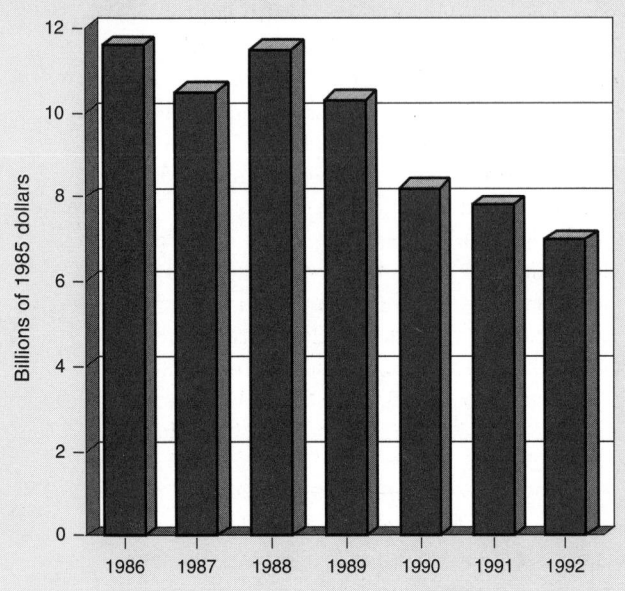

Figure 6.2
Aid to Agriculture from All Sources
1986-1992

Billions of 1985 dollars

Sources: FAO; Energy and Environmental Study Institute.

1.5 billion in 2000. Most of these poor people will live in these same low-income countries.[4]

The drop in overall aid comes at a time of increased demand for emergency assistance, due primarily to armed conflicts. Bilateral emergency assistance (including food aid and aid to refugees) totaled $3.6 billion, accounting for 11 percent of bilateral ODA in 1993. This was up sharply from $1 billion – less than 6 percent of ODA – in the 1980s (see Figure 6.3).

According to James Michel, chairman of the Development Assistance Committee of the Organisation for Economic Co-operation and Development:

Multilateral institutions have been similarly affected. The United Nations saw the share of its assistance going to help refugees and assist in humanitarian emergencies increase massively. In addition, U.N. expenditures on peacekeeping escalated to new levels in 1993.[5]

Emergency operations budgets of agencies such as the U.N. High Commissioner for Refugees, UNICEF and the U.N. World Food Programme (WFP) have increased over the past decade, and emergency assistance now accounts for 50 percent

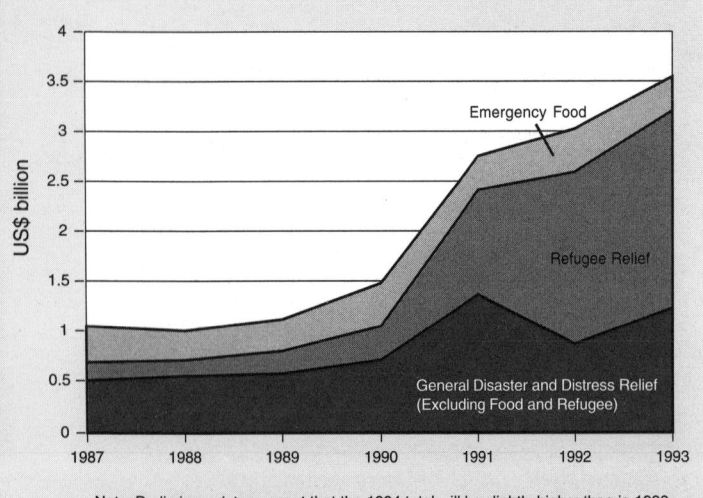

Figure 6.3
Industrial Countries' Bilateral Emergency and Refugee Aid
1987-1993

US$ billion

Emergency Food

Refugee Relief

General Disaster and Distress Relief
(Excluding Food and Refugee)

Note: Preliminary data suggest that the 1994 total will be slightly higher than in 1993.
Source: OECD.

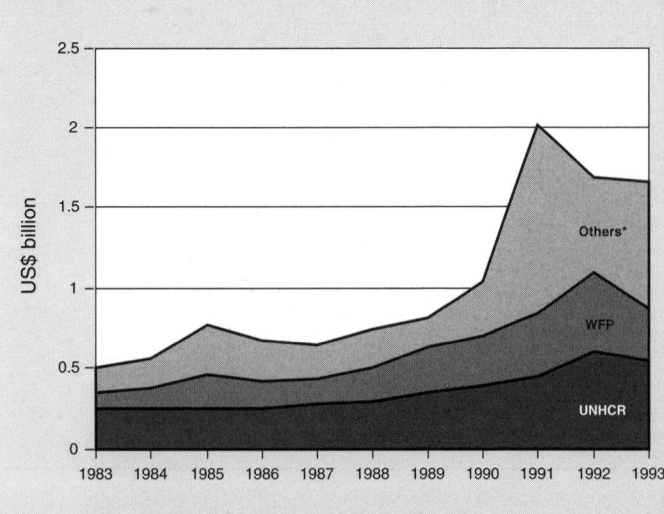

Figure 6.4
Industrial Country Contributions to International Agencies for Emergency and Refugee Aid
1983-1993

US$ billion

Others*

WFP

UNHCR

*Includes UNRWA, European Community, UNICEF.
Source: OECD.

of all U.N. aid. WFP devoted 25 percent of its resources to emergencies in 1989, but 70 percent in 1993. During this same period, development budgets for agencies such as the U.N. Development Programme (UNDP) have declined (see Figure 6.4).

After emergency aid and administrative costs are subtracted, bilateral funds actually available for investment in long-term development in poor countries amounted to $33.2 billion in 1993, down more than 8 percent from the year before.

It is important to note that many relief activities have development or rehabilitation components built into them. This is particularly true of food-for-work projects in which people affected by humanitarian emergencies are employed in reconstruction efforts and paid wholly or partly with food aid commodities. Forging such linkages in a creative manner becomes ever more important as funds decline and crises multiply.

Trends in many individual donors' aid mirror the global patterns. The European Union's (EU) humanitarian aid doubled between 1986 and 1991. Dutch emergency aid increased nearly fivefold between

1990 and 1993, while total ODA remained flat (and fell by 9 percent between 1992 and 1993). In 1992, Australia provided NGOs with 240 percent more funds for emergency and refugee activities than for development projects. In 1991, EU funding of NGO emergency and refugee programs exceeded development grants by 290 percent.[6]

Overall U.S. aid resources (again, with military and other non-ODA included) declined by 24 percent between FY 1985 and FY 1995. Aid is a popular target for budget cutters, although it amounts to less than 1 percent of total federal spending. Aid to agriculture dropped 37 percent from FY 1992 to FY 1995[7], and support for agricultural research has declined precipitously.

Total emergency aid (disaster assistance, emergency food aid and refugee assistance) ballooned from $786 million in FY 1989 to $2.2 billion in FY 1993, representing 23 percent of ODA (see Figure 6.5). In order to meet emergency needs, U.S. policymakers have diverted resources budgeted for child survival activities worldwide and sustainable development in Africa; the lost funds have not been restored. The Clinton administration has reduced non-emergency food aid spending substantially, and recently cut by half the U.S. pledge (the world's largest) to the global Food Aid Convention.

Legislation before the U.S. Congress would cut bilateral development assistance by 35 percent, while maintaining current levels of humanitarian assistance, and aid to Israel and Egypt. Some proposals would eliminate the $800 million Development Fund for Africa, which targets assistance to poor people in poor African countries. There are also plans for steep reductions in U.S. support for multilateral assistance institutions that focus on poor countries such as UNDP and the International Development Association (the soft loan branch of the World Bank). Other proposals call for abolishing the U.S. Agency for International Development (USAID) and putting the State Department in charge of aid. Such a move would further politicize development assistance.

Bread for the World and other U.S. NGOs that lobby on aid issues are working to preserve aid for sustainable development in poor countries. They argue that U.S. withdrawal from leadership in the international development arena will have ripple effects: other donors will certainly cut their aid in response to U.S. reductions, further shrinking total ODA. Moreover, aid can clearly contribute to improvements in people's well-being. As Norwegian Prime Minister Gro Harlem Brundtland has put it,

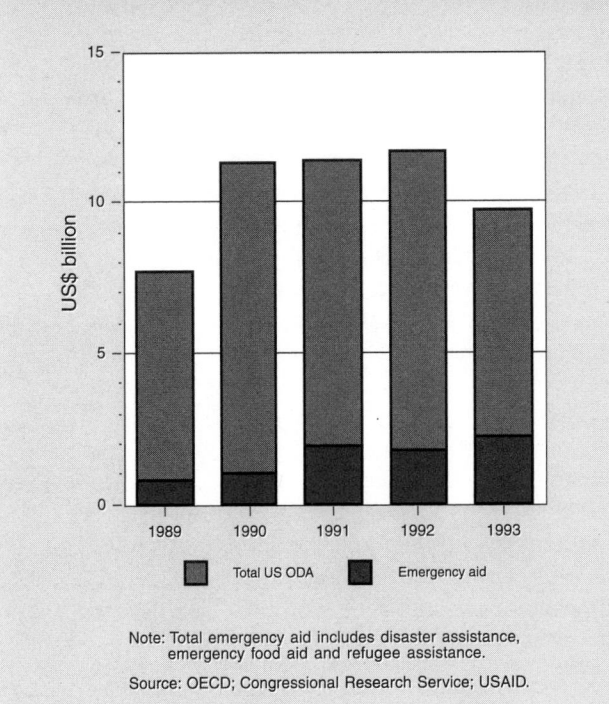

Figure 6.5
Total U.S. Official Development Assistance and Emergency Aid
1989-1993

US$ billion

Total US ODA   Emergency aid

Note: Total emergency aid includes disaster assistance, emergency food aid and refugee assistance.

Source: OECD; Congressional Research Service; USAID.

. . . 2.5 million fewer children will die in 1996 than in 1990, because of increased efforts in primary health care. Guinea worm disease may soon be eradicated, and many regions are free from polio. Countries like Bangladesh, India and Pakistan are now able to feed their populations. Even though it is difficult to estimate how many of these major achievements can be attributed to aid, they suggest that international cooperation can work.[8]

While trade and private investment flows from the industrial to the developing world are considerably larger than the volume of ODA, aid remains the most significant channel of funds for poor countries.

Globally, the squeeze on development resources and proliferation of emergency needs is likely to continue. According to the U.S. Central Intelligence Agency, ethnic, religious and other civil conflicts have put 30 million Africans at risk of malnutrition or death unless they receive emergency humanitarian aid. Similar struggles in Central and South Asia will affect another 10 million people. But "growing reluctance by donor nations to become involved in protracted conflicts and a breakdown in social structures in these regions will substantially constrain relief efforts."[9]

Ironically, many policy-makers now recognize that development assistance can prevent crises. As Mahbub ul Haq of UNDP says, "An ounce of prevention is generally worth more than a ton of punishment. Two billion dollars spent on soldiers in Somalia today buys much less security than the same investment would have 10 years ago in socio-economic development."[10] Adds USAID Administrator J. Brian Atwood, "Sustainable development that creates chains of enterprise, respects the environment, and enlarges the range of freedom and opportunity over generations should be pursued as the principal antidote to social disarray."[11] Yet current directions in "aid giving" virtually guarantee that developing countries will need more emergency aid. Development aid can help societies become less prone to conflict, human rights abuse and hunger, but that sort of aid is rapidly declining.

The aid funding crisis stems in part from strong consensus in the international community on the duty to respond to humanitarian need – a "consensual norm," according to Brown University Professor Peter Uvin.[12] This is strengthened by media tendencies to give greater attention to emergencies than long-term development, pricking public consciences and leading to pressures on governments to act.

The widespread assumption that citizens in donor countries have little interest in development contributes to politicians' willingness to cut development aid. But surveys suggest that popular support for aid remains strong in Europe, especially in the Netherlands and Scandinavia, and in Japan.[13]

Even in the United States, where it is often asserted that foreign aid is wildly unpopular, recent surveys have shown strong levels of support for development assistance. A January 1995 University of Maryland poll found a widespread misperception that aid accounts for 15 percent or more of federal government spending. But 68 percent of respondents supported the United States giving the same percentage of its GNP in aid as other industrial countries. Sixty-seven percent agreed that "as one of the world's rich nations, the United States has a moral responsibility toward poor nations," and 58 percent were willing to pay more in taxes to support aid if it "was going to the poor people who really need it." Fully 91 percent wanted to maintain or increase spending on child survival activities.[14] This and other polls have consistently found majority support for "combating world hunger" as an important goal of U.S. foreign policy.[15]

The polls suggest that politicians in donor countries do not have the mandate they claim for slashing aid. Appeals to save aid should include strong moral arguments, as well as self-interested ones, e.g., aid recipient countries are the export markets of the future. Committed supporters of aid – anti-hunger and environmental advocates, nongovernmental relief and development organizations, concerned people in the academic and religious communities, ethnic organizations and businesses that directly benefit from aid programs – need to organize and mobilize existing but passive public good will into a coherent constituency.

The resources are available. It is a question of where donor nations choose to invest their wealth. Even within foreign aid budgets, most resources go to purposes other than sustainable development and humanitarian assistance. Those who support humanitarian and sustainable development aid must redouble efforts to strengthen the constituency for it. Otherwise, funding will continue to dwindle, while the world's crisis zones continue to require humanitarian relief. ∎

Dr. Marc J. Cohen is senior research associate at Bread for the World Institute and editor of *Countries in Crisis*. Bread for the World Institute intern Jashinta D'Costa provided research assistance.

Creating Secure Livelihoods
in the United States

by Lucilla L. Tan and Don Reeves

U.S. workers protest trade-related job losses.

If . . . the economic success of a nation is judged only by income and by other traditional indicators of opulence and financial soundness, . . . the important goal of well-being is missed.

— Amartya Sen[1]

The United States is not experiencing open civil strife, civilian deaths, displacement and economic and social disruption on the same scale as Rwanda or Bosnia. However, it does face a humanitarian crisis in which the livelihoods and physical safety of millions of families are threatened.

Emergency food needs have increased steadily in major cities in recent years, with a sizeable portion of those needs going unmet.

Drug trafficking, crime and violence have taken over too many U.S. urban neighborhoods. African-American men over 40 years of age in Harlem are less likely to reach 65 than men the same age in Bangladesh.[2] As in Afghanistan (see Chapter 1), crime gangs and the drug trade increasingly seem to offer the only avenues to a decent standard of living for low-skilled young men. Violence is not only a major threat to the health of adolescents, but youths increasingly perpetrate violence: between 1985 and 1993, the number of homicides committed by 14- to 17-year-old males increased

165 percent.[3] The American Medical Association calls violence in the United States "a public health emergency."[4]

When opportunities for secure livelihood – the ability to meet basic needs without tradeoffs – seem beyond reach, the resulting despair and hopelessness may translate or be manipulated into violence and crime.[5] Despair respects no geographic or demographic boundaries. It undermines the well-being of families, communities and eventually whole societies.

Economic insecurity cannot justify violence, nor is it the sole cause. But in any nation, limited chances to earn a living aggravate social problems. People with little education and few job skills face diminishing opportunities for secure livelihoods in the United States, as around the world. These people already face a crisis; and because we live in an interdependent society, we are all affected.

The United States could, and should, end widespread hunger among its people within a few years by ensuring more adequate safety nets. It could, and should, also assure more economic opportunities for livelihood through socially productive activities for many people now in poverty. Useful work is not only a link to a livelihood. It is a source of dignity that is integral to feeling part of society. Only when there is such a sense of belonging do people have a vested interest in contributing to and preserving society's well-being.

The U.S. Congress has adopted some of the rhetoric of providing work opportunities, but is in fact in the process of slashing both the safety nets and programs that would increase work opportunities – nutrition, Head Start (an early childhood education program), job training and other anti-poverty programs. Members of Congress and too many other Americans seem ready to write off millions of low-income people, especially members of minority groups. The results will be yet more poverty, hunger and violence.

Growing Hunger, Poverty and Inequality

Limited economic opportunities and an unraveling social fabric have led directly to increasing poverty and hunger in the United States, despite an improving overall economy. Since 1993, the U.S. economy has grown an average of 3.6 percent a year with modest inflation. In 1994, real disposable income rose 4.3 percent, and the United States regained its rank as the most competitive economy in the world.[6] Official unemployment in June 1995 was 5.6 percent (considerably lower than in most European countries).

However, the gap between rich and poor has grown in the United States in the 1990s.[7] The Food Research and Action Center found in 1995 that 4 million U.S. children under 12 were hungry and 9.6 million were at risk of hunger. The need for emergency food grows faster than the resources available. Underemployment remains high (unemployed, discouraged and involuntary part-time workers; see Figures U.S. 1, U.S. 2 and U.S. 3). Declining job quality, low wages, widening inequality, falling family incomes, hunger and social tension are all connected.

1993 U.S. Poverty Statistics[8]

- 39.3 million people in the United States (15.1 percent of the population) lived below the poverty line (see "The Federal Poverty Measure," p. 69), 1.3 million more than in 1992 and 6.9 million more than in 1989. Subtracting government benefits from the official definition of income would have increased the 1993 poverty rate to 23.4 percent.

- 8.4 million families were poor (12.3 percent). Married-couple families had a poverty rate of 6.5 percent. For single-parent, female-headed families, the rate was 35.6 percent.

- 15.1 percent of poor families had a householder who worked year-round and full-time.

- 9.9 percent of non-Hispanic whites, 33.1 percent of blacks, 30.6 percent of Hispanics and 15.3 percent of Asians and Pacific Islanders were poor.

- 22.7 percent of children under 18 were poor; 63.7 percent of children under age 6 living in female-headed households were poor.

- 41 percent of poor people lived in families whose total 1993 income was less than half of the poverty line.

- The South had the highest poverty rate (17.1 percent); 39.2 percent of all poor people lived in that region.

U.S. Poverty Dynamics[9]

- 10.6 million people (4.5 percent of the population) were poor all 24 months of 1990 and 1991.

- 21 percent of people who were poor in 1990 were not poor in 1991.

- In the early 1990s, children were less likely to leave poverty than non-elderly adults.

- People without high school diplomas were more likely to be poor, and more likely to have longer spells of poverty.

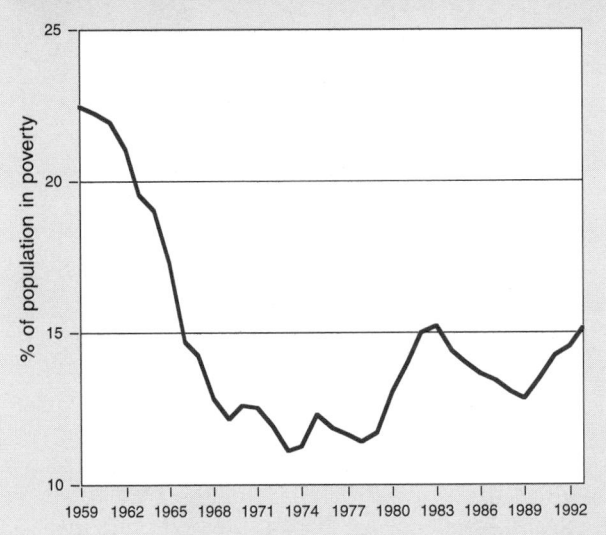

Figure U.S. 1
Official U.S. Poverty Rate
1959-1993

Source: U.S. Bureau of the Census.

percent of all households utilizing emergency feeding programs had no adult working and 19 percent of all clients had not worked for one year or more. About one-third of unemployed clients were last employed in skilled positions (skilled worker, sales, crafts, technical, secretarial, managerial, professional or self-employed).[13]

The U.S. Conference of Mayors reported that in 1994, 83 percent of the 30 cities surveyed registered an increase in requests for emergency food assistance, by an average of 12 percent. On average, 15

Use of Emergency Food Programs

There is presently no official survey of the exact number of hungry people in the United States. Indirect indicators of hunger are food stamp participation and use of emergency food providers.[10] In 1993, Second Harvest found that length of usage increased by 56 percent in soup kitchens, 27 percent in food pantries and 16 percent in emergency shelters, as compared to a year earlier. Forty-six percent of clients had received food stamps for more than two years.

Respondents named unemployment as the dominant reason for seeking food assistance. Sixty-eight

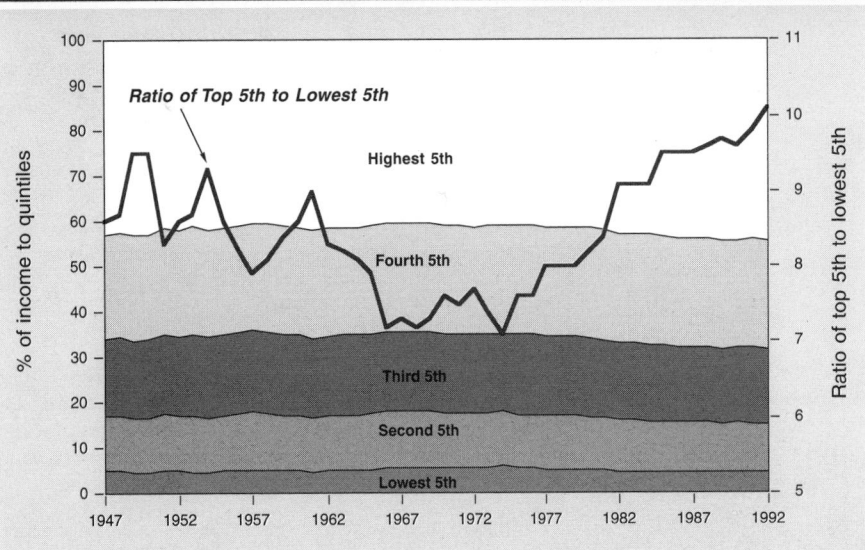

Figure U.S. 2
Distribution of U.S. Household Income
1947-1992

Source: U.S. Bureau of the Census.

percent of the requests went unmet. Of the adults requesting assistance, 23 percent were employed. Unemployment was cited as the primary cause of hunger in 26 of the 30 cities; other causes cited were poverty (18 cities), high cost of housing (15 cities), low public assistance benefit levels (12 cities), high cost of living (7 cities), substance abuse (3 cities) and mental illness (2 cities).[14]

Food Stamp Participation

Before the 1990 recession, the number of food stamp participants hovered below 20 million. As the economy worsened then recovered over the next four years, the number of recipients climbed, reaching 28 million – 10 percent of the people in the United States – in March 1994. The Food Stamp Program cost $28.1 billion in 1994, but only served 60 percent of those eligible. Eighty-two percent of recipient households were families with children.

By May 1995, the number of program participants fell to 26.5 million. Some experts suggest the decline is due to improving economic conditions, while others speculate the trend is due to welfare reforms.[15]

Declining Incomes for Low-Skill Workers

Demand for less-educated and less-skilled workers has declined – most dramatically within manufacturing, where semi-skilled jobs have declined much faster than overall employment.[16] The U.S. Bureau of Labor Statistics reports that two-thirds of the 5.6 million workers displaced (i.e., those who lost jobs because of plant closings, slack work or the elimination of their positions) since 1987 found new jobs by January 1992, but barely a quarter earned as much or

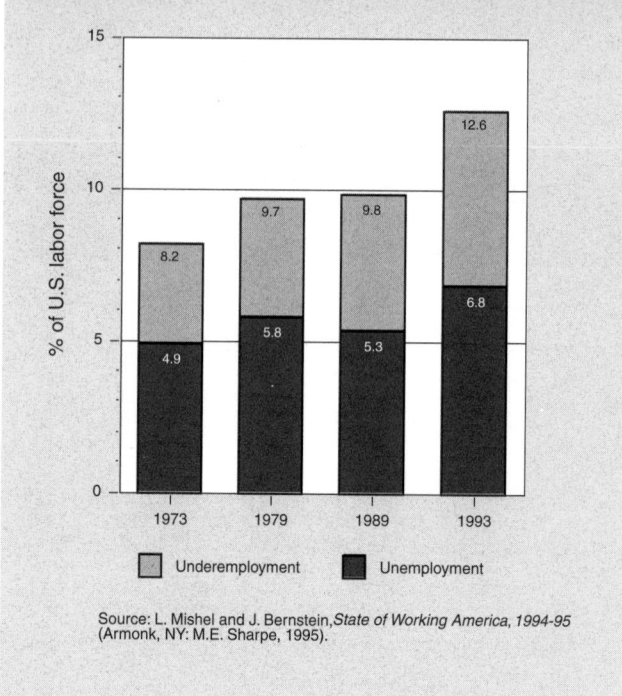

Figure U.S. 3
U.S. Rates of Unemployment and Underemployment 1973-1993

Source: L. Mishel and J. Bernstein, *State of Working America, 1994-95* (Armonk, NY: M.E. Sharpe, 1995).

more as at the lost job.[17] Manufacturing workers were still the largest category of displaced workers, but the lost-job gap between white-collar and blue-collar workers has narrowed over the past decade, reflecting the more widespread nature of job loss.

Shirley Martin, 52, of Maryville, TN, worked at a Levi Strauss plant for 11 years, but lost her job when

---

World SHARE –
Building Community Through Social Businesses

By Elisa Sabatini

World SHARE (Self-Help and Resource Exchange) calls itself a "social business." Social service agencies provide resources to needy people. In contrast, SHARE works *with* and enlists as participants those who are served.

In the United States, SHARE purchases food with participants' advance payments. This purchasing power makes it possible for SHARE to offer $30 worth of food in exchange for $14 in cash or food stamps and two hours of volunteer service. The volunteer

service is a factor in the savings. Service hours are used to accomplish the monthly distribution of food packages to 350,000 families, through 7,500 community-based organizations from 26 warehouses nationwide.

The monthly package contains fresh fruits and vegetables, frozen meats and staples such as beans, rice or pasta. SHARE provides this source of low-cost food for anyone who chooses to participate. However, more than half of SHARE's participants have incomes

below 150 percent of the poverty line and/or live on fixed incomes. Another 41 percent are "middle class."

Volunteer activities include more than just food distribution. Volunteers give thousands of hours to a vast array of community activities, including delivering food to shut-ins, serving on community boards and removing graffiti – all focused on building community one hour at a time.

Elisa Sabatini is World SHARE's regional director for Latin America.

it closed. She found work at a smaller sewing factory after two years, but the job paid $4.25 an hour instead of the $8 an hour she earned at Levi's.[18] Displaced workers like Martin compete directly with entry-level workers, further squeezing workers with no experience and low skills.

Structural Changes in the Economy

Changing technology and increased trade have both contributed to the declining economic position of workers with low skills and little education (see Figures U.S. 4 and U.S. 5). Economists differ on the balance between trade or technological change as causes.

The market for workers carrying out routine tasks, and even that for skilled and technical labor, has become global. The costs of transportation and communications have fallen, developing countries now welcome foreign investment and their work forces have gained education. By 1990:

* American Airlines employed over 1,000 data processors in Barbados and the Dominican Republic to enter names and flight numbers from used airline tickets (flown daily to Barbados) into a computer bank located in Dallas, TX; and

* With a large number of skilled, English-speaking engineers and scientists, India had created a niche for itself in computer programming. Texas Instruments (TI) maintained a software development facility in Bangalore, linking 50 Indian programmers by satellite to TI's Dallas headquarters.[19]

Persistent U.S. trade deficits in manufactured goods since the 1970s have contributed to the decline of U.S. manufacturing and lowered demand for less-skilled U.S. workers who traditionally looked to the manufacturing sector for good-paying jobs.

The large decline in the real value of the federal minimum wage since 1981 and declining union clout have also contributed to growing wage differences.[20]

Impact on the Labor Market

Employment Growth in Low-Wage Sectors[21]

Between 1975 and 1990, the proportion of the labor force employed in goods-producing industries with historically stable, high wages fell nearly 23 percent. During this period, service industries increased their employment, but mainly in low-wage areas such as retail sales (see "Discount Stores," p. 73). In 1994, almost 85 percent of the 3.5 million new jobs were concentrated in services.

Demand for Temporary and Part-Time Workers

Temporary and part-time workers are cheaper to employ, since they generally receive no benefits and can be employed on an "as needed" basis. At a Ford Motor Co. plant in St. Louis, MO, 3,400 full-time employees earn an average of $57,000 a year with overtime. Two hundred temps do essentially the same type of work two to three days a week for $20,000 a year. Temporary workers accounted for 1.6 percent of the labor force in 1993. The total payroll for temps tripled to $19.6 billion between 1985 and 1993. Part-time workers constituted 19 percent of the total work force in 1993, and a third of them worked part-time involuntarily.[22]

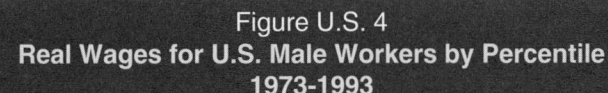

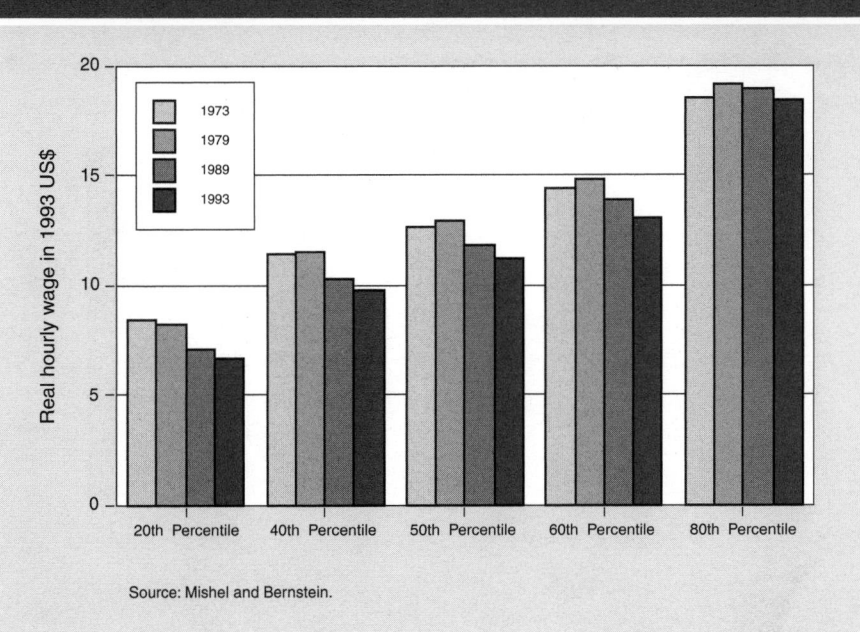

Figure U.S. 4
Real Wages for U.S. Male Workers by Percentile 1973-1993

Real hourly wage in 1993 US$

1973
1979
1989
1993

20th Percentile 40th Percentile 50th Percentile 60th Percentile 80th Percentile

Source: Mishel and Bernstein.

Demand for Technologically Skilled Workers[23]

High-tech companies are hiring more graduates with technical backgrounds, as businesses demand better information systems and consumer interest in linking to cyberspace increases. Computer-related help-wanted ads in *The Washington Post* increased by 79 percent during 1994, and now make up one-quarter of all its employment advertising. Skilled white-collar clerical workers are also in demand. The National Association of Temporary Staffing Services recently predicted a continued shortage of skilled workers for the more demanding office jobs: "As companies . . . eliminate layers of management . . . they want someone who can be a receptionist but also handle a spreadsheet, . . . type fast . . . and also do a mail merge."[24]

Workers with lower levels of skill and education face worsening job prospects and declining wages, since technology, education, innovation and flexibility are now highly needed and rewarded in the U.S. economy. As Labor Secretary Robert Reich puts it:

Most of the good-paying jobs created in the last two years require some technical know-how. . . . [W]hile a gas station attendant might be lucky to earn $12,000 a year, an auto mechanic who understands computer diagnostics can earn as much as $70,000.[25]

Enhancing Livelihood Opportunities for Poor People

Government programs that provide food and other assistance to hungry and poor people are vitally important. Some of these programs certainly need reform, but funding should not be slashed.

Nearly everyone – liberal or conservative – believes that poor people should, wherever possible, find work that enables them to support themselves. This has long been a stated U.S. policy goal. The rest of this chapter focuses on policies that would help the nation actually achieve it.

Strengthening Incentives for Work

At present, a full-time minimum wage worker earns a gross annual income of $8,500, or just 88 percent of the 1994 poverty threshold for a two-person household. If the head of a family receiving Aid to Families with Dependent Children (AFDC, the main welfare program) takes a full-time minimum wage job, the family loses AFDC, food stamps, housing subsidies and access to health care through Medicaid, and must pay income and Social Security taxes, as well as transportation and child care costs. The job may not provide health benefits. These losses amount to a 77 percent tax on whatever income a welfare recipient earns.[26]

The United States should enhance its policies to "make work pay":

- **Maintain or expand the Earned Income Credit (EIC).** First enacted in 1975, EIC supplements the earnings of low-income workers by reducing their taxes and providing a credit to those who owe no taxes. For those not in the labor market or who have low earnings, EIC presents a clear incentive to increase work hours since it raises the effective wage received. Because it is paid out of government tax receipts, there is no employer disincentive.[27]

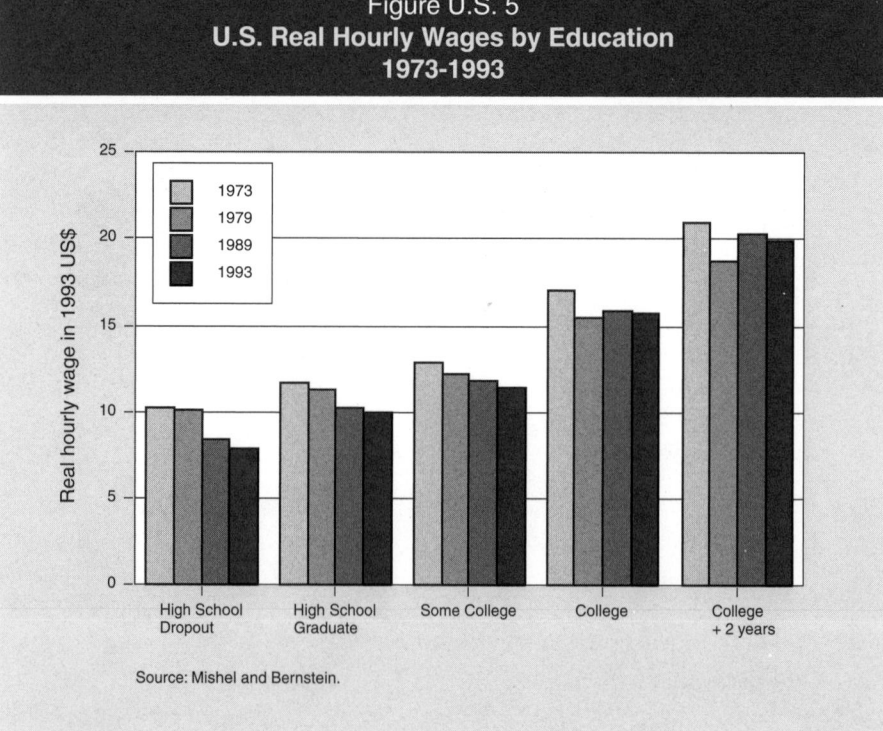

Figure U.S. 5
U.S. Real Hourly Wages by Education 1973-1993

Source: Mishel and Bernstein.

Discount Stores: Factories of the '90s[28]

Discount retail stores have become a major source of new jobs. Wal-Mart, the discount chain and the nation's second largest private employer, added 153,000 of the 1.9 million net new jobs in the first 30 months of the recovery from the 1990 to 1991 recession. The other 165 discount retail chains accounted for an additional 186,000 jobs.

Discount retailers generally pay $5 an hour to $9 an hour compared to the $15 an hour to $20 an hour in traditionally high-paying blue-collar jobs. Benefits generally include profit-sharing, medical and dental care, life insurance and paid vacations.

Full-time work at discounters means 28 to 30 hours per week, not the 35 to 40 hours still standard in manufacturing. This gives the retailers flexibility to raise a worker's hours in busy periods without paying a premium for overtime.

Many local retailers argue that they cannot compete against large discount retailers' low prices and larger selection of goods. A study of Wal-Mart in Iowa found that three to four years after the chain opened a store, smaller retailers shut down.

Restaurants, health care and temporary employment have generated even more jobs than the discounters, but most lack comparable benefits.

- **Raise the minimum wage.** The Clinton administration has proposed raising the minimum wage from $4.25 to $5.15 an hour. Opponents argue that raising the minimum wage might hurt those the legislation is intended to help because employers may cut back on labor to contain the higher costs. Studies testing this theory are inconclusive. Also, critics claim large numbers of teenagers will quit school for low-wage jobs, displacing marginally qualified workers and increasing unemployment.[29] But proponents – including Bread for the World – argue an increased minimum wage could boost morale, increase productivity, reduce turnover and increase the incentive for work.

- **Introduce wage subsidies for "low income" earners.** One study shows that a wage subsidy of $32 per week to a worker working 20 hours at $5 an hour (phasing out slowly as earnings increase) would attract 850,000 non-working single mothers into the labor force. The subsidy would save the government money because it would reduce AFDC costs as recipients take jobs, and the cost of the subsidy would be lower than AFDC benefits. It also makes work more attractive than AFDC. The subsidy would be less costly than EIC because most EIC dollars go to full-time workers who might have worked anyway.[30]

Government Employment and Training Programs

Publicly funded job training programs must be a component of any effort to help disadvantaged people make the transition from the declining low-skill labor market to the expanding high-skill market. Business is unlikely to make such a large-scale investment on its own.

The U.S. Department of Labor recently evaluated the impact of various approaches to jobs training. Among the findings:[31]

- **Short-term (three to six months) classroom training.** Most short-term training programs have not produced significant earnings gains for participants, especially youth. A notable exception is the Center for Employment and Training (CET) in San Jose, CA. There, participants sustained annual earnings gains of 40 percent over a control group of non-participants in the third and fourth years after entry into the program. The elements that set CET apart from other training programs are: a focus on job placement, the integration of basic education with vocational skills training, a curriculum tailored to the needs of individual students and highly experienced staff with knowledge of the local labor market.

- **Long-term classroom training.** Disadvantaged youth have benefitted from Job Corps (see "Major Federal Government Employment and Training Programs," p. 74). A study of long-term community college training for displaced workers in Pennsylvania found "earnings increases" of roughly 6 percent to 7 percent per year of training.

- **Subsidized employment approaches.** In some programs, a government agency pays a private-sector employer to hire and provide informal training to disadvantaged individuals, or offers

Job Corps[32]

Job Corps is an intensive "boarding school" program providing basic education, vocational skills, a wide range of support services and job placement. It takes about a year to complete and costs an average of $15,000 per student. Job Corps enrolled 62,000 new youth in 1993, with total outlays of $970 million.

The difficulty of the training and the strict code of conduct cause a substantial number of enrollees to drop out or be dismissed within the first three months. In 1993, 70 percent of those who completed the program moved on to jobs or further education, about the same as in 1978. Participation improves the future earnings of participants, while reducing welfare dependency and involvement in serious crime.

Job Training Partnership Act (JTPA) Title II Training for Adults[33]

Passage of JTPA in 1983 marked a shift in the federal government's training strategy from work experience to on-the-job training. Primary services provided are classroom training, job search assistance and on-the-job training. In 1993, JTPA Title II enrolled 550,000 new participants (310,000 of whom were adults) at a cost of $1.7 billion. About 30 percent of adult JTPA trainees have not received high school diplomas, and 28 percent get AFDC. The average adult trainee stays in the program for four months. Total training costs per adult are about $3,300.

Although the program's impact on youth has been disappointing, disadvantaged adults have achieved improvements in earnings – increases of 10 percent for men and 15 percent for women. These programs have been cost-effective: JTPA services for adults produced earnings gains 50 percent greater than the total additional training costs within 30 months after enrollment. However, these earnings gains did not significantly reduce welfare participation, and resulted mainly from increased work hours, not increased wages.

Job Opportunities and Basic Skills Training Program (JOBS)[34]

The Family Support Act of 1988 expanded welfare-to-work mandates for AFDC participants. JOBS provides basic education, training, extensive job search assistance and support services. Fiscal year (FY) 1993 spending totaled $1.1 billion. States are accountable for the number and type of AFDC recipients participating, but not for the number who get jobs or earn their way off AFDC. Of the more than 4 million parents receiving AFDC checks each month, JOBS served on average only about 11 percent between FY 1991 and FY 1993. JOBS has not widely served AFDC recipients who most need help in avoiding long-term dependence such as teen parents and people with learning disabilities or emotional problems. Program administrators report that they lack the resources to provide current participants with the services and assistance they need. Programs generally do not focus on recipients' employment as the ultimate goal.

participants extensive support services during a year of subsidized employment. When the subsidized job is over, participants may stay with their employer without a subsidy, or receive assistance in finding new work. This approach has been "remarkably successful" for single mothers on welfare. Recipients showed average annual gains in earnings of 40 percent to 50 percent. This approach alone has been less successful in creating long-term benefits for disadvantaged youth.

- **Job Search Assistance (JSA).** JSA produced moderate long-term earnings gains of $300 to $700 for welfare recipients. JSA, together with on-the-job training, led to annual gains in earnings of more than $1,100 for adults. The impact of JSA for disadvantaged youth is mixed. It helped youths find jobs more quickly, but did not improve long-term employment prospects.

Successful job training programs provide participants with a range of support services (see "Cleveland Works," p. 76).

Temporary subsidized work experience for disadvantaged youth typically does not result in long-term improvements in employment and earnings.[35] The difficulty of succeeding with school dropouts points to the importance of dropout prevention efforts. The United States needs to enhance post-secondary training for youths who do not go to college. Compared to Germany and Japan, such opportunities are limited in the United States.

Corporate Training Efforts

The best companies of the 21st century will bring together brain power wherever it is, around the country or around the globe.

– Jerry Jasinowski, president, National Association of Manufacturers[36]

Corporations that have profited from increased competitiveness could retrain their older workers for new, high-tech jobs. Some are already moving in this direction. Motorola requires employees to attend 40 hours of classes annually at the company university, which offers science, liberal arts and language. Motorola management recognizes that its workers are key to product quality and innovation, and should understand the global economy in which the company operates. Motorola estimates it earns $30 for every $1 invested in employee training. At NYNEX, a communications firm, workers can take unpaid sabbaticals to pursue a degree, while continuing to receive benefits.[37]

In addition to retraining current workers, corporations could also offer joint training or internship programs for participants in government job programs. The Kenosha Job Center in Wisconsin found that putting trainees in "real job situations" showed them how to apply their training productively.[38] Such partnerships not only benefit trainees, but also give corporations the opportunity to screen potential employees.

Job Creation

The government can stimulate the economy, encourage business growth and create more jobs by lowering taxes, increasing spending or lowering interest rates to make it cheaper to borrow money for investment and consumption. The U.S. government reduced unemployment in these ways in the 1960s and early 1970s. But high inflation in the late 1970s and continued deficit spending throughout the years have made these approaches less feasible now. It should be possible to increase jobs somewhat by reducing the costs of regulation to employers without abandoning the social purposes for which regulations were established – worker rights, product safety and environmental protection, for example.

The nation still faces pressing unmet social needs such as quality child care, infrastructure repair and basic preventive health care. A government-financed jobs program would be expensive, but joblessness is financially and socially costly, too. Unemployment entails higher income-assistance expenditures, reduced tax revenues, lost goods and services and the costs of coping with the social problems increased joblessness spawns.

A jobs creation program providing employment for every job seeker unable to find work in the regular labor market, and which paid an average wage of $17,500 annually, would have cost almost $200 billion a year to operate between 1977 and 1986.[39] That is less than the current annual military budget.

If we linked national priorities to a large scale jobs program, we might be able to build a political base for the program and help to ensure that public funds are spent responsibly.[40]

Governments could also help poor people start small businesses. Developing countries pioneered successful microenterprise credit and training approaches, and these have now been shown to work in the United States, too.

A recent study shows that self-employment of AFDC recipients through microenterprise ventures contributes to their families' economic well-being and is a source of personal gratification. The bulk of the microenterprises provide services such as hairdressing, cosmetology, cleaning and child care. The average annual earnings are nearly $9,000 (in January 1990 dollars). This is not enough to bring families out of poverty, and these businesses also take time to succeed. So self-employment can only help welfare families escape poverty if they can also continue to receive some benefits. Welfare rules also need to be modified so that microentrepreneurs can accumulate assets.[41]

Whatever the mechanisms or programs, policies must remain focused on work opportunities that would help disadvantaged, low-skilled people make the transition to better lives for themselves and their children.

The Need to Preserve the Safety Net

The returns from investing in education and skills training do not occur overnight. Because of low earnings available to less-skilled workers, "training programs alone often cannot lift disadvantaged participants entirely out of poverty," says Secretary Reich.[42] Without government intervention to protect the nutrition and health of poor people, the goal of moving them toward self-sufficiency through training programs will be undermined. The Cleveland Works program illustrates the importance of providing adequate support services for trainees to make a successful transition into the labor force.

Congress is moving toward time limits on AFDC benefits to encourage welfare recipients to seek employment. This reflects the widespread perception among working Americans that AFDC allows unwed mothers to avoid work in a world where it has become common for mothers to work.[43]

However, not everyone in the welfare population is unemployed because of inadequate job skills. About a third of the welfare population is hampered by learning disabilities, substance abuse and depression. Job skills training is doomed to failure unless such persons are first equipped with basic "life skills" such as coping with conflict, responsibility and self-esteem. Toby Herr, director of Project Match, a welfare-to-work program at the Cabrini-Green public housing development in Chicago, advocates broadening the definition of work to include other positive activities such as volunteering and good parenting.[44] This way, people who are not yet ready for training, but are making the effort to become employable, can continue to receive benefits and feel that society supports their efforts to make the transition to self-reliance.

Cleveland Works [45]

Cleveland Works (CW) is a training program based in Ohio. Critical elements of its success are a focus on employment as the ultimate goal and the range of support services for participants. According to director David Roth, more than 50 percent of those who complete the program are placed in full-time jobs. Eighty percent of those placed have not returned to welfare or poverty. Roth attributes CW's success to:

- **Range of training.** CW recognizes the different skill needs of participants. It teaches skills ranging from the basics of how to complete job applications, dress for interviews and write thank you letters afterward to computer use.

- **Services.** To enable trainees to focus on learning skills, the program provides a great variety of support services, including day care, access to Head Start, advice on buying work clothes and lawyers who help deal with legal problems that may interfere with getting a job.

- **Standards.** CW teaches trainees the importance of basic job values (such as punctuality and regular attendance), and the program enforces a dress code (skirts and dresses for women, ties for men).

- **Jobs with benefits**. CW places its trainees only in jobs that provide health benefits for workers and their families.

- **Cost-effectiveness.** Funding comes from a variety of government training programs, foundations and private contributions; trainees and businesses who recruit CW graduates pay no fees. It costs CW $5,300 to train and place a student in a job. This is cost-effective, since for every $1 the program spends, it "gives the government back" $3 in welfare savings.

Individual Responsibility

Smart isn't something that you are, it is something you can get.

— Jeff Howard, Efficacy Institute, Lexington, MA[46]

Getting smart requires persistent hard work. We all need to recognize the value of education, cultivate our abilities and teach our children the value of work. Education and skills do not by themselves guarantee job security, but without them, finding a job that pays well is much more difficult.

Ultimately, all adults are responsible for their own choices, no matter what the circumstances. This responsibility extends to our duties as citizens to support positive employment policies and programs.

Despite best efforts, some people will never be able to fully support their families because of disabilities and debilitating health problems. They, as well as people facing shorter-term family emergencies, must have access to publicly funded social services. The government must always meet the education and health needs of disadvantaged children to give them the best start toward a life out of poverty.

Conclusion

Every person deserves the opportunity to develop to the fullest and to participate constructively in society. Providing disadvantaged people with opportunities to participate in productive work is more than a means of saving taxpayers money. It is about ensuring that society offers everyone, especially disadvantaged people, a basis to believe that individual efforts to nurture talents and dreams are not futile.

The best hope for assuring that current social and economic problems in the United States do not degenerate into a full-fledged crisis is to provide everyone the chance to achieve a sustainable livelihood – a dignified and worthwhile life. ∎

Dr. Lucilla L. Tan is research assistant and Don Reeves is economic policy analyst at Bread for the World Institute.

Appendix

TABLE 1: Global Hunger – Life and Death Indicators

	Total Population (millions) 1995	Projected Population (millions) 2025	Average population growth rate (%) 1995-2000	Total fertility rate 1995	% age <15 1995	% urban 1995	Life expectancy at birth (years) 1995 M/F	Infant (under 1) mortality rate per 1,000 live births 1993	Under-5 mortality rate per 1,000 live births 1960	Under-5 mortality rate per 1,000 live births 1993	Maternal mortality rate per 100,000 live births 1980-1992
Developing Countries	..	..	..	..	..	..	../..	69	216	102	351
Africa (sub-Saharan)	..	..	..	..	46	..	../..	109	255	179	616
Angola	11.1	26.6	3.3	6.9	45	32	47.4/50.6	170	345	292	..
Benin	5.4	12.3	2.9	6.9	47	31	47.2/50.5	87	310	144	160
Botswana	1.5	3.0	2.9	4.7	43	28	65.3/69.2	43	170	56	250
Burkina Faso	10.3	21.7	2.5	6.3	48	27	45.3/48.1	99	318	175	810
Burundi	6.4	13.5	2.8	6.5	46	8	49.4/52.9	107	255	178	..
Cameroon	13.2	29.2	2.8	5.5	44	45	57.0/60.0	71	264	113	430
Cape Verde	0.4	0.7	..	4.1	45	54	65.5/67.5	54	164	73	..
Central African Republic	3.3	6.4	2.4	5.5	43	39	47.8/52.5	104	294	177	600
Chad	6.4	12.9	2.8	5.7	41	21	47.9/51.1	121	325	206	960
Comoros	0.7	1.6	..	6.8	48	31	57.5/58.5	88	248	128	..
Congo	2.6	5.7	2.7	6.1	44	59	47.8/52.0	82	220	109	900
Côte d'Ivoire	14.3	36.8	3.2	7.1	47	44	48.6/50.5	89	300	120	..
Djibouti	0.6	1.1	..	5.6	41	83	48.7/52.0	113	289	158	..
Equatorial Guinea	0.4	0.8	..	5.7	43	42	48.4/51.6	116	316	180	..
Eritrea	3.5	7.0	2.6	5.6	..	17	51.3/54.6	120	294	204	..
Ethiopia	55.1	126.9	2.9	6.8	49	13	48.4/51.6	120	294	204	560 x
Gabon	1.3	2.7	2.8	5.5	39	50	53.9/57.2	93	287	154	190
Gambia	1.1	2.1	..	5.4	45	26	45.4/48.7	131	375	216	..
Ghana	17.5	38.0	2.9	5.8	45	36	56.2/59.9	103	215	170	1,000
Guinea	6.7	15.1	2.9	6.8	44	30	46.0/47.0	133	337	226	800
Guinea-Bissau	1.1	2.0	2.1	5.6	43	22	43.9/47.1	139	336	235	700 x
Kenya	28.3	63.4	2.8	6.0	48	28	53.0/55.4	61	202	90	170 x
Lesotho	2.1	4.2	2.6	5.0	41	23	60.5/65.5	107	204	156	..
Liberia	3.0	7.2	3.2	6.6	46	45	56.0/59.0	145	288	217	..
Madagascar	14.8	34.4	3.1	5.9	46	27	57.5/60.5	100	364	164	570
Malawi	11.1	22.3	1.8	6.9	48	14	44.3/45.3	141	365	223	400
Mali	10.8	24.6	3.0	6.9	46	27	46.4/49.7	120	400	217	2,000
Mauritania	2.3	4.4	2.5	5.2	45	54	51.9/55.1	116	321	202	..
Mauritius	1.1	1.5	1.1	2.3	30	41	68.3/75.0	19	84	22	99
Mozambique	16.0	35.1	3.4	6.3	46	34	45.4/48.3	164	331	282	300
Namibia	1.5	3.0	2.6	5.1	42	37	60.0/62.5	62	206	79	370 x
Niger	9.2	22.4	3.3	7.3	49	17	46.9/50.2	191	320	320	700
Nigeria	111.7	238.4	2.8	6.2	45	39	50.8/54.0	114	204	191	800
Rwanda	8.0	15.8	2.6	6.3	48	6	45.2/48.0	81	191	141	210
Senegal	8.3	16.9	2.7	5.8	45	42	50.3/52.3	63	303	120	600
Sierra Leone	4.5	8.7	2.3	6.3	44	36	39.5/42.6	164	385	284	450
Somalia	9.3	21.3	3.1	6.8	48	26	47.4/50.6	125	294	211	1,100
South Africa	41.5	71.0	2.2	4.0	37	51	62.3/68.3	53	126	69	84 x
Sudan	28.1	58.4	2.7	5.6	46	25	53.6/56.4	77	292	128	550
Swaziland	0.9	1.6	..	4.7	46	31	57.7/62.3	74	223	107	..
Tanzania	29.7	62.9	2.8	5.7	47	24	50.2/52.9	108	249	167	340 x
Togo	4.1	9.4	3.0	6.3	49	31	55.2/58.8	84	264	135	420
Uganda	21.3	48.1	2.9	7.0	47	13	42.2/44.3	111	218	185	550
Zaire	43.9	104.6	3.0	6.5	48	29	50.4/53.4	120	286	187	800
Zambia	9.5	19.1	2.6	5.7	50	43	45.4/46.8	114	220	203	150
Zimbabwe	11.3	19.6	2.1	4.8	44	32	49.8/51.8	58	181	83	..

TABLE 1, continued: Global Hunger – Life and Death Indicators

	Total Population (millions) 1995	Projected Population (millions) 2025	Average population growth rate (%) 1995-2000	Total fertility rate 1995	% age <15 1995	% urban 1995	Life expectancy at birth (years) 1995 M/F	Infant (under 1) mortality rate per 1,000 live births 1993	Under-5 mortality rate per 1,000 live births 1960	Under-5 mortality rate per 1,000 live births 1993	Maternal mortality rate per 100,000 live births 1980-1992
South Asia	..	..	..	..	..	..	../..	87	238	127	492
Afghanistan	20.1	45.3	5.6	6.6	41	20	45.0/46.0	165	360	257	640
Bangladesh	120.4	196.1	2.2	4.1	42	18	58.1/58.2	94	247	122	600
Bhutan	1.6	3.1	2.3	5.7	39	6	51.6/54.9	128	324	197	1,310
India	935.7	1,392.1	1.8	3.6	36	27	62.6/62.9	81	236	122	460
Nepal	21.9	40.7	2.5	5.2	42	14	56.5/56.5	90	279	128	830
Pakistan	140.5	284.8	2.8	5.9	41	35	62.9/65.1	95	221	137	500
Sri Lanka	18.4	25.0	1.2	2.4	35	22	70.9/75.4	15	130	19	80
East Asia and the Pacific	..	..	..	..	..	..	../..	42	200	56	159
Burma (Myanmar)	46.5	75.6	2.1	4.0	36	26	58.5/61.8	81	237	111	460
Cambodia	10.3	19.7	2.5	5.1	46	21	52.6/55.4	115	217	181	500
China	1,221.5	1,526.1	1.0	2.0	27	30	68.2/71.7	35	209	43	95
Fiji	0.8	1.2	..	2.9	38	41	70.6/74.9	23	97	28	..
Hong Kong	5.9	5.9	0.3	1.2	20	95	76.2/82.3	6	52	7	6
Indonesia	197.6	275.6	1.5	2.8	37	35	63.3/67.0	71	216	111	450
Korea, N.	23.9	33.4	1.6	2.3	30	61	68.7/75.2	24	120	32	41
Korea, S.	45.0	54.4	0.9	1.8	24	81	68.8/76.1	8	124	9	26
Laos	4.9	9.7	2.8	6.4	45	22	52.0/55.0	96	233	141	300
Malaysia	20.1	31.6	2.0	3.4	36	54	69.9/74.3	13	105	17	59
Mongolia	2.4	3.8	2.0	3.4	40	61	64.4/67.3	59	185	78	200
Papua New Guinea	4.3	7.5	2.2	4.8	40	16	57.2/58.7	67	248	95	900
Philippines	67.6	104.5	2.0	3.8	40	54	66.6/70.2	45	102	59	100
Singapore	2.8	3.4	0.8	1.7	23	100	73.5/78.6	5	40	6	10
Solomon Islands	0.4	0.8	..	5.2	47	17	69.7/73.9	27	185	33	..
Thailand	58.8	73.6	1.0	2.1	31	20	65.2/71.6	27	146	33	50
Vietnam	74.5	118.2	2.1	3.7	39	21	64.9/69.6	36	219	48	120
Latin America and the Caribbean	482.0	709.8	1.7	3.0	34	74	67.2/72.4	38	157	48	189
Argentina	34.6	46.1	1.2	2.7	30	88	69.7/76.8	24	68	27	140
Belize	0.2	0.4	2.6	3.9	44	47	73.4/76.1	33	104	42	..
Bolivia	7.4	13.1	2.3	4.6	41	61	59.8/63.2	78	252	114	600
Brazil	161.8	230.3	1.5	2.8	32	78	65.5/70.1	52	181	63	200
Chile	14.3	19.8	1.4	2.5	31	84	71.1/78.1	15	138	17	35
Colombia	35.1	49.4	1.5	2.6	33	73	67.4/73.3	16	132	19	200
Costa Rica	3.4	5.6	2.1	3.1	35	50	74.5/79.2	14	112	16	36
Cuba	11.0	12.7	0.6	1.8	22	76	74.2/78.0	9	50	10	39
Dominican Republic	7.8	11.2	1.6	2.9	35	65	68.9/73.1	40	152	48	..
Ecuador	11.5	17.8	2.0	3.3	38	58	67.3/72.5	45	180	57	170
El Salvador	5.8	9.7	2.2	3.8	40	45	65.8/70.8	45	210	60	..
Guatemala	10.6	21.7	2.8	5.1	45	42	64.7/69.8	53	205	73	200
Guyana	0.8	1.1	..	2.4	32	36	64.4/69.5	47	126	63	..
Haiti	7.2	13.1	2.1	4.7	40	32	56.7/60.2	85	270	130	600
Honduras	5.7	10.7	2.8	4.6	47	44	67.5/72.3	43	203	56	220
Jamaica	2.4	3.3	0.8	2.2	33	54	72.4/76.8	11	76	13	120
Mexico	93.7	136.6	1.8	3.0	36	75	68.9/75.0	27	141	32	110
Nicaragua	4.4	9.1	3.1	4.8	46	63	66.6/70.3	51	209	72	..
Panama	2.6	3.8	1.6	2.8	34	53	71.8/76.3	18	104	20	60
Paraguay	5.0	9.0	2.5	4.1	40	53	69.4/73.1	28	90	34	300
Peru	23.8	36.7	1.9	3.3	36	72	65.5/69.4	43	236	62	300
Suriname	0.4	0.6	..	2.5	35	50	69.0/74.0	28	96	34	..
Trinidad & Tobago	1.3	1.8	1.1	2.3	31	72	70.5/75.1	18	73	21	110
Uruguay	3.2	3.7	0.6	2.3	26	90	69.7/76.2	19	47	21	36
Venezuela	21.8	34.8	2.0	3.1	38	93	70.0/75.7	20	70	24	..

TABLE 1, continued: Global Hunger – Life and Death Indicators

	Total Population (millions) 1995	Projected Population (millions) 2025	Average population growth rate (%) 1995-2000	Total fertility rate 1995	% age <15 1995	% urban 1995	Life expectancy at birth (years) 1995 M/F	Infant (under 1) mortality rate per 1,000 live births 1993	Under-5 mortality rate per 1,000 live births 1960	Under-5 mortality rate per 1,000 live births 1993	Maternal mortality rate per 100,000 live births 1980-1992
Middle East and North Africa	..	..	..	..	..	..	.. /..	53	240	70	202
Algeria	27.9	45.5	2.2	3.6	39	56	67.5/70.3	57	243	68	140 x
Bahrain	0.6	0.9	..	3.6	32	90	71.1/75.3	18	208	22	..
Cyprus	0.7	0.9	..	2.4	25	54	75.6/80.0	9	36	10	..
Egypt	62.9	97.3	1.9	3.7	40	45	64.7/67.3	46	258	59	270
Iran	67.3	123.5	2.1	4.8	44	59	69.0/70.3	42	233	54	120
Iraq	20.4	42.7	3.0	5.5	47	75	66.5/69.5	57	171	71	120
Jordan	5.4	12.0	3.3	5.4	43	72	67.7/71.8	23	149	27	48 x
Kuwait	1.5	2.8	3.2	3.0	34	97	74.1/78.2	11	128	13	6
Lebanon	3.0	4.4	1.8	2.9	33	87	68.1/71.7	33	85	40	..
Libya	5.4	12.9	3.3	6.2	48	86	63.9/67.5	67	269	100	70 x
Morocco	27.0	40.7	1.8	3.4	40	48	63.9/67.5	48	215	59	330
Oman	2.2	6.1	3.9	6.9	36	13	68.9/73.3	23	300	29	..
Qatar	0.6	0.8	..	4.1	30	91	70.0/75.4	20	239	25	..
Saudi Arabia	17.9	42.7	3.5	6.2	43	80	69.9/73.4	33	292	38	41
Syria	14.7	33.5	3.3	5.6	49	52	66.7/71.2	33	201	39	140
Tunisia	8.9	13.3	1.7	3.0	37	57	68.4/70.7	30	244	36	70
Turkey	61.9	90.9	1.8	3.2	33	69	66.5/70.7	67	217	84	150
United Arab Emirates	1.9	3.0	2.0	4.1	32	84	73.9/76.5	18	240	21	..
Yemen	14.5	33.7	3.2	7.4	52	34	51.9/52.4	91	378	137	..
Industrial Countries	..	..	..	..	..	..	.. /..	9	43	10	10
Albania	3.4	4.7	1.0	2.8	33	37	70.0/75.8	34	151	41	..
Armenia	3.6	4.7	1.2	2.5	31	69	70.3/76.3	28	..	33	..
Australia	18.1	24.7	1.2	1.9	22	85	75.4/81.2	7	24	8	3
Austria	8.0	8.3	0.4	1.6	18	56	73.9/80.1	7	43	8	8
Azerbaijan	7.6	10.1	1.1	2.4	33	56	68.0/75.5	36	..	52	..
Belarus	10.1	9.9	-0.1	1.7	22	71	64.5/75.1	19	..	22	..
Belgium	10.1	10.4	0.3	1.7	18	97	74.1/80.6	8	35	10	3
Bosnia & Herzegovina	3.5	4.5	4.5	1.6	23	49	70.5/75.9	..	..	..	..
Bulgaria	8.8	7.8	-0.4	1.5	19	71	67.8/74.8	16	70	19	9
Canada	29.5	38.3	1.0	1.9	21	77	75.0/81.2	7	33	8	5
Croatia	4.5	4.2	-0.3	1.7	19	64	68.1/76.5	..	..	..	..
Czech Republic	10.3	10.6	0.1	1.8	21	65	67.8/74.9	9	..	10	..
Denmark	5.2	5.1	0.1	1.7	17	85	73.0/78.7	6	25	7	3
Estonia	1.5	1.4	-0.5	1.6	21	73	63.8/74.8	20	..	23	..
Finland	5.1	5.4	0.4	1.9	19	63	72.7/80.2	4	28	5	11
France	58.0	61.2	0.4	1.7	20	73	73.8/81.3	7	34	9	9
Georgia	5.5	6.1	0.3	2.1	25	59	69.5/77.6	24	..	28	..
Germany	81.6	76.4	0.0	1.3	16	87	73.5/79.8	6	40	7	5
Greece	10.5	9.9	0.2	1.4	19	65	75.6/80.6	9	64	10	5
Hungary	10.1	9.4	-0.3	1.7	19	65	64.5/73.8	13	57	15	15
Ireland	3.6	3.9	0.3	2.1	26	58	73.4/78.9	6	36	7	2
Israel	5.6	7.8	1.5	2.8	30	91	75.4/79.2	7	39	9	3
Italy	57.2	52.3	0.0	1.3	16	67	75.1/81.4	7	50	9	4
Japan	125.1	121.6	0.2	1.5	16	78	76.8/82.9	5	40	6	11
Kazakhstan	17.1	21.7	0.7	2.4	31	60	66.5/75.0	42	..	49	..
Kyrgyzstan	4.7	7.1	1.6	3.5	38	39	66.5/73.8	48	..	58	..
Latvia	2.6	2.3	-0.7	1.6	21	73	63.3/74.9	22	..	26	..
Lithuania	3.7	3.8	0.0	1.8	22	72	64.9/76.0	17	..	20	..
Macedonia	2.2	2.6	0.8	2.0	26	60	69.8/75.8	..	..	..	..
Moldova	4.4	5.1	0.3	2.1	28	52	63.5/71.6	31	..	36	..
Netherlands	15.5	16.3	0.6	1.6	18	89	75.1/80.8	6	22	8	10
New Zealand	3.6	4.4	1.0	2.1	23	86	73.4/79.4	7	26	9	13
Norway	4.3	4.7	0.4	2.0	19	73	74.1/80.6	6	23	8	3
Poland	38.4	41.5	0.2	1.9	24	65	66.7/75.7	13	70	15	11

TABLE 1, continued: Global Hunger – Life and Death Indicators

	Total Population (millions) 1995	Projected Population (millions) 2025	Average population growth rate (%) 1995-2000	Total fertility rate 1995	% age <15 1995	% urban 1995	Life expectancy at birth (years) 1995 M/F	Infant (under 1) mortality rate per 1,000 live births 1993	Under-5 mortality rate per 1,000 live births 1960	Under-5 mortality rate per 1,000 live births 1993	Maternal mortality rate per 100,000 live births 1980-1992
Portugal	9.8	9.7	0.0	1.6	18	36	72.1/78.9	9	112	11	10
Romania	22.8	21.7	-0.2	1.5	22	55	66.6/73.3	23	82	29	72
Russian Federation	147.0	138.5	-0.2	1.5	22	76	61.5/73.6	28	..	31	..
Slovakia	5.4	6.0	0.4	1.9	25	59	66.5/75.4	16	..	18	..
Slovenia	1.9	1.8	0.0	1.5	19	64	68.8/78.1	7	..	..	..
Spain	39.6	37.6	0.1	1.2	17	76	75.3/81.0	8	57	9	5
Sweden	8.8	9.8	0.4	2.1	19	83	76.2/81.9	5	20	6	5
Switzerland	7.2	7.8	0.8	1.6	16	61	75.4/81.7	6	27	8	5
Tajikistan	6.1	11.8	2.7	4.7	43	32	68.8/74.0	64	..	83	..
Turkmenistan	4.1	6.7	2.1	3.8	41	45	63.5/70.0	71	..	89	..
Ukraine	51.4	48.7	-0.2	1.6	21	70	64.2/74.2	21	..	25	..
United Kingdom	58.3	61.5	0.3	1.8	19	90	74.4/79.4	7	27	8	8
USA	263.3	331.2	0.9	2.1	22	76	73.4/80.1	9	30	10	8
Uzbekistan	22.8	37.7	2.1	3.7	41	41	67.5/73.2	54	..	66	..
Yugoslavia	10.8	11.5	-0.3	2.0	23	57	70.3/75.3	..	..	..	..
World	**5,716.4**	**8,294.3**	**1.5**	**3.0**	**32**	**45**	**63.7/67.8**	..	..	..	..

x Data that refer to years or periods other than those specified in the column heading, differ from the standard definition or refer to only part of a country.

.. Data not available.

TABLE 2: Global Health, Nutrition and Welfare Indicators

	Human development rank 1995	Refugees by country of asylum (thousands) 1994	Gross school enrollment rate (%)[1] total 1992	Gross school enrollment rate (%)[1] male 1992	Gross school enrollment rate(%)[1] female 1992	% of infants with low birthweight 1990	% 1-year-old children fully immunized (measles) 1990-1993	Food production per capita (index 1979-81=100) 1993	Daily per capita calorie supply as a % of requirements 1988-1990	% annual deforestation (total forest) 1981-1990
Developing Countries	..	..	**54**	..	..	**19**	**78**	**116**	**107**	..
Africa (sub-Saharan)	..	..	**42**	..	..	**16**	**49**	**93**	**93**	..
Angola	164	10.7	33	35.6	30.5	19	47	70	80	0.7
Benin	155	70.0	34	46.0	22.0	..	67	121	104	1.2
Botswana	74	..	71	68.6	73.4	8	60	68	97	0.5
Burkina Faso	169	49.5	19	23.1	14.1	21x	42	132	94	0.7
Burundi	165	300.0	31	34.6	27.4	..	61	87	84	0.6
Cameroon	127	42.9	50	55.3	44.4	13	33	76	95	0.6
Cape Verde	123	..	59	60.5	57.6	..	95x	94	..	0.0
Central African Republic	149	47.4	37	47.6	27.2	15	69	97	82	0.4
Chad	162	..	28	38.5	16.5	..	19	99	73	0.7
Comoros	139	..	37	39.5	34.4	..	56x	83	..	..
Congo	122	14.8	56	..	..	16	55	79	103	0.2
Côte d'Ivoire	145	359.4	39	47.2	30.6	14x	52	85	111	1.0
Djibouti	154	33.2	18	20.4	15.6	..	42x	..	..	0.0
Equatorial Guinea	142	..	60	..	..	..	53x	..	..	0.4
Eritrea	..	0.7	..	..	..	..	23	..	..	..
Ethiopia	171	347.7	14	15.6	11.8	16	22	84x	73	0.3
Gabon	114	..	47	..	..	..	65	80	104	0.6
Gambia	161	2.0	33	40.0	26.3	..	87x	73	..	0.8
Ghana	129	113.6	45	50.6	39.0	17	50	115	93	1.3
Guinea	168	553.2	22	30.4	13.4	21	57	106	97	1.1
Guinea-Bissau	163	23.6	28	35.7	19.7	20	46	110	97	0.7
Kenya	130	248.9	57	59.1	55.7	16	76	82	89	0.5
Lesotho	131	..	57	51.5	62.8	11	77	68	93	..
Liberia	159	120.0	17	..	..	..	38	44	98	0.5
Madagascar	135	..	35	35.5	33.7	10	52	84	95	0.8
Malawi	157	88.9	46	48.3	42.7	20	92	74	88	1.3
Mali	172	..	15	18.9	11.1	17	51	95	96	0.8
Mauritania	150	82.2	32	36.7	26.5	11	49	81	106	0.0
Mauritius	60	..	59	58.6	59.1	9	84	99	128	..
Mozambique	167	..	25	28.7	20.9	20	62	76	77	0.7
Namibia	108	1.1	81	..	..	12	71	76	..	0.3
Niger	174	15.0	14	18.0	10.2	15	20	80	95	0.0
Nigeria	141	5.4	51	55.5	47.3	16	34	134	93	0.7
Rwanda	156	6.0	39	..	..	17	81	73	82	0.2
Senegal	152	72.8	31	36.6	25.0	11	46	112	98	0.6
Sierra Leone	173	15.9	28	33.5	22.0	17	67	87	83	0.6
Somalia	166	..	7	..	..	16	30x	56	81	0.4
South Africa	95	91.4	76	..	..	..	85	74	128	..
Sudan	144	726.9	31	34.8	27.0	15	49	77	87	1.0
Swaziland	124	0.1	70	71.7	68.4	..	85x	84	..	..
Tanzania	147	882.4	34	35.0	32.9	14	79	77	95	1.2
Togo	140	12.2	60	75.1	43.9	20	48	110	99	1.4
Uganda	158	283.8	37	41.6	32.0	..	73	102	93	0.9
Zaire	143	1,724.3	39	45.7	31.5	15	33	99	96	0.6
Zambia	136	137.3	49	53.3	45.5	13	62	101	87	1.0
Zimbabwe	121	1.4	70	72.8	66.4	14	73	80	94	0.6
South Asia	..	..	..	..	..	**34**	**78**	..	**99**	**0.8**
Afghanistan	170	18.8	14	18.7	9.6	20	42	69	72	..
Bangladesh	146	116.0	38	43.1	32.8	50	71	99	88	3.3
Bhutan	160	..	31	..	..	..	68	85	128	0.6
India	134	257.4	55	63.8	45.8	33	82	123	101	0.6
Nepal	151	103.3	55	68.4	41.4	..	59	118	100	1.0
Pakistan	128	1,055.1	25	32.6	16.3	25	71	109	99	2.9
Sri Lanka	97	..	66	65.6	67.1	25	89	81	101	1.3

TABLE 2, continued: Global Health, Nutrition and Welfare Indicators

	Human development rank 1995	Refugees by country of asylum (thousands) 1994	Gross school enrollment rate (%)[1] total 1992	Gross school enrollment rate (%)[1] male 1992	Gross school enrollment rate(%)[1] female 1992	% of infants with low birthweight 1990	% 1-year-old children fully immunized (measles) 1990-1993	Food production per capita (index 1979-81=100) 1993	Daily per capita calorie supply as a % of requirements 1988-1990	% annual deforestation (total forest) 1981-1990
East Asia and the Pacific	..	..	..	..	..	11	91	..	112	..
Burma (Myanmar)	132	..	47	48.2	46.6	16	71	104	114	1.2
Cambodia	153	..	30	..	..	..	37	124	96	1.0
China	111	287.1	55	58.0	51.8	9	94	142x	112	..
Fiji	46	..	78	78.4	77.1	..	96x	95	..	..
Hong Kong	24	24.3	70	70.2	69.7	8	75	89	125	..
Indonesia	104	6.6	60	63.5	57.1	14	90	143	121	1.0
Korea, N	83	..	75	..	..	..	99	78	121	..
Korea, S	31	..	79	83.5	75.0	9	89	96	120	..
Laos	138	..	48	56.4	40.2	18	46	115	111	0.9
Malaysia	59	10.5	60	59.6	61.1	10	80	160	120	1.8
Mongolia	110	..	60	56.2	62.9	10	84	69	97	..
Papua New Guinea	126	8.5	34	37.3	30.3	23	30	103	114	0.3
Philippines	100	0.7	77	76.6	78.2	15	87	89	104	2.9
Singapore	35	..	68	68.9	66.3	7	89	36	136	0.0
Solomon Islands	125	..	44	..	..	..	64x	83	..	..
Thailand	58	100.4	53	53.1	52.8	13	86	108	103	2.9
Vietnam	120	45.0	49	50.0	47.4	17	93	131	103	1.4
Latin America and the Caribbean	..	..	..	..	..	11	85	98	114	..
Argentina	30	..	79	75.2	81.8	8	95	92	131	..
Belize	29	8.1	76	..	..	..	80x	96	..	0.2
Bolivia	113	..	66	71.6	60.9	12	81	110	84	1.1
Brazil	63	0.8	70	71.1	69.7	11	84	109	114	0.6
Chile	33	..	71	71.3	70.5	7	93	120	102	..
Colombia	57	..	67	64.9	69.0	10	94	110	106	0.6
Costa Rica	28	23.7	66	67.9	65.7	6	82	101	121	2.6
Cuba	72	1.5	65	62.2	67.7	8	93	69	135	0.9
Dominican Republic	96	1.2	72	70.0	73.8	16	99	97	102	2.5
Ecuador	68	..	71	72.1	70.3	11	73	116	105	1.7
El Salvador	115	..	54	54.1	53.5	11	86	78	102	2.1
Guatemala	112	4.6	43	46.8	39.2	14	71	87	103	1.6
Guyana	105	..	68	68.1	68.2	..	80 x	90	..	0.1
Haiti	148	..	30	30.5	28.4	15	24	66	89	3.9
Honduras	116	..	59	57.0	60.5	9	94	94	98	1.9
Jamaica	88	..	65	64.5	64.6	11	72	106	114	5.3
Mexico	53	46.7	65	66.0	64.0	12	93	90	131	1.2
Nicaragua	109	0.3	61	61.1	61.1	15	83	54	99	1.7
Panama	49	..	68	67.2	69.5	10	83	89	98	1.7
Paraguay	87	..	59	59.3	58.0	8	96	114	116	2.4
Peru	93	..	79	83.9	73.6	11	75	..	87	0.4
Suriname	77	..	71	69.2	72.5	..	61 x	94	..	0.1
Trinidad & Tobago	39	..	68	67.9	67.8	10	87	90	114	1.9
Uruguay	32	..	77	71.8	81.9	8	80	111	101	..
Venezuela	47	1.8	71	69.7	71.6	9	63	98	99	1.2
Middle East and North Africa	..	..	..	..	..	10	80	101	124	..
Algeria	85	219.0	66	71.2	59.9	9	69	123	123	..
Bahrain	44	..	84	81.3	85.8	..	90x	..	..	..
Cyprus	23	..	75	..	..	..	83x	117	..	0.1
Egypt	107	6.9	67	73.9	60.5	10	89	114	132	..
Iran	70	2,236.3	68	73.6	61.3	9	96	123	125	..
Iraq	106	119.6	55	61.8	47.9	15	81	89	128	..
Jordan	80	..	66	..	..	7	88	131	110	..

TABLE 2, continued: Global Health, Nutrition and Welfare Indicators

	Human development rank 1995	Refugees by country of asylum (thousands) 1994	Gross school enrollment rate (%)[1] total 1992	Gross school enrollment rate (%)[1] male 1992	Gross school enrollment rate(%)[1] female 1992	% of infants with low birthweight 1990	% 1-year-old children fully immunized (measles) 1990-1993	Food production per capita (index 1979-81=100) 1993	Daily per capita calorie supply as a % of requirements 1988-1990	% annual deforestation (total forest) 1981-1990
Kuwait	61	174.0	47	47.0	47.6	7	93	..	..	..
Lebanon	101	11.2	73	73.9	71.2	10	65	183	127	..
Libya	73	1.2	66	66.0	66.4	..	89	50	140	..
Morocco	117	..	43	49.8	35.4	9	83	112	125	..
Oman	91	..	59	..	..	10	95	..	..	..
Qatar	56	..	75	71.5	77.9	..	86 x	..	..	..
Saudi Arabia	76	18.0	52	55.0	49.3	7	92	328	121	..
Syria	78	37.9	67	71.4	61.5	11	86	90	126	..
Tunisia	75	..	64	68.4	60.2	8	89	126	131	..
Turkey	66	24.7	61	68.3	54.1	8	74	101	127	0.0
United Arab Emirates	45	..	80	76.3	83.9	6	90	..	..	..
Yemen	137	12.8	44	64.6	22.5	19	51	76	..	..
Industrial Countries	..	..	80	..	..	6	80	..	134	..
Albania	82	3.0	69	..	..	7	76	97	107	0.0
Armenia	90	304.0	78	..	..	..	93	..	..	..
Australia	11	..	79	77.5	80.3	6	86	105	124	0.0
Austria	14	24.2	84	85.9	82.0	6	60	107	133	0.4
Azerbaijan	99	230.4	68	..	..	..	84	..	..	..
Belarus	42	1.6	74	..	..	..	96	..	..	0.5
Belgium	12	5.6	84	84.1	84.3	6	77	..	149	0.3
Bosnia & Herzegovina	..	1,456.7	..	..	..	..	..	..	..	..
Bulgaria	65	..	67	..	..	6	92	66	148	0.2
Canada	1	..	100	100.0	100.0	6	85x	108	122	..
Croatia	..	183.6	..	..	..	..	..	..	..	..
Czech Republic	38	1.2	68	67.6	69.0	..	97	..	..	..
Denmark	16	18.0	84	82.3	85.6	6	81	129	135	0.2
Estonia	43	..	70	68.9	72.0	..	74	..	..	..
Finland	5	..	96	90.6	100.0	4	99	101	113	0.0
France	8	36.0	86	83.5	87.5	5	76	99	143	0.1
Georgia	92	..	78	..	..	..	58	..	..	..
Germany	15	350.0	81	..	..	..	70	102	..	0.5
Greece	22	6.4	78	77.4	77.6	6	76	103	151	0.0
Hungary	50	10.5	67	66.1	66.9	9	100	87	137	0.5
Ireland	19	..	83	80.6	84.6	4	78	121	157	1.3
Israel	21	..	77	..	..	7	96	82	125	..
Italy	20	46.1	70	69.0	70.3	5	50	101	139	..
Japan	3	9.0	77	78.4	76.3	6	66	77	125	0.0
Kazakhstan	64	4.7	67	..	..	..	91	..	..	..
Kyrgyzstan	89	21.2	77	..	..	..	94	..	..	..
Latvia	48	..	68	66.0	69.2	..	80	..	..	..
Lithuania	71	..	67	65.6	67.5	..	94	..	..	..
Macedonia	..	14.8	..	..	..	..	..	..	..	..
Moldova	81	..	76	..	..	..	92	..	..	..
Netherlands	4	..	88	89.4	86.5	..	95	118	114	0.3
New Zealand	17	..	85	83.5	85.6	6	82	95	131	..
Norway	7	..	88	86.4	88.6	4	94	109	120	..
Poland	51	..	75	74.4	76.4	..	96	103	131	0.1
Portugal	36	..	77	70.2	84.3	5	99	122	136	0.5
Romania	98	..	61	..	..	7	91	82	116	0.0
Russian Federation	52	48.9	69	67.3	69.7	..	83	..	..	..
Slovakia	40	1.8	71	70.7	72.1	..	96	..	..	..
Slovenia	..	29.2	..	..	..	..	..	..	..	..
Spain	9	1.3	86	83.0	88.7	4	83	107	141	0.0
Sweden	10	..	78	76.7	79.3	5	95	91	111	..
Switzerland	13	44.9	74	76.8	70.8	5	83	98	130	0.6
Tajikistan	103	0.6	67	..	..	..	97	..	..	..
Turkmenistan	86	..	77	..	..	..	98	..	..	..

TABLE 2, continued: Global Health, Nutrition and Welfare Indicators

	Human development rank 1995	Refugees by country of asylum (thousands) 1994	Gross school enrollment rate (%)[1] total 1992	Gross school enrollment rate (%)[1] male 1992	Gross school enrollment rate(%)[1] female 1992	% of infants with low birthweight 1990	% 1-year-old children fully immunized (measles) 1990-1993	Food production per capita (index 1979-81=100) 1993	Daily per capita calorie supply as a % of requirements 1988-1990	% annual deforestation (total forest) 1981-1990
Ukraine	54	3.9	70	..	..	..	90	..	..	0.3
United Kingdom	18	2.0	77	76.1	77.4	7	92	100	130	1.1
USA	2	..	95	91.9	98.1	7	83	90	138	0.1
Uzbekistan	94	7.9	77	..	..	..	91	..	..	..
Yugoslavia	..	..	..	..	..	..	..	..	..	..
World	..	**14,488.7**	**58**	..	..	..	..	**102**	..	..

[1] Gross school enrollment rate compares the enrollment of all schools and colleges with the population of the relevant age groups.
x Data refer to a year or period than that specified in the column heading.
.. Data not available.

TABLE 3: Global Economic Indicators

	GNP per capita (US$) 1993	GNP per capita real growth rate (%) 1985-1993	Real GDP per capita (PPP$) 1993	Military expenditure (as % of combined education & health expenditure) 1990-1991	Total Debt (US$ billions) 1993	Debt servicing (as % of exports) 1993	Food as % of total imports 1993	Food as % of total exports 1993	Food as % of household consumption 1980-1985	Per capita energy consumption (kg. of oil equivalent) 1993
Developing Countries	..	..	..	**60**	..	..	**6.2**	**5.7**	**41**	..
Africa (sub-Saharan)	..	..	..	**43**	..	..	**14.5**	**9.6**	**38**	..
Angola	c	-0.9	..	208	9.7	7	19.7	..	..	..
Benin	420	-1.1	1,630	..	1.5	6	11.8	3.0	37	20
Botswana	2,590	5.7	4,650	22	0.7	4	11.3	3.0	25	388
Burkina Faso	300	0.0	800	30	1.1	7	13.9	20.4	..	16
Burundi	180	0.6	660	42	1.1	35	10.1	0.2	..	24
Cameroon	770	-7.3	2,060	48	6.6	19	13.2	12.2	24	87
Cape Verde	870	2.1	1,830	..	0.2	7	24.1	8.6	..	..
Central African Republic	390	-3.0	1,060	33	0.9	7	21.6	16.4	..	29
Chad	200	0.5	710	74	0.8	5	5.7	24.2	..	16
Comoros	520	-2.2	1,320	..	0.2	8	28.3	84.3	..	..
Congo	920	-1.9	2,430	37	5.1	16	24.1	0.8	37	165
Côte d'Ivoire	630	-5.2	1,420	14	19.1	33	18.5	33.5	39	109
Djibouti	780	..	..	..	0.2	3	21.5	19.7	..	..
Equatorial Guinea	360	1.5	..	..	0.3	5	15.9	6.6	..	..
Eritrea/e	b	..	..	..	..	..	..	..	..	..
Ethiopia/e	100	-1.8	380	190	4.7	14	..	..	49	..
Gabon	4,050	-1.7	..	51	3.8	11	11.9	0.1	..	769
Gambia	360	1.0	1,280	11	0.4	13	28.8	11.0	..	57
Ghana	430	1.3	2,160	12	4.6	25	14.2	32.1	50	96
Guinea	510	1.3	..	37	2.9	14	18.1	3.5	..	66
Guinea-Bissau	220	1.6	790	..	0.8	15	41.3	83.3	..	37
Kenya	270	0.3	1,310	24	7.0	31	12.0	7.1	38	99
Lesotho	660	0.8	1,800	48	0.5	5	11.7	4.1	..	..
Liberia	b	..	..	47	1.9	2	51.8	0.7	..	..
Madagascar	240	-1.7	700	37	4.6	22	9.8	30.9	59	34
Malawi	220	0.4	780	24	1.8	24	23.4	5.9	30	35
Mali	300	-4.3	530	53	2.7	6	11.9	29.3	57	20
Mauritania	510	-0.1	1,590	40	2.2	20	29.8	9.0	..	105

	GNP per capita (US$) 1993	GNP per capita real growth rate (%) 1985-1993	Real GDP per capita (PPP$) 1993	Military expenditure (as % of combined education & health expenditure) 1990-1991	Total Debt (US$ billions) 1993	Debt servicing (as % of exports) 1993	Food as % of total imports 1993	Food as % of total exports 1993	Food as % of household consumption 1980-1985	Per capita energy consumption (kg. of oil equivalent) 1993
Mauritius	2,980	5.8	12,450	4	1.0	8	10.8	28.3	24	391
Mozambique	80	1.9	380	121	5.3	17	17.6	15.2	..	43
Namibia	1,660	2.3	3,930	23	..	..	7.5	10.1	..	..
Niger	270	-2.1	810	11	1.7	24	20.3	16.1	..	38
Nigeria	310	3.2	1,480	33	32.5	24	11.6	1.5	48	141
Rwanda	200	-3.5	640	25	0.9	15	19.2	0.2	29	27
Senegal	730	-0.3	1,640	33	3.8	15	29.0	9.0	49	115
Sierra Leone	140	-0.6	770	23	1.4	14	50.8	2.9	56	74
Somalia	b	-2.3	..	200	2.5	..	51.5	68.0	..	..
South Africa	2,900	-1.5	..	41	..	..	5.3	5.2	34	2,399
Sudan	b	-0.2	..	44	16.6	5	15.9	50.7	60	..
Swaziland	1,050	3.8	1,690	11	0.2	3	8.0	38.3	..	..
Tanzania/h	100	1.4	..	77	7.5	36	7.4	9.2	64	35
Togo	330	-3.4	1,040	39	1.3	8	9.5	8.8	..	47
Uganda	190	1.9	840	18	3.1	84	6.7	17.9	..	21
Zaire	b	-0.8	..	71	11.3	5	41.9	1.3	..	..
Zambia	370	1.8	1,170	63	6.8	38	8.3	1.6	36	146
Zimbabwe	540	-1.1	1,900	66	4.2	31	10.0	5.5	40	471
South Asia	..	..	..	72	..	..	7.8	5.6	51	..
Afghanistan	b	..	..	..	..	..	14.1	17.9	..	..
Bangladesh	220	1.8	1,290	41	13.9	16	15.0	0.5	59	59
Bhutan	170	4.5	..	..	a	7	8.8	13.7	..	..
India	290	3.0	1,250	65	91.8	29	3.9	6.0	52	242
Nepal	160	1.8	1,150	35	2.0	12	9.0	13.0	57	22
Pakistan	430	1.5	2,110	125	26.1	23	12.8	6.8	37	209
Sri Lanka	600	-2.6	3,030	107	6.8	12	10.1	2.8	43	110
East Asia and the Pacific	..	..	..	..	..	..	..	..	45	..
Burma (Myanmar)	b	..	..	222	5.5	11	12.7	35.8	..	39
Cambodia	b	..	..	..	0.4	6	10.5	0.3	..	..
China	490	6.5	2,120	114	83.8	11	1.9	7.2	61	623
Fiji	2,140	-2.5	5,220	37	0.3	9	12.9	38.4	..	..
Hong Kong/g	17,860	5.3	21,670	10	..	..	3.0	1.1	12	2,278
Indonesia	730	4.8	3,140	49	89.5	32	4.8	4.3	48	321
Korea, N.	c	..	..	..	..	..	11.2	0.7	..	..
Korea, S.	7,670	8.1	9,810	60	47.2	8	4.1	0.8	35	2,863
Laos	290	2.1	..	..	2.0	7	3.9	17.8	..	39
Malaysia	3,160	5.7	8,630	38	23.3	7	4.5	7.7	23	1,529
Mongolia	400	-0.3	..	..	0.4	7	17.2	7.4	..	1,089
Papua New Guinea	1,120	1.1	2,470	41	3.2	30	14.3	6.1	..	238
Philippines	830	1.6	2,660	41	35.3	24	5.2	10.3	51	328
Solomon Islands	750	2.5	..	..	0.1	8	9.8	16.8	..	..
Singapore	19,310	6.1	20,470	129	..	..	3.4	2.0	19	5,563
Thailand	2,040	8.4	6,390	71	45.8	15	1.5	9.9	30	678
Vietnam	170	4.8	1,040	..	24.2	13	3.3	18.0	..	77
Latin America and the Caribbean	..	..	..	25	..	..	8.5	15.5	34	..
Argentina	7,290	1.4	9,130	51	74.5	39	4.1	36.9	35	1,351
Bolivia	770	1.4	2,400	57	4.2	44	9.6	11.3	33	310
Belize	2,440	5.7	..	..	0.2	8	13.1	60.8	..	..
Brazil	3,020	-0.6	5,470	23	132.7	24	7.7	13.4	35	666
Chile	3,070	6.1	8,380	68	20.6	23	4.6	13.2	29	911
Colombia	1,400	2.3	5,630	57	17.2	34	7.9	10.1	29	694
Costa Rica	2,160	-2.6	5,580	5	3.9	19	6.6	38.7	33	558

TABLE 3, continued: Global Economic Indicators

	GNP per capita (US$) 1993	GNP per capita real growth rate (%) 1985-1993	Real GDP per capita (PPP$) 1993	Military expenditure (as % of combined education & health expenditure) 1990-1991	Total Debt (US$ billions) 1993	Debt servicing (as % of exports) 1993	Food as % of total imports 1993	Food as % of total exports 1993	Food as % of household consumption 1980-1985	Per capita energy consumption (kg. of oil equivalent) 1993
Cuba	c	..	..	125	..	..	23.3	76.6	..	..
Dominican Republic	1,080	0.3	3,240	22	4.6	12	14.6	47.0	46	340
Ecuador	1,170	0.8	4,260	26	14.1	28	5.6	23.8	30	561
El Salvador	1,320	1.2	2,360	66	2.0	15	12.0	10.9	33	222
Guatemala	1,110	0.8	3,390	31	3.0	18	10.0	33.1	36	159
Guyana	350	0.6	1,710	21	1.9	28	8.0	36.9	..	..
Haiti	b	-3.4	..	30	0.8	2	54.1	10.2	..	..
Honduras	580	0.0	1,890	92	3.9	32	11.4	41.7	39	180
Jamaica	1,390	3.1	3,000	8	4.3	24	10.7	18.5	36	1,096
Mexico	3,750	0.9	7,100	5	118.0	30	9.0	8.9	35	1,439
Nicaragua	360	-6.2	2,070	97	10.4	66	19.1	46.4	..	241
Panama	2,580	-0.7	5,940	34	6.8	19	7.6	51.2	38	599
Paraguay	1,500	1.3	3,490	42	1.6	21	4.2	46.1	30	214
Peru	1,490	-3.5	3,130	39	20.3	39	14.5	4.5	35	332
Suriname	1,210	2.2	3,670	27	..	..	14.0	11.4	..	..
Trinidad & Tobago	3,730	-2.7	8,850	9	2.1	25	13.5	4.7	19	4,696
Uruguay	3,910	3.0	6,350	38	7.3	38	5.2	35.7	31	715
Venezuela	2,840	1.0	8,130	33	37.5	20	8.3	1.5	23	2,369
Middle East and North Africa	..	..	..	91	..	..	..	..	39	..
Algeria	1,650	-2.2	4,390	11	25.8	72	26.6	0.6	..	955
Bahrain	7,870	-1.0	13,480	41	..	..	6.3	0.4	..	..
Cyprus	10,380	5.2	15,470	17	..	..	7.7	15.7	..	..
Egypt	660	0.7	3,530	52	40.6	16	21.8	12.1	49	539
Iran	..	-0.7	..	38	20.6	5	13.9	2.5	37	1,235
Iraq	c	..	..	271	..	..	18.4	0.1	..	..
Jordan	1,190	-5.9	4,010	138	7.0	17	18.6	12.8	35	766
Kuwait	23,350	0.8	..	88	..	..	12.0	0.1	..	4,217
Lebanon	c	..	..	..	1.4	7	15.3	17.9	..	..
Libya	i	..	..	71	..	..	17.0	0.2	..	..
Morocco	1,030	0.9	3,270	72	21.4	26	13.1	11.8	38	299
Oman	5,600	1.2	10,720	293	2.7	15	11.8	1.3	..	2,408
Qatar	15,140	-0.7	22,910	192	..	..	12.7	0.2	..	..
Saudi Arabia	..	-0.9	..	151	..	..	12.8	1.1	..	4,552
Syria	c	-2.1	..	373	20.0	7	12.7	11.5	..	..
Tunisia	1,780	2.2	5,070	31	8.7	21	6.3	7.9	37	582
Turkey	2,120	3.0	5,550	87	67.9	31	3.6	18.2	40	983
United Arab Emirates	22,470	0.5	23,390	44	..	..	7.2	2.0	..	16,878
Yemen	b	..	..	197	5.9	9	24.2	2.3	..	285
Industrial Countries	..	..	..	33	..	..	6.1	6.2	14	..
Albania	340	-7.0	..	51	0.8	2	47.3	4.2	..	455
Armenia/d	660	-11.7	2,080	..	0.1	0	60.0	..	..	958
Australia	17,510	1.1	18,490	24	..	..	2.9	17.0	13	5,316
Austria	23,120	2.1	18,800	9	..	..	3.9	2.5	16	3,277
Azerbaijan/d	730	-9.4	2,230	..	a	..	29.1	..	..	2,470
Belarus/d	2,840	-0.2	6,360	..	1.0	0	39.8	9.1	..	3,427
Belgium	21,210	2.4	18,490	20	..	..	..	..	15	4,989
Bosnia & Herzegovina	b	..	..	..	..	..	..	..	..	..
Bulgaria	1,160	-2.8	3,730	29	12.3	7	5.5	9.1	..	1,954
Canada	20,670	0.4	20,410	15	..	..	4.5	5.3	11	7,821
Croatia	c	..	..	..	3.0	..	6.6	7.6	..	..
Czech Republic	2,730	-2.0	7,700	17	8.7	11	4.9	5.2	..	..
Denmark	26,510	1.1	18,940	18	..	..	5.8	16.2	13	3,861
Estonia/d	3,040	-5.2	6,860	..	0.2	2	10.3	15.1	..	..

TABLE 3, continued: Global Economic Indicators

	GNP per capita (US$) 1993	GNP per capita real growth rate (%) 1985-1993	Real GDP per capita (PPP$) 1993	Military expenditure (as % of combined education & health expenditure) 1990-1991	Total Debt (US$ billions) 1993	Debt servicing (as % of exports) 1993	Food as % of total imports 1993	Food as % of total exports 1993	Food as % of household consumption 1980-1985	Per capita energy consumption (kg. of oil equivalent) 1993
Finland	18,970	-0.3	15,230	15	..	..	4.3	2.5	16	5,635
France	22,360	1.8	19,440	29	..	..	6.9	10.9	16	4,031
Georgia/d	560	-16.4	1,410	..	0.6	3	..		..	891
Germany/f	23,560	1.9	20,980	29	..	..	6.9	3.8	12	..
Greece	7,390	1.3	8,360	71	..	..	9.4	19.9	30	2,160
Hungary	3,330	0.0	6,260	18	24.8	37	3.4	17.8	25	2,385
Ireland	12,580	4.8	11,850	12	..	..	7.3	17.4	22	3,016
Israel	13,760	2.3	14,890	106	..	..	5.1	5.3	21	2,607
Italy	19,620	1.9	18,070	21	..	..	9.5	5.3	19	2,697
Japan	31,450	3.6	21,090	12	..	..	8.7	0.2	17	3,642
Kazakhstan/d	1,540	-4.6	3,770	..	1.6	0	7.5	10.2	..	4,435
Kyrgyzstan/d	830	-2.1	2,420	..	0.3	1	14.3	..	..	965
Latvia/d	2,030	-4.5	5,170	..	0.2	3	4.0	8.6	..	1,717
Lithuania/d	1,310	-6.4	3,160	..	0.3	1	..	..	..	2,596
Macedonia	780	..	..	..	0.9	..	13.7	10.7	..	..
Moldova/d	1,180	-5.4	3,210	..	0.3	0	17.3	5.2	..	1,345
Netherlands	20,710	2.0	18,050	22	..	..	8.8	14.3	13	4,533
New Zealand	12,900	0.2	15,390	16	..	..	5.2	36.6	12	4,299
Norway	26,340	0.5	19,130	22	..	..	3.9	0.7	15	5,096
Poland	2,270	-1.8	5,010	30	45.3	9	8.0	8.8	29	2,390
Portugal	7,890	4.7	9,890	32	36.9	18	8.3	2.3	34	1,781
Romania	1,120	-6.5	2,910	25	4.5	6	10.6	4.3	..	1,765
Russian Federation/d	2,350	-5.0	5,240	132	83.1	12	14.9	0.2	..	4,438
Slovakia	1,900	-2.6	6,450	..	3.3	8	..	..	..	..
Slovenia	6,310	..	..	..	1.9	..	6.3	3.4	..	1,531
Spain	13,650	3.1	13,310	18	..	..	7.7	13.7	24	2,373
Sweden	24,830	0.1	17,560	16	..	..	4.6	1.4	13	5,385
Switzerland	36,410	0.7	23,620	14	..	..	4.4	2.1	17	3,491
Tajikistan/d	470	-7.8	1,430	..	a	..	19.8	..	..	634
Turkmenistan/d	..	-1.6	..	..	a	..	30.7	..	..	2,268
Ukraine/d	1,910	-3.9	4,030	..	3.6	0	20.4	22.5	..	3,960
United Kingdom	17,970	1.3	17,750	40	..	..	6.9	3.7	12	3,718
USA	24,750	1.2	24,750	46	..	..	2.9	7.0	10	7,918
Uzbekistan/d	960	-1.6	2,580	..	0.7	4	74.2	..	..	2,033
Yugoslavia	c	..	..	..	..	..	..	..	..	..
World	..	..	..	37	..	..	6.3	6.0	..	1,421

a   Indicates less than 50 million.
b   GNP per capita estimated to be low-income ($695 or less).
c   GNP per capita estimated to be lower-middle-income ($696 to $2,785).
d   GNP per capita estimates for the economies of the former Soviet Union are preliminary.
e   GNP per capita data for Eritrea and Ethiopia are not yet desegregated and are included in Ethiopia.
f   PPP estimate of GNP per capita and data on share in GDP refer to the former West Germany.
g   References GNP relate to GDP.
h   Data cover mainland Tanzania only.
i   GNP per capita estimated to be upper-middle-income ($2,786-$8,625)
..   Data not available.

TABLE 4: Malnutrition and Poverty Indicators – Developing Countries

	% of under-5 suffering from underweight (moderate & severe) 1980-93	% of under-5 suffering from underweight (severe) 1980-1993	% of under-5 suffering from wasting (moderate and severe) 1980-1993	% of under-5 suffering from stunting (moderate and severe) 1980-1993	% of population with access to health services 1985-1993	% of population with access to safe water 1988-1993 total	% of population with access to safe water 1988-1993 urban	% of population with access to safe water 1988-1993 rural	Adult literacy rate (%)* 1992 total	Adult literacy rate (%)* 1992 male	Adult literacy rate (%)* 1992 female
Africa (sub-Saharan)	**31**	**9**	**7**	**42**	**56**	**42**	**73**	**35**	**54**	**63**	**40**
Angola	..	..	..	..	30x	41	71	20	43	57	29
Benin	..	..	..	..	18	51	66	46	33	35	17
Botswana	15x	..	..	44	89x	89	100	77	67	85	66
Burkina Faso	30	8	13	29	49x	56	51	72	17	31	10
Burundi	38x	10x	6x	48x	80	57	99	54	33	63	42
Cameroon	14	3	3	24	41	50	57	43	60	70	45
Cape Verde	..	..	..	..	..	..	..	..	66	..	..
Central African Republic	..	..	..	..	45	24	19	26	54	55	26
Chad	..	..	..	..	30	..	30	..	45	46	20
Comoros	..	..	..	..	..	..	..	..	56	..	..
Congo	24	..	5	27	83	38	92	2	71	72	45
Côte d'Ivoire	12	2	9	17	30x	76	70	81	37	69	41
Djibouti	..	..	..	..	..	..	..	..	43	..	..
Equatorial Guinea	..	..	..	..	..	..	..	..	75	66	38
Eritrea	..	..	..	..	..	..	..	..	..	..	..
Ethiopia	48x	16x	8x	64x	46	25	91	19	33	..	..
Gabon	..	..	..	..	90x	68	90	50	59	76	50
Gambia	17	..	..	..	..	..	..	..	36	43	18
Ghana	27	6	7	31	60	52	93	35	61	74	54
Guinea	..	..	..	..	80	55	50	56	33	39	15
Guinea-Bissau	23x	..	..	..	40	41	56	35	52	53	25
Kenya	22	6	6	33	77	49	74	43	75	82	60
Lesotho	16	2	5	26	80	47	59	45	69	..	..
Liberia	20x	..	3x	37x	39	50	93	22	35	53	31
Madagascar	39	9	5	51	65	23	55	9	81	90	74
Malawi	27	8	5	49	80	56x	97x	50x	54	..	..
Mali	31x	9x	11x	24x	..	41	53	38	36	48	22
Mauritania	48	..	16	57	45	66	67	65	36	48	22
Mauritius	24	..	16	22	100	97	98	96	81	85	75
Mozambique	..	..	..	..	39	22	44	17	37	46	21
Namibia	26	6	9	28	72	52	98	35	40	..	..
Niger	36	12	16	32	32	59	60	59	12	44	18
Nigeria	36	12	9	43	66	36	81	30	53	63	41
Rwanda	29	6	4	48	80	66	75	62	57	67	39
Senegal	20	5	9	22	40	48	84	26	31	55	26
Sierra Leone	29	..	9x	35	38	37	33	37	29	35	12
Somalia	..	..	..	..	27x	37	50	29	27	41	16
South Africa	..	..	..	..	..	..	..	..	81	..	..
Sudan	20	..	14	32	51	48	55	43	43	45	13
Swaziland	..	..	..	..	..	..	..	..	74	..	..
Tanzania	29	7	6	47	76x	50	67	46	64	..	..
Togo	24x	6x	5x	30x	61	60	77	53	48	59	33
Uganda	23	5	2	45	49x	31	58	28	59	65	37
Zaire	28x	..	5x	43x	26	39	68	24	74	86	63
Zambia	25	6	5	40	75x	53	70	28	75	83	67
Zimbabwe	12x	2x	1x	29x	85	84	95	80	83	76	61
South Asia	**64**	**24**	**12**	**63**	**77**	**77**	**84**	**74**	**48**	**61**	**33**
Afghanistan	..	..	..	..	29	23	40	19	29	48	15
Bangladesh	66x	27x	16x	65x	45	84	82	85	36	49	23
Bhutan	38	..	4	56	65	34	60	30	39	55	26
India	69x	27x	..	65x	85	79	85	78	50	64	35
Nepal	70x	5x	14x	69x	..	42	67	39	26	39	14
Pakistan	40	14	9	50	55	68	85	50	36	49	22
Sri Lanka	29x	2x	18	36	93x	60	80	55	89	94	85

TABLE 4, continued: Malnutrition and Poverty Indicators – Developing Countries

	% of under-5 suffering from underweight (moderate & severe) 1980-93	% of under-5 suffering from underweight (severe) 1980-1993	% of under-5 suffering from wasting (moderate and severe) 1980-1993	% of under-5 suffering from stunting (moderate and severe) 1980-1993	% of population with access to health services 1985-1993	% of population with access to safe water 1988-1993 total	% of population with access to safe water 1988-1993 urban	% of population with access to safe water 1988-1993 rural	Adult literacy rate (%)* 1992 total	Adult literacy rate (%)* 1992 male	Adult literacy rate (%)* 1992 female
East Asia and the Pacific	**27**	..	..	..	**87**	**66**	**91**	**57**	..	..	..
Burma (Myanmar)	32x	9x	..	..	48	32	37	..	82	90	72
Cambodia	..	..	..	..	53	36	65	33	38	52	24
China	21x	3x	4x	32x	90	69	99	60	79	92	68
Fiji	..	..	..	..	..	..	..	..	90	..	..
Hong Kong	..	..	..	..	99x	100	100	96	91	..	..
Indonesia	40	..	..	..	80	51	68	43	83	91	77
Korea, N.	..	..	..	..	..	..	..	..	95	..	..
Korea, S.	..	..	..	..	100	93	100	76	97	99	95
Laos	37	..	11	40	67	36	54	33	54	..	..
Malaysia	..	..	..	..	..	78	96	66	82	89	72
Mongolia	12x.	..	2x	26x	95	80	100	58	81	..	..
Papua New Guinea	35	..	..	..	96	33	94	20	70	82	48
Philippines	34	5	6	37	76	82	85	79	94	90	90
Singapore	14x	..	4x	11x	100	100	100	..	90	..	..
Solomon Islands	..	..	..	..	..	..	..	..	24	..	..
Thailand	26x	4x	6x	22x	90	77	87	72	94	96	92
Vietnam	52	14	7	60	90	24	39	21	92	93	84
Latin America and the Caribbean	**11**	**2**	**3**	**21**	**74**	**80**	**90**	**55**	**86**	**88**	**84**
Argentina	..	..	..	..	71	71	77	29	96	97	96
Belize	..	..	..	..	..	..	..	..	96	..	..
Bolivia	13x	3x	2x	38x	67	54	81	19	81	86	72
Brazil	7	1	2	16	..	87	95	61	82	84	81
Chile	3x	..	1x	10x	97	86	98	75	95	95	94
Colombia	10	2	3	17	60	86	87	82	90	88	86
Costa Rica	6	..	2	8	80x	93	100	86	94	93	93
Cuba	..	..	1	..	98	98	100	91	95	96	94
Dominican Republic	10	2	1	19	80	59	75	35	81	86	83
Ecuador	17	0	2	34	88	55	63	43	88	89	85
El Salvador	15	..	5	30	40	47	85	19	70	80	70
Guatemala	34x	8x	1x	58x	34	62	92	43	54	65	48
Guyana	..	..	..	..	..	..	..	..	98	99	96
Haiti	37x	3x	9x	40x	50	39	55	33	43	61	49
Honduras	21	4	2	34	66	68	89	51	71	78	73
Jamaica	7	1	3	9	90	100	100	100	84	99	99
Mexico	14	..	6	22	78	84	94	66	89	91	86
Nicaragua	11	1	1	22	83	54	76	21	65	..	..
Panama	16	..	6	22	80x	84	100	66	90	90	90
Paraguay	4	1	0	17	63	35	50	24	91	93	89
Peru	11	2	1	37	75x	72	75	18	87	93	80
Suriname	..	..	..	..	..	..	..	..	92	96	96
Trinidad & Tobago	7x	0x	4x	5x	100	97	99	91	97	..	..
Uruguay	7	2	..	16	82	75	85	5	97	98	97
Venezuela	6	..	2	6	..	89	89	89	90	88	91
Middle East and North Africa	**13**	..	**6**	**25**	**82**	**77**	**93**	**61**	**54**	**70**	**45**
Algeria	9	..	6	18	88	68x	85x	55x	57	74	49
Bahrain	..	..	..	..	..	..	..	..	84	84	71
Cyprus	..	..	..	..	..	..	..	..	..	..	..
Egypt	9	2	3	24	99	90	95	86	49	66	35
Iran	..	..	..	..	80	89	100	75	65	67	45
Iraq	12	2	3	22	93	77	93	41	55	73	51
Jordan	6	1	3	19	97	99	100	97	84	91	72
Kuwait	6	..	3	12	100	..	100	..	77	78	68

	% of under-5 suffering from underweight (moderate & severe) 1980-93	% of under-5 suffering from underweight (severe) 1980-1993	% of under-5 suffering from wasting (moderate and severe) 1980-1993	% of under-5 suffering from stunting (moderate and severe) 1980-1993	% of population with access to health services 1985-1993	% of population with access to safe water 1988-1993 total	% of population with access to safe water 1988-1993 urban	% of population with access to safe water 1988-1993 rural	Adult literacy rate (%)* 1992 total	Adult literacy rate (%)* 1992 male	Adult literacy rate (%)* 1992 female
Lebanon	..	..	..	..	95	92	95	85	91	89	74
Libya	..	..	..	..	..	97	100	80	72	78	52
Morocco	9	2	2	23	70	54	92	14	41	64	40
Oman	..	..	..	..	96	84	91	77	35	..	..
Qatar	..	..	..	..	..	..	..	..	78	..	..
Saudi Arabia	..	..	..	..	97	95	100	74	61	76	50
Syria	..	..	..	..	90	74	90	58	68	82	53
Tunisia	10x	2x	3x	18x	90x	99	100	99	63	77	59
Turkey	..	..	..	..	..	78x	95x	63x	81	91	72
United Arab Emirates	..	..	..	..	99	95	..	..	78	..	..
Yemen	30	4	13	44	38	36	61	30	41	56	28
Developing Countries	**37**	**12**	**6**	**43**	**79**	**69**	**88**	**60**	**68**	**79**	**58**

x Data that refer to years or periods other than those specified in the column heading, differ from the standard definition, or refer to only part of a country.

* Due to use of different sources for total adult literacy vs. male and female rates, there may be discrepancies for some countries.

.. Data not available.

TABLE 5: U.S. National Hunger and Poverty Trends

	1970	1980	1982	1984	1985	1986	1987	1988	1989	1990	1991	1992	1993	1994	1995
Total Population (millions)	205.1	227.8	232.5	237	239.3	241.6	243.9	246.3	248.3	248.7	252.2	255.1	257.9	260.7	263.4
Total hungry population (millions)	..	..	..	..	..	..	..	..	..	..	30.0	..	..	..	..
Children under 18 hungry (millions)	..	..	..	..	..	..	..	..	..	..	12.1	..	..	..	..
Children under 12 hungry (millions)	..	..	..	..	..	..	..	..	..	..	4.0			..	8.8
Children under 12 at-risk of hunger (millions)	..	..	..	..	..	..	..	..	..	..	9.6	..	..	..	21.2
Total poverty rate (%)*	12.6	13.0	15.0	14.4	14.0	13.6	13.4	13.1	12.8	13.5	14.2	14.8	15.1	..	..
White poverty rate (%)	9.9	10.2	12.0	11.5	11.4	11.0	10.4	10.1	10.0	10.7	11.3	11.9	12.2	..	..
Black poverty rate (%)	33.5	32.5	35.6	33.8	31.1	31.1	32.6	31.6	30.7	31.9	32.7	33.4	33.1	..	..
Hispanic poverty rate (%)	..	25.7	29.9	28.4	29.0	27.3	28.1	26.8	26.2	28.1	28.7	29.6	30.6	..	..
Elderly poverty rate (%)	24.6	15.7	14.6	12.4	12.6	12.4	12.5	12.0	11.4	12.2	12.4	12.9	12.2	..	..
Total child poverty rate (%)*	15.1	18.3	21.9	21.5	20.7	20.5	20.5	19.7	19.6	20.6	21.1	22.3	22.7	..	..
White child poverty rate (%)	..	13.9	17.0	16.7	16.2	16.1	15.4	14.6	14.8	15.9	16.1	17.4	17.8	..	..
Black child poverty rate (%)	..	42.3	47.6	46.6	43.6	43.1	45.6	44.2	43.7	44.8	45.6	46.6	46.1	..	..
Hispanic child poverty rate (%)	..	33.2	39.5	39.2	40.3	37.7	39.6	37.9	36.2	38.4	39.8	40.0	40.9	..	..
Poverty rate of people in female-headed households (%)*	38.1	36.7	40.6	38.4	37.6	38.3	38.3	37.2	32.2	33.4	39.7	39.0	38.7	..	..
Percent of federal budget spent on food assistance	0.5	2.4	2.1	2.1	2.0	1.9	1.9	1.9	1.9	1.9	2.0	2.3	2.5	2.5b	2.5b
Total infant mortality rate[1] (per 1,000 live births)	20.0	12.6	11.5	10.8	10.6	10.4	10.1	10.0	9.7	9.1	8.9	8.5	8.3	..	..
White infant mortality rate	17.8	11.0	10.1	9.4	9.3	8.9	8.6	8.5	8.5	7.7	7.3	6.9	..	..	..
Black infant mortality rate	32.6	21.4	19.6	18.4	18.2	18.0	17.9	17.6	17.6	17.0	17.6	16.8	..	..	..
Hispanic infant mortality rate	..	..	..	..	..	..	7.9	8.1	8.5	7.8	7.5	6.8	..	..	..
Unemployment rate (%)	4.9	7.1	9.7	7.5	7.2	7.0	6.2	5.5	5.3	5.5	6.7	7.4	6.8	6.1	..
White unemployment rate (%)	4.5	6.3	8.6	6.5	6.2	6.0	5.3	4.7	4.5	4.7	6.0	6.5	6.0	5.3	..
Black unemployment rate (%)	10.4a	14.3	18.9	15.9	15.1	14.5	13.0	11.7	11.4	11.3	12.4	14.1	12.9	11.5	..
Hispanic unemployment rate (%)	..	10.1	13.8	10.7	10.5	10.6	8.8	8.2	8.0	8.0	9.9	11.4	10.6	9.9	..
Household Income Distribution (per quintile in percentages)															
Lowest 20 percent	..	5.0	4.5	4.4	4.4	4.3	4.3	4.4	3.8	3.9	3.8	3.8	3.6	..	..
Second quintile	..	11.6	11.0	10.7	10.8	10.8	10.6	10.7	9.5	9.6	9.6	9.4	9.1	..	..
Third quintile	..	17.3	16.9	16.7	16.7	16.7	16.6	16.7	15.8	15.9	15.9	15.8	15.3	..	..
Fourth quintile	..	24.5	24.2	24.1	24.1	24.2	24.1	24.2	24	24	24.2	24.2	23.8	..	..
Highest 20 percent	..	41.5	43.5	44.2	44.1	44.2	44.4	44.1	46.8	46.6	46.5	46.9	48.2	..	..
Ratio of highest 20 percent to lowest 20 percent	..	8.3	9.7	10.0	10.0	10.3	10.3	10.0	12.3	11.9	12.2	12.3	13.4	..	..

* Data for 1992 are revised.
[1] Data for 1993 are provisional.
a 1972 data.
b Estimates.
.. Data not available .

ERRATUM
Table 5, p. 92, lines 3-5

	1991	1995
Children under 12 hungry (millions)	5.5 (12.8%)	4.0 (8.8%)
Children under 12 at-risk of hunger (millions)	6.0 (14.0%)	9.6 (21.2%)

TABLE 6: United States – State Hunger and Poverty Statistics

	Total population (millions) July 1994	% of population in poverty 1993	Unemployment rate (seasonally adjusted) May 1995	AFDC and food stamp benefits as % of poverty level (one-parent family of 4 persons) 1994	Infant mortality rate per 1,000 live births 1994	% of children under 12 hungry 1995	% of children under 12 hungry or at-risk 1991	% of children under 12 hungry or at-risk 1995	% of population all ages hungry 1991
Alabama	4.22	17.4	5.9	46.1	9.9	8.6	35.0	29.5	15.8
Alaska	0.61	9.1	6.4	89.8	5.9	5.5	17.7	20.3	9.9
Arizona	4.08	15.4	5.6	62.4	8.6	9.0	25.8	30.4	12.4
Arkansas	2.45	20.0	4.1	50.4	8.0	10.0	38.5	36.1	14.5
California	31.43	18.2	8.5	79.6	6.7	11.8	27.8	37.1	13.2
Colorado	3.66	9.9	3.9	63.1	6.6	6.0	21.0	21.0	8.7
Connecticut	3.28	8.5	5.1	83.5	..	6.1	16.2	19.4	7.2
Delaware	0.71	10.2	4.3	61.7	7.0	5.9	21.8	21.8	6.3
District of Columbia	0.57	26.4	8.6	67.7	17.8	11.3	33.7	40.0	15.6
Florida	13.95	17.8	5.1	59.3	8.1	11.8	27.5	39.5	12.9
Georgia	7.06	13.5	4.8	57.2	9.7	7.3	27.1	24.5	14.4
Hawaii	1.18	8.0	5.1	96.6	6.5	5.4	23.7	19.1	6.5
Idaho	1.13	13.1	5.1	60.2	7.3	8.2	34.4	30.6	11.7
Illinois	11.75	13.6	5.5	62.5	9.1	7.9	28.0	26.3	11.3
Indiana	5.75	12.2	4.7	58.2	9.5	7.2	25.3	28.1	13.2
Iowa	2.83	10.3	3.3	66.6	7.0	6.4	31.7	23.2	8.0
Kansas	2.55	13.1	4.7	68.7	8.8	8.1	22.8	29.1	10.3
Kentucky	3.83	20.4	5.0	53.5	7.7	9.2	29.8	33.7	15.8
Louisiana	4.32	26.4	7.1	49.4	9.5	12.1	32.1	39.1	15.9
Maine	1.24	15.4	6.2	68.4	6.3	9.9	24.3	35.0	11.8
Maryland	5.01	9.7	5.0	65.4	8.9	5.9	16.4	19.9	7.6
Massachusetts	6.04	10.7	5.0	76.5	5.7	6.5	19.3	22.5	9.2
Michigan	9.50	15.4	5.7	71.4	8.6	8.4	27.6	29.9	11.8
Minnesota	4.57	11.6	3.9	73.9	6.6	6.7	21.2	24.4	10.8
Mississippi	2.67	24.7	6.0	42.1	10.1	10.3	38.7	37.3	19.9
Missouri	5.28	16.1	5.1	58.0	8.1	9.2	26.9	32.4	12.4
Montana	0.86	14.9	5.5	66.9	8.2	7.9	31.5	30.3	12.9
Nebraska	1.62	10.3	2.6	63.2	7.9	6.9	28.6	24.8	8.0
Nevada	1.46	9.8	5.9	61.8	6.2	6.7	27.9	22.9	9.6
New Hampshire	1.14	9.9	3.8	73.4	6.6	6.3	12.6	22.8	6.1
New Jersey	7.90	10.9	6.5	67.0	7.9	7.1	20.3	22.7	8.1
New Mexico	1.65	17.4	5.7	64.6	8.9	8.7	36.1	31.4	18.8
New York	18.17	16.4	6.3	83.1	8.5	9.5	29.7	30.7	12.8
North Carolina	7.07	14.4	4.3	54.5	10.0	8.3	26.3	29.5	12.2
North Dakota	0.64	11.2	3.3	67.9	6.3	5.3	27.9	21.2	12.2
Ohio	11.10	13.0	4.7	62.5	8.9	7.1	24.3	26.5	11.2
Oklahoma	3.26	19.9	4.6	61.4	9.4	10.6	28.7	38.7	14.2
Oregon	3.09	11.8	5.2	73.5	7.0	6.9	24.1	25.2	11.3
Pennsylvania	12.05	13.2	5.7	67.8	7.6	7.6	25.6	28.1	9.2
Rhode Island	1.00	11.2	6.4	78.0	6.0	6.9	25.6	25.8	8.7
South Carolina	3.66	18.7	4.9	49.9	8.9	10.0	31.3	35.8	13.7
South Dakota	0.72	14.2	2.3	65.8	11.8	8.0	28.6	29.9	11.7
Tennessee	5.18	19.6	4.6	48.7	8.8	10.6	30.7	36.8	13.0
Texas	18.38	17.4	6.0	48.7	7.2	10.1	28.6	30.6	14.7
Utah	1.91	10.7	3.7	66.1	6.0	7.0	25.5	24.7	10.8
Vermont	0.58	10.0	3.9	80.1	6.7	5.2	20.5	21.9	10.6
Virginia	6.55	9.7	4.5	61.9	8.0	5.8	20.5	20.7	8.3
Washington	5.34	12.1	6.1	77.5	5.4	7.4	22.7	27.5	8.0
West Virginia	1.82	22.2	7.6	55.7	6.8	10.2	38.6	37.3	15.0
Wisconsin	5.08	12.6	3.9	73.6	7.7	7.8	24.7	28.6	8.3
Wyoming	0.48	13.3	4.8	60.7	8.0	8.9	22.6	28.9	8.3
United States	**260.34**	**15.1**	**5.7**	**65.4**	**7.7**	**12.8**	**26.8**	**30.1**	**12.0**

Sources for Tables

**TABLE 1: Global Hunger –
Life and Death Indicators**
Total population, projected population, average annual population growth rate, fertility rate, urban population, life expectancy: U.N. Population Fund, *The State of World Population 1995* (Oxford: New Internationalist Publications, 1995).

Population under age 15: Population Reference Bureau, *World Population Data Sheet 1995* (Washington: Population Reference Bureau, 1995).

Infant mortality, under-5 mortality, maternal mortality: UNICEF, *The State of the World's Children 1995* (New York: Oxford University Press, 1995) ("*SWC*").

TABLE 2: Global Health, Nutrition and Welfare Indicators
Human development rank, gross enrollment data: U.N. Development Programme, *Human Development Report 1995* (New York: Oxford University Press, 1995) ("*HDR*").

Refugees by country of asylum: U.N. High Commissioner for Refugees, *Populations of Concern to UNHCR*, June 1995.

Low birthweight, percent immunized (measles), daily per capita calorie supply: *SWC*.

Food production per capita: Food and Agriculture Organization of the United Nations (FAO), FAOSTAT TS software, 1994, Rome.

Total deforestation: World Resources Institute, *World Resources 1994-95* (New York: Oxford University Press, 1994).

TABLE 3: Global Economic Indicators
GNP per capita, GNP growth rate, real GDP per capita: The World Bank, *The World Bank Atlas 1995* (Washington: The World Bank, 1994).

Military expenditure as percent of combined education and health expenditure: *HDR*.

Total Debt, debt servicing as percent of exports: The World Bank, *World Debt Tables, 1994-95, Vol. I* (Washington: The World Bank, 1994).

Food as percent of total imports, exports: FAO.

Food as percent of household consumption: *SWC*.

Per capita energy consumption: The World Bank, *World Development Report 1995* (New York: Oxford University Press, 1995).

TABLE 4: Malnutrition and Poverty Indicators – Developing Countries
Underweight, wasting, stunting, health services, safe water data: *SWC*.

Literacy data: *HDR, 1994*.

TABLE 5: U.S. National Hunger and Poverty Trends
Total hungry population, total children hungry: Center on Hunger, Poverty and Nutrition·Policy, Tufts University.

Children under 12 hungry, at-risk of hunger: Food Research and Action Center (FRAC), Washington, DC.

Poverty data, household income distribution: U.S. Bureau of the Census.

Percent of federal budget spent on food assistance: *Budget of the United States Government Fiscal Year 1995* (Washington: U.S. Government Printing Office, 1994).

Infant mortality: U.S. National Center for Health Statistics.

Unemployment: U.S. Bureau of Labor Statistics.

TABLE 6: United States – State Hunger and Poverty Statistics
Total population, population in poverty: U.S. Bureau of the Census.

Unemployment: U.S. Bureau of Labor Statistics.

AFDC and food stamp benefits as percent of poverty level: The Annie E. Casey Foundation, *Kids Count Data Book 1995* (Baltimore: The Annie E. Casey Foundation).

Infant mortality: U.S. National Center for Health Statistics, *Monthly Vital Statistics Report* 43:12 (June 1995).

Children under 12 hungry, at risk of hunger: FRAC.

Population all ages hungry: Center on Hunger, Poverty and Nutrition Policy, Tufts University.

Abbreviations

AFDC	–	Aid to Families with Dependent Children
ANC	–	African National Congress (South Africa)
CNN	–	Cable News Network
DHA	–	U.N. Department of Humanitarian Affairs
EIC	–	Earned Income Credit
EU	–	European Union
FAO	–	Food and Agriculture Organization of the United Nations
FY	–	Fiscal Year
HDI	–	Human Development Index
ICN	–	International Conference on Nutrition
IDS	–	Institute of Development Studies, University of Sussex, U.K.
InterAction	–	American Council for Voluntary International Action
IOM	–	International Organization for Migration
LTTE	–	Liberation Tigers of Tamil Eelam (Sri Lanka)
LWR	–	Lutheran World Relief
MECC	–	Middle East Council of Churches
NGO	–	Nongovernmental Organization
NIS	–	Newly Independent States of the former Soviet Union
OECD	–	Organisation for Economic Co-operation and Development
RENAMO	–	National Resistance Movement (Mozambique)
U.K.	–	United Kingdom
U.N.	–	United Nations
UNDP	–	U.N. Development Programme
UNESCO	–	U.N. Educational, Scientific and Cultural Organization
UNHCR	–	U.N. High Commissioner for Refugees
UNICEF	–	U.N. Children's Fund
UNRWA	–	U.N. Relief and Works Agency for Palestine Refugees in the Near East
U.S.	–	United States
USA for Africa	–	United Support of Artists for Africa
USAID	–	U.S. Agency for International Development
USDA	–	U.S. Department of Agriculture
U.S.S.R.	–	Union of Soviet Socialist Republics
UXO	–	Unexploded Ordinance
WFP	–	U.N. World Food Programme

Glossary

Anemia – A condition in which the hemoglobin concentration (the number of red blood cells) is lower than normal as a result of a deficiency of one or more essential nutrients such as iron or due to disease.

Apartheid – The former legally enforced system of racial segregation and discrimination against blacks and others of colored descent in South Africa.

Asylum – Protection given by one country to refugees from another.

Autonomy – Self-government with respect to local or internal affairs.

Bilateral aid – Financial or material assistance provided to an individual developing country by a donor country (as distinguished from multilateral aid).

Cold War – The global state of tension and military rivalry that existed from 1945 to 1990 between the United States and the former Soviet Union and their respective allies.

Complex humanitarian emergencies – Crises arising from conflicts within nation-states leading to large-scale displacement of people, mass famine, and fragile or failing economic, political and social institutions.

Daily calorie requirement – The average number of calories needed to sustain normal levels of activity and health, taking into account age, sex, body weight and climate: roughly 2,350 calories per person per day.

Debt service – The sum of repayments of principal and payments of interest on debt.

Developing countries – Countries in which most people have a low economic standard of living. Also known as the "Third World," the "South" and the "less-developed countries."

Ethnicity – Identifying characteristics shared by a group of people such as culture, custom, race, language, religion or other social distinctions.

Famine – A situation of extreme scarcity of food, potentially leading to widespread starvation.

Fertility rate – The average number of children born by a woman during her lifetime; a measure of long-term population changes.

Food security – Assured access for every person, primarily by production or purchase, to enough nutritious food to sustain productive human life.

Genocide – The systematic and planned extermination of an entire national, racial, political or ethnic group. International law requires collective action to oppose genocide.

Green revolution – A term used to describe technological changes in agricultural production methods since World War II. The technologies rely on the use of improved seeds, known as high-yielding varieties, often with irrigation, chemical fertilizers and pesticides.

Gross domestic product (GDP) – The value of all goods and services produced within a nation during a specified period, usually a year.

Gross national product (GNP) – The value of all goods and services produced by a country's citizens, wherever they are located.

Human development – A measure of well-being devised by the U.N. Development Programme, based on economic growth, educational attainment and health.

Human rights – The basic rights and freedoms of all human beings, including, but not limited to, the right to life and liberty, freedom of thought and expression and equality before the law.

Humanitarian intervention – The delivery of emergency aid by outside parties, including official aid agencies and non-governmental organizations.

Hunger – A condition in which people lack the basic food intake to provide them with the energy and nutrients for fully productive, active and healthy lives.

Industrial countries – Countries in which most people have a high economic standard of living (though there are often significant poverty populations). Also called the "developed countries" or the "North."

Infant mortality rate (IMR) – The annual number of deaths of infants under one year of age per 1,000 live births.

Infectious disease – A disease caused by invasion of body tissue by microorganisms.

Inflation – An increase in overall prices, which leads to a decrease in purchasing power.

Infrastructure – The basic facilities, services and installations needed for the functioning of a community or society such as transportation, communications, financial, educational and health care systems.

Livelihood security – The ability of a household to meet all of its basic needs – for food, shelter, water, sanitation, health care and education – without making tradeoffs.

Low birthweight infants – Babies born weighing 2,500 grams (5 pounds, 8 ounces) or less who are especially vulnerable to illness and death during the first months of life.

Malnutrition – Failure to achieve nutrient requirements, which can impair physical and/or mental health. Malnutrition may result from consuming too little food or a shortage or imbalance of key nutrients, e.g., micronutrient deficiencies or excess consumption of refined sugar and fat.

Microenterprises – Very small economic ventures owned and managed by one entrepreneur and employing fewer than five people.

Micronutrients – Vitamins, major minerals and trace elements needed for a healthy, balanced diet. Often contrasted with "macronutrients" – protein and calories. Micronutrient deficiencies are also called "hidden hunger."

Multilateral aid – Financial or material assistance channeled to developing countries via international organizations such as the World Bank, the European Union or U.N. agencies (as distinguished from bilateral aid).

Official Development Assistance (ODA) – Aid provided by donor governments and intergovernmental organizations to developing countries. At least 25 percent is a grant, with promotion of economic development or welfare as the main objective.

Population at risk – People who are in need of or dependent on outside aid to avoid large-scale malnutrition and deaths as a result of complex humanitarian emergencies. These people include refugees, internally displaced people and others in need.

Poverty line – An official measure of poverty defined by national governments. In the United States, it is based on ability to afford the U.S. Department of Agriculture's "Thrifty Food Plan," which provides a less-than-adequate diet.

Purchasing Power Parity (PPP) – An estimate of the amount of money required to purchase comparable goods in different countries, expressed in U.S. dollars.

Recession – A period during which a country's GDP declines in two or more consecutive three-month periods. The reduction in economic activity is less severe than during a "depression."

Repatriation – Sending refugees and other migrants back to their home countries.

Resettlement – Permitting refugees to remain in an asylum country on a permanent basis; permitting internally displaced people to settle permanently in a new community.

Sovereignty – Supreme independent political authority, generally residing in national governments.

Starvation – Suffering or death from extreme or prolonged lack of food.

Stunting – Failure to grow to normal height caused by chronic undernutrition during the formative years of childhood.

Sustainability – Society's ability to shape its economic and social systems so as to maintain both natural resources and human life.

Sustainable development – The reduction of hunger and poverty in environmentally sound ways. It includes four objectives: meeting basic human needs, expanding economic opportunities, protecting and enhancing the environment, and promoting pluralism and democratic participation.

Underemployment – The situation of not being fully employed year round. Underemployed people include unemployed, discouraged and involuntary part-time workers.

Under-five mortality rate – The annual number of deaths of children under five years of age per 1,000 live births; a high rate correlates closely with hunger and malnutrition.

Undernutrition – A form of mild, chronic or acute malnutrition characterized by inadequate intake of food energy (measured by calories), usually due to eating too little. Stunting, wasting and underweight are common forms of undernutrition.

Underweight – A condition in which a person is seriously below normal weight for her or his age.

Uprooted people – People displaced against their will from their communities and means of survival. This includes refugees who flee their homelands, people displaced within their own countries and people living in "refugee-like" circumstances who are not legally recognized as refugees.

Vulnerability to hunger – Individuals, households, communities or nations who have enough to eat most of the time, but whose poverty makes them especially susceptible to hunger due to changes in the economy, climate or political conditions.

Wasting – A condition in which a person is seriously below the normal weight for her or his height due to acute undernutrition.

World Bank – An intergovernmental agency – formally called The International Bank for Reconstruction and Development – that makes long-term loans to the governments of developing nations.

Notes and Bibliography

Introduction

1. Richard J. Barnet, "The Global War Against the Poor," March 23, 1995 (draft manuscript), Institute for Policy Studies, Washington, DC.

2. David C. Korten, "NGO Strategic Networks: From Community Projects to Global Transformation," Paper prepared for the Asian Regional Workshop on Strategic Networking for Sustainable Development and Environmental Action, Bangkok, Thailand, November 26-30, 1990, p. 2.

Chapter 1

1. Arthur Simon, *Harvesting Peace: The Arms Race and Human Need* (Kansas City, MO: Sheed and Ward, 1990); Anthony Lake *et al.*, eds., *After the Wars* (New Brunswick, NJ and Oxford: Transaction Books for the Overseas Development Council, 1990).

2. U.S. Mission to the United Nations, *Global Humanitarian Emergencies, 1995* (New York: U.S. Mission to the United Nations, January 1995), p. 1.

3. Bais Karolien, *Development and Conflict* (Amsterdam: NCO, 1994); United Nations Development Programme, *Human Development Report 1994* (New York: Oxford University Press, 1994); Kevin Watkins, *The Oxfam Poverty Report* (Oxford: Oxfam, 1995), p. 43.

4. *Ibid.*, p. 47.

5. Karen Jacobsen, *The Impact of Refugees on the Environment: A Review of Evidence* (Washington: Refugee Policy Group, 1994); Ellen Messer with Thomas Marchione and Marc J. Cohen, "Food from Peace," Draft 2020 Vision Discussion Paper prepared for the International Food Policy Research Institute, August 1995.

6. Larry Minear and Thomas G. Weiss, *Mercy Under Fire: War and the Global Humanitarian Community* (Boulder, CO: Westview Press, 1995); Watkins.

7. Eleanor Noss Whitney *et al.*, *Understanding Nutrition*, 5th ed. (St. Paul, MN: West Publishing Company, 1990).

8. Frances Stewart, "War and Underdevelopment: Can Economic Analysis Help Reduce the Costs?," *Centro Studi Luca D'Agliano-Queen Elizabeth House Development Studies Working Papers* No. 56 (April 1993).

9. U.S. Centers for Disease Control and Prevention, *Morbidity and Mortality Weekly Supplement on Refugee and Famine-Affected Public Health Measures* (Atlanta: CDC, 1993).

10. *World Declaration and Plan of Action for Nutrition*, Plan paragraphs 37, 37a, 43f, 43m.

11. Refugee Policy Group estimates; see also Hal Kane, "The Hour of Departure: Forces that Create Refugees and Migrants," *Worldwatch Paper* No. 125 (Washington: Worldwatch Institute, 1995).

12. Food and Agriculture Organization of the United Nations, *Sixth World Food Survey* (Rome: FAO, forthcoming).

13. World Health Organization, *The World Health Report 1995* (Geneva: WHO, 1995); Stewart.

14. Food and Agriculture Organization of the United Nations, *World Declaration and Plan of Action for Nutrition* (Rome: FAO, 1992), Declaration paragraph 19.

15. John Sommer, *Hope Restored? Humanitarian Aid in Somalia, 1990-1994* (Washington: RPG, 1994).

16. Quoted in John Darnton, "Forgotten by World, Afghans Plunge Into Misery," *New York Times*, August 11, 1994.

17. Quoted in John F. Burns, "As U.S. Aid Ends, Need of Afghan War Victims Persists," *New York Times*, February 22, 1995.

18. G. Rose, *The Strategy of Preventive Medicine* (Oxford: Oxford Medical Publications, 1993); Steven Hansch *et al.*, *Lives Lost, Lives Saved* (Washington: RPG, 1994).

19. *Sudanese Rebels at a Crossroads: Opportunities for Building Peace in a Shattered Land* (Washington: Center of Concern, 1994); see also Human Rights Watch, *Abuses by All Parties in the War in Southern Sudan* (New York: Human Rights Watch, 1994).

20. Barbara Herwaldt *et al.*, "Crisis in the Sudan: Where is the World?," *The Lancet* 342 (July 10, 1993): 119-120.

21. Messer, Marchione and Cohen; Peter Uvin, "The Political Ecology of Conflict in Rwanda," 1995 (unpublished manuscript), Brown University; U.S. Committee for Refugees, *World Refugee Survey 1995* (Washington: Immigration and Refugee Services of America, 1995); Stephen Buckley, "At Least 2,000 Refugees Die in Rwandan Violence," *Washington Post*, April 24, 1995; Matt Bigg, "Foreigners Flee Fighting in Burundi," *Washington Post*, March 30, 1995.

Additional Sources (Afghanistan) –

Anderson, John Ward. 1994. "New Fighting Dashes Hope of Peace in Afghanistan." *Washington Post*, August 30.

De Neufville, Peter. 1995. "Religious Zeal Drives Afghani Youth Army to Swift, Dubious Win." *Christian Science Monitor*, March 29.

Far Eastern Economic Review. 1994-1995. Weekly.

Food and Agriculture Organization of the United Nations. 1995. *Foodcrops and Shortages* No. 1 (January-February).

_____. 1994. *Afghanistan: ESN Nutrition Country Profile.* July.

Harrison, Selig S. 1990. "Afghanistan." In *After the Wars*, pp. 45-74. Edited by Anthony Lake *et al.* New Brunswick, NJ: Transaction Books for the Overseas Development Council.

McCoy, Alfred W. 1991. *The Politics of Heroin: CIA Complicity in the Global Drug Trade.* Brooklyn: Lawrence Hill Books.

Moore, Molly and John Ward Anderson. 1995. "Children Bear Brunt of Modern Wars." *Washington Post,* April 16.

Rubin, Barnett R. 1994. "Afghanistan in 1993: Abandoned but Surviving." *Asian Survey* 34:2 (February): 185-190.

_____. 1995. *The Fragmentation of Afghanistan: State Formation and Collapse in the International System.* New Haven and London: Yale University Press.

_____. Personal Interview. Washington, DC. April 10, 1995.

United Nations Administrative Committee on Coordination/Subcommittee on Nutrition. 1994-1995. *Refugee Nutrition Information System: Report on the Nutrition Situation of Refugee and Displaced Populations* Nos. 8-10. December 19, 1994; February 21, 1995 and April 28, 1995.

United Nations Children's Fund. 1994a. *1994 UNICEF Annual Report.* New York: UNICEF.

_____. 1994b. *The Progress of Nations 1994.* New York: UNICEF.

_____. 1995a. *The Progress of Nations 1995.* New York: UNICEF.

_____. 1995b. *The State of the World's Children 1995.* New York: Oxford University Press.

Chapter 2

1. J. Brian Atwood, Speech delivered at the International Development Conference, Washington, DC, January 17, 1995.

2. Kevin Watkins, *The Oxfam Poverty Report* (Oxford: Oxfam, 1995), p. 68.

3. John G. Sommer, *Hope Restored? Humanitarian Aid in Somalia 1990-1994* (Washington: Refugee Policy Group, 1994).

4. Timothy R. Frankenberger, *Conceptual Issues Related to Food Security* (Atlanta: CARE Food Security Unit Publications, no date – mimeo).

5. Larry Minear *et al.*, *Humanitarianism Under Siege: A Critical Review of Operation Lifeline Sudan* (Trenton, NJ: Red Sea Press and Washington: Bread for the World Institute, 1991); John Prendergast, "Peace, Development and People of the Horn of Africa," *Occasional Paper* No. 1 (Washington: Bread for the World Institute and Center of Concern, 1992).

6. Larry Minear, U.B.P. Chelliah, Jeff Crisp, John Mackinlay and Thomas G. Weiss, "United Nations Coordination of the International Humanitarian Response to the Gulf Crisis," *Occasional Paper Series* No. 13 (Providence, RI: The Thomas J. Watson Jr. Institute of International Studies, Brown University, 1992).

7. Watkins, p. 59.

8. Hiram Ruiz, *People Want Peace: Repatriation and Reintegration in War-Torn Sri Lanka* (Washington: Immigration and Refugee Services of America, 1994).

9. David Little, *Sri Lanka: The Invention of Enmity* (Washington: United States Institute of Peace Press, 1994); Barnett R. Rubin, *Cycles of Violence: Human Rights in Sri Lanka Since the Indo-Sri Lanka Agreement* (Washington: Asia Watch, 1987).

10. The World Bank, *Sri Lanka: Poverty Assessment* (Washington: The World Bank, 1995).

11. John M. Richardson and S.W.R. de Samarasinghe, "Measuring the Economic Dimensions of Sri Lanka's Ethnic Conflict," in S.W.R. de Samarasinghe and Reed Cougham, eds., *Economic Dimensions of Ethnic Conflict* (New York: St. Martin's Press, 1991), pp. 194-223.

12. Mohan Samarasinghe, "Sri Lanka: Economy Poised for Take Off," Inter Press Service, Harare, Zimbabwe, April 17, 1995.

13. Jean Drèze and Amartya Sen, eds., *The Political Economy of Hunger*, vol III. Endemic Hunger (Oxford: Clarendon Press, 1990), p. 5.

14. U.N. Children's Fund, "Sri Lanka: Tough Lessons," *Profiles in Success: People's Progress in Africa, Asia and Latin America* (New York: UNICEF, 1995), p. 23.

15. Kalinga Seneviratne, "Sri Lanka: Social Miracle Passes Unnoticed at Copenhagen Summit," Inter Press Service, Harare, Zimbabwe, March 15, 1995.

16. UNICEF.

17. Ruiz.

18. John Ward Anderson, "Cut-off Sri Lankans Gain Reprieve from War," *Washington Post*, February 4, 1995.

19. Food and Agriculture Organization of the United Nations, *The State of Food and Agriculture 1994* (Rome: FAO, 1994).

20. Ruiz.

21. Molly Moore, "Sri Lanka, Tamil Rebels Agree to Tentative Two-Week Truce," *Washington Post*, January 4, 1995.

22. *Ibid.*

23. John-Thor Dahlburg, "War Returns with Fury to Sri Lanka: Military Determined to End Rebels' Stand," *Washington Post*, July 14, 1995.

24. This is a summary of the author's paper, "Refugees and Internally Displaced Women," in *Closing the Gender Gap* (Washington: The World Bank, forthcoming).

25. *IDS Policy Briefing* Issue 3, April 1995.

26. U.S. Agency for International Development, "Breaking the Cycle of Despair: President Clinton's Initiative on the Horn of Africa," June 1994 (mimeo); revised and expanded November 1994.

27. J. Brian Atwood, Speech delivered at the Constituency for Africa Summit on African Aid, Washington, DC, February 3, 1995.

Additional Sources (General) –

American Red Cross Newsletter. 1990. HIS 0106, September.

Anderson, Mary and Peter Woodrow. 1989. *Rising from the Ashes: Disaster Response Toward Development*. Boulder, CO: Westview Press.

Bennett, Jon *et al.* 1995. *Meeting Needs: NGO Coordination in Practice*. London: Earthscan for the International Council of Voluntary Agencies.

Benthall, Jonathan. 1993. *Disasters, Relief and the Media*. New York: St. Martin's Press.

Boutros-Ghali, Boutros. 1992. *An Agenda for Peace*. New York: United Nations.

_____. 1994a. *An Agenda for Development*. New York: United Nations.

_____. 1994b. *Building Peace and Development*. New York: United Nations.

_____. 1994c. *Improving the Capacity of the United Nations for Peacekeeping*. New York: United Nations.

Chelala, César A. 1994. "A New Perspective for the Assessment of Children's Health" (unpublished manuscript). Pan American Health Organization, Washington, DC.

Chelliah, U.B.P. 1993. "War Breeds Hunger: Feeding the Victims." *Forum for Applied Research and Public Policy*. Winter.

_____. 1994. "Violence and Militarism." In *Causes of Hunger: Hunger 1995*, pp. 35-46. Edited by Marc J. Cohen. Silver Spring, MD: Bread for the World Institute.

Cohen, Marc J., ed. 1992. *Hunger 1993: Uprooted People*. Washington: Bread for the World Institute.

_____. 1994. *Causes of Hunger: Hunger 1995*. Silver Spring, MD: Bread for the World Institute.

Connelly, Matthew and Paul Kennedy. 1994. "Must It Be the Rest Against the West?" *The Atlantic Monthly*, December.

Cranna, Michael, ed. 1994. *The True Cost of Conflict*. London: Earthscan for Saferworld.

Cuny, Fredrick C. 1991. *Carnegie Special Report: Northern Iraq*.

Deng, Francis M. 1993. *Protecting the Dispossessed: A Challenge for the International Community*. Washington: The Brookings Institution.

Deng, Francis M. and Larry Minear. 1992. *The Challenges of Famine Relief: Emergency Operations in the Sudan*. Washington: The Brookings Institution.

D'Silva, Brian. 1995. "Food Security in Complex Emergencies." Presentation at Bread for the World, Silver Spring, MD, February.

Development Assistance Committee. 1995. *Development Co-operation Review Series: United States, 1995* No. 8. Paris: Organisation for Economic Co-operation and Development.

Drèze, Jean and Amartya Sen. 1989. *Hunger and Public Action*. Oxford: Clarendon Press.

Freeman, Bowyer. 1994. "Five Weeks in Africa with the United Methodist Committee on Relief." Presentation at Bread for the World, Silver Spring, MD, October.

Gurr, Ted Robert. 1993. *Minorities at Risk: A Global View of Ethnopolitical Conflicts*. Washington: United States Institute of Peace.

Gurr, Ted Robert and Barbara Harff, eds. 1994a. "Early Warning of Communal Conflicts and Humanitarian Crises." Proceedings of a workshop held at the Center for International Development and Conflict Management, University of Maryland, November 5-6, 1993. In *The Journal of Ethno-Development* 4:1.

_____. 1994b. *Ethnic Conflict in World Politics*. Boulder: Westview Press.

Huntington, Samuel P. 1993. "The Clash of Civilizations." *Foreign Affairs* 72:3 (Summer): 21-49.

Holt, Victoria K. 1995. *Briefing Book on Peacekeeping: The U.S. Role in United Nations Peace Operations*. Washington: Council for a Liveable World Education Fund.

Humanitarianism and War Project. 1994. *Status Report* No. 15. Providence, RI: The Thomas J. Watson Jr. Institute for International Studies, Brown University.

Independent Working Group on the Future of the United Nations. 1995. *The United Nations in Its Second Half-Century*. New York: Ford Foundation.

InterAction. 1995. *InterAction Member Profiles, 1995-1996*. Washington: American Council for Voluntary International Action.

International Council of Voluntary Agencies. No date. *NGO Statement to the 45th Session of the Executive Committee of the U.N. High Commissioner for Refugees' Programme*. Geneva: ICVA.

_____. 1995. *Position Paper for the World Summit for Social Development*. Geneva: ICVA.

International Federation of Red Cross and Red Crescent Societies. 1995. *World Disasters Report 1995*. Geneva: International Federation of Red Cross and Red Crescent Societies.

Kaplan, Robert D. 1988. *Surrender or Starve: The Wars Behind the Famine*. Boulder: Westview Press.

_____. 1994. "The Coming Anarchy." *The Atlantic Monthly*, February, pp. 44-76.

Karolien, Bais. 1994. *Development and Conflict*. Amsterdam: NCO.

Lake, Anthony *et al.*, eds. 1990. *After the Wars*. New Brunswick, NJ and Oxford: Transaction Books for the Overseas Development Council.

Lappé, Frances Moore and Joseph Collins. 1977. *Food First: Beyond the Myth of Scarcity*. Boston: Houghton-Mifflin.

Liaison Committee of Development NGOs to the European Union. 1994. *Conflict, Development and Military Intervention: The Role, Position and Experience of the NGOs*. Brussels: Liaison Committee.

Maxwell, Simon and Margaret Buchanan-Smith, eds. "Linking Relief and Development." *ids bulletin* 25:4 (October 1994).

Mehretu, Assefa. 1993. "Geographic Distributional Incongruities between Density and Land Potential in Sub-Saharan Africa: the Case of Zimbabwe" (unpublished manuscript). Michigan State University.

Messer, Ellen. 1989. "The Ecology and Politics of Food Availability." In *African Food Systems in Crisis. Part One: Microperspectives*. Edited by R. Huss-Ashmore and S.H. Katz. New York: Gordon and Breach.

_____. 1991. *Food Wars: Hunger as a Weapon of War in 1990*. Providence, RI: World Hunger Program, Brown University, RR-91-3.

_____. 1994. "Food Wars: Hunger as a Weapon of War in 1993." In *The Hunger Report 1993*, pp. 43-69. Edited by Peter Uvin. Langhorne, PA: Gordon and Breach for the Alan Shawn Feinstein World Hunger Program, Brown University.

Minear, Larry and Thomas G. Weiss. 1993. *Humanitarian Action in Times of War*. Boulder: Lynn Rienner Publishers.

_____. 1995. *Mercy Under Fire: War and the Global Humanitarian Community*. Boulder: Westview Press.

Minear, Larry, Thomas G. Weiss and Kurt M. Campbell. 1991. "Humanitarianism and War: Learning the Lessons from Recent Armed Conflicts." *Occasional Paper Series* No. 8. Providence, RI: The Thomas J. Watson Jr. Institute of International Studies, Brown University.

Ottaway, Marina. 1994. "Democratization and Ethnic Nationalism: African and East European Experiences." *Policy Essay* No. 14. Washington: Overseas Development Council.

Refugee Policy Group. 1992. *Cambodia: A Time to Return, Reconciliation and Reconstruction*. Washington: RPG.

Riley, Stephen. 1994. "Wars and Famine in Africa." *Conflict Studies* No. 268. London: The Research Institute for the Study of Conflict and Terrorism.

Robinson, Clive *et al.* 1994. *Food Security Beyond 2000*. Brussels: Liaison Committee of Development NGOs to the European Community.

Rondos, Alexander. 1994. "The Collapsing State and International Security." In *Global Engagement: Cooperation and Security in the 21st Century*. Edited by Janne Nolan. Washington: The Brookings Institution.

Rubenstein, Richard E. and Jarle Crocker. 1994. "Challenging Huntington." *Foreign Policy* No. 96 (Fall): 113-128.

Rupesinghe, Kumar. 1993. "Humanitarian Agencies and Armed Conflicts." *International Alert*.

Sen, Amartya. 1981. *Poverty and Famines: An Essay on Entitlement and Deprivation*. Oxford: Clarendon Press.

_____. 1993. "The Political Economy of Hunger: On Reasoning and Participation." Paper presented at the World Bank Conference on Overcoming Global Hunger, The American University, Washington, DC.

Sahnoun, Mohamed. 1994. *Somalia: The Missed Opportunities*. Washington: U.S. Institute of Peace Press.

Smillie, Ian and Henny Helmich, eds. 1993. *Non-Governmental Organisations and Governments: Stakeholders for Development*. Paris: Organisation for Economic Co-operation and Development.

Stewart, Frances. 1993. "War and Underdevelopment." *Centro Studi Luca D'Agliano-Queen Elizabeth House Development Studies Working Papers* No. 56 (April).

Talal, Crown Prince Hassan Bin. 1992. "Humanitarian Intervention and Global Humanitarian Regime." Position paper presented at the Humanitas Conference, 21-23 February.

Taylor, William C. 1994. "Control in an Age of Chaos." *Harvard Business Review*, December.

Thomas, William. 1994. "Cashing in Chaos." *Business*, December.

Thompson, W. Scott, James Lane, Brian Urquhart and Chester Crocker. No date. *On International Conflict and Conflict Resolution*. Washington: United States Institute of Peace.

Unidad Coordinadora Post Cosecha. 1993. *Post Cosecha: Plan Operativo, Fase 1993-1995*. Tegucigalpa: UCPC.

United Nations Children's Fund. 1994. *Realidad Socioeconomico de Guatemala*. Guatemala City: UNICEF and SEGEPLAN.

United Nations Development Programme. 1992, 1994. *Human Development Report 1992, 1994*. New York: Oxford University Press.

United Nations High Commissioner for Refugees. 1994. "Evaluation of Activities." Paper submitted to 45th General Assembly. 20 July.

_____. 1995. *Directory of Nongovernmental Organizations*. Geneva: UNHCR.

"UN Security Council: The Need for Reform." *Resurgence*. No. 56 (January 1995): 6738.

U.S. Agency for International Development. 1993. *The World Food Day Report 1993: The President's Report to the U.S. Congress*. Washington: USAID.

_____. 1994a. *Terms of Reference – Evaluation of Emergency Assistance to Rwanda*. Washington: USAID.

_____. 1994b. *The World Food Day Report 1994: The President's Report to the U.S. Congress*. Washington: USAID.

U.S. Centers for Disease Control and Prevention. 1993. *Morbidity and Mortality Weekly Supplement on Refugee and Famine-Affected Public Health Measures*. Atlanta: CDC.

U.S. Committee for Refugees. 1992-1995. *World Refugee Surveys*. Washington: Immigration and Refugee Services of America.

Weiss, Thomas G. 1994. "Interventions: Whither the United Nations?" *The Washington Quarterly* 17:1 (Winter): 109-128.

Additional Sources (Sri Lanka) –

Chambers, Robert. 1989. "Editorial Introduction: Vulnerability, Coping and Policy." *ids bulletin* 20 (2): 1-7.

De Silva, Kingsley. 1992. "Ethnic Conflict, the Search for Peace, and the Development Process." *CASID Distinguished Speaker Series* No. 11. East Lansing: Michigan State University.

Dyson, Anthony, ed. 1988. "Sri Lanka." *Asia 1988 Yearbook*, pp. 235-240. Hong Kong: Far Eastern Economic Review.

Keerawella, Gamini and Rohan Samarajiva. 1994. "Sri Lanka in 1993." *Asian Survey*, 34:2 (February): 168-174.

Sen, Amartya. 1987. "Food and Freedom." *Sir John Crawford Lecture.* Washington: The World Bank.

Watts, Michael J. and Hans Bohle. 1992. "Hunger, Famine and the Space of Vulnerability." *GeoJournal* 30 (2): 117-125.

Chapter 3

1. "Statement by Senator Patrick Leahy," *Congressional Record*, July 22, 1993, p. S9290.

2. Michael Renner, "Budgeting for Disarmament: The Costs of War and Peace," *Worldwatch Paper* No. 122 (Washington: Worldwatch Institute, 1994).

3. Anthony Lake *et al.*, eds., *After the Wars* (New Brunswick, NJ: and Oxford: Transaction Books for the Overseas Development Council, 1990).

4. John Darnton, "U.N. Faces Refugee Crisis that Never Ends," *New York Times*, August 8, 1994; Hal Kane, "Refugee Flows Swelling," in Lester Brown *et al.*, *Vital Signs 1992* (New York and London: W.W. Norton, 1992).

5. Undated IOM brochure.

6. Number of mines from James P. Grant, Executive Director, UNICEF, statement before U.S. Senate Appropriations Committee, Subcommittee on Foreign Operations, Hearing on the Global Land Mine Crisis, May 13, 1994; percentage of civilian victims from Cyrus Vance and Herbert Okun, statement before Land Mine Hearing; monthly casualties from U.N. General Assembly, "Moratorium on the Export of Anti-personnel Land Mines, Report of the Secretary-General," July 27, 1994; number of mines from Human Rights Watch/Arms Project and Physicians for Human Rights (HRW and PHR), *Landmines: A Deadly Legacy* (New York: HRW, 1993); mines-to-people ratio estimated by Renner based on U.S. Department of State, *Hidden Killers: The Global Problem with Uncleared Landmines* (Washington: Department of State, 1993); production figures from Kenneth Anderson, HRW/Arms Project, statement before Land Mine Hearing and United Nations, "UNHCR Calls for International Ban on Land Mines," Press Release REF/1084, May 26, 1994.

7. HRW and PHR; Donovan Webster, "One Leg, One Life at a Time," *New York Times Magazine*, January 23, 1994; U.N. Department of Humanitarian Affairs, "Secretary-General Reports to Economic and Social Council on Strengthening Coordination of Emergency Humanitarian Assistance," *Briefing Note*, July 5, 1994.

8. "Moratorium…."

9. Jesuit Refugee Service, "Land Mine Updates," *the mustard seed*, Winter/Spring 1995.

10. Byron Peachey, "Laos Report," March 2, 1995 (unpublished report), Mennonite Central Committee, Washington, DC.

11. Lake.

12. "Cambodia Emerges from Isolation as Economic Reforms Take Hold," *IMF Survey*, September 26, 1994.

13. Phillip Shemon, "Rebels Still Torment Cambodia 20 Years after Their Rampage," *New York Times*, February 6, 1995.

14. Nayan Chanda and Nate Thayer, "Cambodia: Things Fall Apart…," *Far Eastern Economic Review*, May 19, 1994.

15. Shemon; Global Witness, *Forests, Famine and War: The Key to Cambodia's Future* (London: Global Witness, 1995).

16. Richard Ehrlich, "Cambodia," *The New Internationalist*, August 1994.

17. United Nations, "The Secretary-General's Consolidated Appeal for Cambodia's Immediate Needs and National Rehabilitation," May 1992; HRW and PHR, *Landmines in Cambodia: The Cowards' War* (New York: HRW, 1991).

18. Paul Donovan, "Opportunity Knocks," *The New Internationalist*, April 1993.

19. Karen Gellen, "U.N. Brokers Peaceful Transitions in Angola, Mozambique," *Africa Recovery*, December 1994.

20. Jim Wurst, "Mozambique: Peace and More," *World Policy Journal*, 1994.

21. UNHCR, *Refugees,* December 1993, p. 22.

22. USAID, *Mozambique: A Success in the Making*, 1995 (mimeo); Gellen.

23. Appropriate Technology International, "Mozambique: Proceeding Pouco a Pouco," *Oilseed Press* Nos. 3 and 4, September 1994.

24. U.S. Department of State.

25. USAID.

26. U.N. Administrative Committee on Coordination/Subcommittee on Nutrition, *Refugee Nutrition Information System Report* No. 9, February 21, 1995.

27. Farhan Haq, "Mozambique-U.N.: Experts Bask in Glory of Relative Success," Inter Press Service, Harare, Zimbabwe, March 28, 1995.

Additional Sources –

Americas Watch. 1991. *El Salvador and Human Rights: The Challenge of Reform.* New York: HRW.

———. 1993. *El Salvador: Accountability and Human Rights: The Report of the United Nations Commission on the Truth for El Salvador.* New York: HRW.

De Soto, Alvaro and Graciana Castillo. 1994. "Obstacles to Peacebuilding." *Foreign Policy* No. 94: 69-83.

Edwards, B. and G. Tovar. 1991. *Places of Origin: The Repopulation of Rural El Salvador.* Boulder, CO: Lynne Rienner.

InterAmerican Development Bank. 1995. *Economic and Social Progress in Latin America, 1994.* Washington: IADB.

MacDonald, M. and M. Gatehouse. 1995. *The Mountains of Morazan: Portrait of a Returned Refugee Community in El Salvador.* London: Latin America Bureau.

Montgomery, Tommie Sue. 1995. *Revolution in El Salvador: From Civil Strife to Civil Peace.* Boulder: Westview Press.

Spence, J., G. Vickers and D. Dye. 1995. *The Salvadoran Peace Accords and Democratization: A Three Year Progress Report and Recommendations.* Cambridge, MA: Hemisphere Initiatives.

UNICEF. 1993. *Child Malnutrition: Country Profiles.* New York: UNICEF.

U.S. Agency for International Development. 1984. *Displaced Persons in El Salvador: An Assessment.* Washington: USAID.

Vio, F. 1993. *Project Analysis of the Health Sector in El Salvador: Food and Nutrition Policy in El Salvador.* San Salvador: USAID.

Chapter 4

1. We use "conflict management" rather than "conflict resolution" based on the assumption that conflict is never "resolved" once and for all.

Sources –

Alfredsson, Gudmundur and Danilo Türk. 1993. "International Mechanisms for the Monitoring and Protection of National Minority Rights: Their Advantages, Disadvantages and Interrelationship." In *Monitoring Human Rights in Europe*, pp. 169-186. Edited by Aric Bloed *et al*. The Netherlands: Kluwer Academic Publishers.

Cohen, Lenard J. 1993. *Broken Bonds: The Disintegration of Yugoslavia*. Boulder, CO: Westview Press.

Gurr, Ted Robert. 1993. *Minorities at Risk*. Washington: United States Institute of Peace Press.

Havel, Vàclav. 1992. *Summer Meditations*. New York: Vintage Books.

Lerner, Natan. 1990. *Group Rights and Discrimination in International Law*. Dordrecht: Martinus Nijhoff.

Linz, Juan J. and Alfred Stepan. 1993. "Political Identities and Electoral Sequence: Spain, the Soviet Union and Yugoslavia." In *Exit from Communism*, pp. 123-140. Edited by Stephen Graubard. New Brunswick, NJ: Transaction Books.

Marks, Shula. 1989. "Patriotism, Patriarchy and Purity: Natal and the Politics of Zulu Ethnic Consciousness." In *The Creation of Tribalism in South Africa*, pp. 215-240. Edited by Leroy Vail. London: James Currey.

Naldi, Gino J. 1989. *The Organization of African Unity: An Analysis of Its Role*. London and New York: Mansell Publishers.

Ottaway, Marina. 1993. *South Africa: The Struggle for a New Order*. Washington: The Brookings Institution.

_____. 1994. "Democratization and Ethnic Nationalism: African and Eastern European Experiences." *Policy Essay* No. 14. Washington: Overseas Development Council.

Stokes, Gale. 1993. *The Walls Came Tumbling Down: The Collapse of Communism in Eastern Europe*. New York: Oxford University Press.

Zaslavsky, Victor. 1993. "Nationalism and Democratic Transition." In *Exit from Communism*. Edited by Stephen Graubard. New Brunswick, NJ: Transaction Books.

Chapter 5

1. Robert J. Berg, President of the International Development Conference, Washington, DC suggested this phrase.

2. Quoted in *Media, Disaster Relief and Images of the Developing World* (Washington: The Annenberg Washington Program, 1994).

3. Quoted in Jonathan Benthall, *Disasters, Relief and the Media* (New York: St. Martin's Press, 1993), p. 187.

4. See, for example, C. Wright Mills, *The Power Elite* (New York: Oxford University Press, 1956).

5. Ben H. Bagdikian, *The Media Monopoly*, 4th Edition (Boston: Beacon Press, 1992), p. 11.

6. *Media & Values*, Spring 1990.

7. Mark Achbar, ed., *Manufacturing Consent: Noam Chomsky and the Media* (Montreal: Black Rose Books, 1994), pp. 85-87.

8. Howard Kurtz, "Pulp Friction: Newsprint Inflation Shakes Up Papers," *Washington Post*, March 8, 1995.

9. Robert I. Rotberg and Thomas G. Weiss, "The Media, Humanitarian Crises, and Policy-making," *WPF Reports* Number 7, Cambridge, MA, 1995, p. 9.

10. "The News At Any Cost: How Journalists Compromise Their Ethics to Shape the News," *Media & Values*, Spring 1990.

11. Bagdikian, pp. 199-201.

12. *Ibid.*, pp. 21-24.

13. Achbar, p. 145.

14. Presentation at UNICEF Information Workshop, Nairobi, June 19, 1991, cited in Benthall, p. 203.

15. Jeff Greenfield, "Making the News Pay," *Media & Values*," Spring 1990.

16. Marvin Kalb, "The CNN Factor in Foreign Policymaking," Presentation at The Woodrow Wilson Center, Smithsonian Institution, March 15, 1994.

17. Greenfield.

18. Michael J. O'Neill, "Who Cares About the Truth?," *Nieman Reports*, Spring 1994, pp. 13-14.

19. *Ibid.*, pp. 11-12.

20. James Davison Hunter, "Before the Shooting Begins," *Columbia Journalism Review* (July-August 1993): 31.

21. "Balance Bias With Critical Questions," *Media & Values*, Spring 1990.

22. "The Global Information Revolution," Keynote Address, Managing Chaos Conference, U.S. Institute of Peace, December 1, 1994.

23. *Ibid.*

24. *Ibid.*

25. Daniel Hallin, "Whatever Happened to the News?," *Media & Values*, Spring 1990.

26. Addresses are: Bread for the World, 1100 Wayne Avenue, Suite 1000, Silver Spring, MD 20910, telephone (301) 608-2400, fax (301) 608-2401, e-mail bread@igc.org; RESULTS, 236 Massachusetts Avenue, N.E., Suite 300, Washington, DC 20002, telephone (202) 543-9340, fax (202) 546-3228.

Sources for "Rock Music" –

"Charity Benefits: Getting Money Out Of Rock," *Rolling Stone*, May 12, 1983, pp. 62ff.

"Farm Aid IV Reaps Bountiful Harvest," *Billboard*, April 21, 1990, pp. 10, 81.

"The George Harrison Bangla Desh Benefit," *Rolling Stone*, September 2, 1971, cover story.

"Live Aid…How It Really Works," *African Business*, September 1985, pp. 8-14.

Parade, May 21, 1995.

"Update on African Aid Groups," *Calendar Magazine of the Los Angeles Times*, December 8, 1985, pp. 4-5.

Scott, Michael and Mutombo Mpanya. 1994. *We Are the World: An Evaluation of Pop Aid for Africa*. Washington: InterAction, 1994.

Chapter 6

1. James H. Michel, *Development Co-operation: Efforts and Policies of the Members of the Development Assistance Committee, 1994 Report* (Paris: Organisation for Economic Co-operation and Development, 1994); J. Brian Atwood, "Suddenly, Chaos," *Washington Post*, July 31, 1994; U.S. Agency for International Development, "Breaking the Cycle of Despair: President Clinton's Initiative on the Horn of Africa, Report of the President's Representative," June 1994 (mimeo), revised and expanded November 1994; "Anguish in Rwanda," Editorial, *Washington Post*, January 25, 1995; Boutros Boutros-Ghali, *An Agenda for Peace* (New York: United Nations, 1992); Will Nixon, "Relief Disaster," *In These Times*, August 22, 1994; David Rohde, "Aid Givers are Troubled by the West's New Neglect of Civil, Ethnic Conflicts," *Christian Science Monitor*, February 22, 1995.

2. The Development Assistance Committee of the Organisation for Economic Co-operation and Development (the intergovernmental organization which monitors aid levels and trends) defines ODA as grants and loans by official governmental and intergovernmental agencies to developing countries. Loans must have a grant element of at least 25 percent and the resources must promote economic development and welfare. Aid to former communist countries in Europe is not counted. Other items which some donors include in their aid budgets are likewise excluded from ODA, e.g., U.S. military aid. Unless otherwise noted, the statistics on aid are taken from Michel. See also Robin Wright, "Foreign Aid Hits Lowest Level in Two Decades," *Los Angeles Times*, June 13, 1995.

3. Adrian Hewitt, ed., *Crisis or Transition in Foreign Aid* (London: Overseas Development Institute; Washington: Overseas Development Council and Ottawa: North-South Institute), pp. 1-2.

4. Gro Harlem Brundtland, "A Shameful Condition," in U.N. Children's Fund, *The Progress of Nations 1995* (New York: UNICEF, 1995), pp. 45-47; Bread for the World Institute, "At the Crossroads: The Future of Foreign Aid," *Occasional Paper* No. 4 (Silver Spring, MD: Bread for the World Institute, 1995), p. 35; Judith Randel and Tony German, eds., *The Reality of Aid 1995: An Independent Review of International Aid* (London: Earthscan for ACTIONAID, the International Council of Voluntary Agencies and Eurostep, 1995), pp. 3, 5.

5. Michel, p. 2.

6. Data on funding of NGO activities from Ian Smillie and Henny Helmich, eds., *Non-Governmental Organisations and Governments: Stakeholders for Development* (Paris: Organisation for Economic Co-operation and Development, 1993), p. 33.

7. "At the Crossroads," p. 45.

8. Brundtland, p. 45.

9. R. Jeffrey Smith, "Demand for Humanitarian Aid May Skyrocket," *Washington Post*, December 17, 1994.

10. Quoted in Judith Randel and Tony German, eds., *The Reality of Aid 1994* (London: ACTIONAID, 1994), p. 32.

11. Atwood.

12. Peter Uvin, *The International Organization of Hunger* (London and New York: Kegan Paul International, 1994).

13. Hewitt.

14. Program on International Policy Attitudes, *Americans and Foreign Aid: A Study of American Public Attitudes* (College Park, MD: University of Maryland, 1995).

15. See, for example, *American Public Opinion and U.S. Foreign Policy 1995* (Chicago: The Chicago Council on Foreign Relations, 1995).

Additional Sources –

Cohen, Marc J. 1995. "The United States." In *The Reality of Aid 1995*, pp. 96-98. Edited by Judith Randel and Tony German. London: Earthscan for ACTIONAID, the International Council of Voluntary Agencies and Eurostep.

Environmental and Energy Study Institute. 1995. *U.S. Development Assistance: A Visual Briefing*. Washington: EESI.

Mathews, Jessica. 1994. "Robbing Development to Pay for Disaster Relief." *Washington Post*, July 5.

_____. 1995. "The Assault on AID." *Washington Post*, February 28.

Nowels, Larry Q. 1995. "Foreign Aid Budget and Policy Issues for the 104th Congress." *CRS Issue Brief* IB95020. Washington: Congressional Research Service of the Library of Congress. February 9.

Bread for the World Institute and RESULTS Educational Fund, "Putting Children First: A Report on the Effectiveness of U.S. Agency for International Development Child Survival Programs in Fiscal Year 1991." *Occasional Paper* No. 3 (January 1995). Silver Spring, MD: Bread for the World Institute and Washington: RESULTS Educational Fund.

Sheehy, Thomas P. 1995. "The Index of Economic Freedom: A Tool for Real Reform of Foreign Aid." *The Heritage Foundation Backgrounder* No. 986 (May 6).

Special Feature

1. Amartya Sen, "The Economics of Life and Death," *Scientific American*, May 1993, p. 40.

2. *Ibid.*, p. 46.

3. Associated Press, "Reported Major Crimes Fell 3% in 1994," *Washington Post*, May 22, 1995 and "Violence Tied to Decline in Teens' Health," *Washington Post*, June 7, 1995.

4. Curt Suplee, "Nation's Violence a 'Public Health Emergency,' AMA Says in Report," *Washington Post*, June 14, 1995.

5. Timothy R. Frankenberger, *Conceptual Issues Related to Food Security* (Atlanta: CARE Food Security Unit Publications, no date – mimeo).

6. *Economic Report of the President* (Washington: U.S. Government Printing Office, 1995); F. Williams, "The Art of Staying Ahead is Adaptation," *Financial Times*, September 30, 1994.

7. Steven Pearlstein, "Widening the Income Gap," *Washington Post*, May 29, 1995.

8. U.S. Bureau of the Census, *Income, Poverty and Valuation of Noncash Benefits: 1993*, U.S. Current Population Report P60-188, February 1995, and *Current Population Survey*, March 1993.

9. Martina Shea, "Dynamics of Economic Well-being: Poverty, 1990 to 1992," *U.S. Bureau of the Census Current Population Reports*, Series P70-42 (Washington: U.S. Government Printing Office, 1995), pp. 2-6.

10. Bill Ayres, *Just the Facts: Hunger, Poverty and Homelessness*, (New York: World Hunger Year, 1994).

11. Patricia Ruggles, *Drawing the Line* (Washington: The Urban Institute, 1993), p. 4.

12. "Income, Poverty,...," Table 7; U.S. Bureau of Census, "Preliminary Estimates of Poverty Threshold in 1994," January 1995.

13. The survey, sponsored by Kraft General Foods, was conducted by the Van Amburg Group. The reported results are based on 8,596 client responses from 3,685 feeding programs at 3,182 agencies served by 28 food banks. Second Harvest is the national food bank association.

14. U.S. Conference of Mayors, *A Status Report on Hunger and Homelessness in America's Cities: 1994* (Washington: U.S. Conference of Mayors, 1994).

15. Jennifer Dixon, "Food Stamp Rolls Down By 1 Million Since 1994," *Washington Post*, June 1, 1995; "Taking Credit for Dip in Food Stamp Rolls," *Washington Post*, July 31, 1995; Colin Greer, "Something is Robbing Our Children of Their Future," *Parade*, March 5, 1995, p. 4.

16. Frank Levy and Richard Murnane, "U.S. Earnings Levels and Earnings Inequality: A Review of Recent Trends and Proposed Explanations," *Journal of Economic Literature* (September 1992): 1372.

17. Jennifer Gardner, "Displaced Workers: 1987-91," *Bureau of Labor Statistics Bulletin*, July 1993, p. 2427.

18. Kenneth Labich, "The New Unemployed," *National Times*, April 1993, p. 39.

19. Robert Reich, *The Work of Nations* (New York: Vintage Books, 1992), p. 211.

20. Jeffrey Sachs and Howard Shatz, "Trade and Jobs in US Manufacturing," *Brookings Papers on Economic Activity* 1 (1994): 1-84; Paul Krugman and Robert Lawrence, "Trade, Jobs and Wages," *Scientific American*, April 1994, pp. 44-49; John DiNardo, Nicole Fortin and Thomas Lemieux, "Labor Market Institutions and the Distribution of Wages, 1973-1992: A Semi-Parametric Approach," January 1994 (unpublished paper), University of California-Irvine; Richard Freeman, "How Much Has De-Unionization Contributed to the Rise in Male Earnings Inequality?," in Sheldon Danziger and Peter Gottschalk, eds., *Uneven Tides: Rising Inequality in America* (New York: Russell Sage Foundation, 1993), pp.133-163; David Card, "The Effect of Unions on the Distribution of Wages: Redistribution or Relabeling?," *NBER Working Paper* No. 4195 (October 1992); Martin Bailey, Gary Burtless and Robert Litan, *Growth with Equity* (Washington: The Brookings Institution, 1993), p. 63.

21. Center on Hunger, Poverty and Nutrition Policy, *Statement on Key Welfare Reform Issues: The Empirical Evidence* (Medford, MA: Center on Hunger, Poverty and Nutrition Policy, Tufts University, 1995), p. 12.; *Economic Report of the President* (Washington: U.S. Government Printing Office, 1995), p. 57.

22. George Church, "We're #1 and It Hurts," *Time,* October 24, 1994; David Segal, "Shortage of Temporary Workers to Hit as Vacation Season Starts," *Washington Post*, May 29, 1995, sec. Washington Business; Susan Leach, "U.S. Part-Time Work Force Changed Only Modestly," *Christian Science Monitor*, June 3, 1994.

23. John Bound and George Johnson, "Changes in the Structure of Wages in the 1980s: An Evaluation of Alternative Approaches," *American Economic Review* (June 1992): 371-392; Chinhui Juhn, Kevin Murphy and Brooks Pierce, "Earnings Losses of Displaced Workers," *Journal of Political Economy* (June 1993): 410-442; Lawrence Katz and Kevin Murphy, "Changes in Relative Wages, 1963-1987: Supply and Demand Factors," *Quarterly Journal of Economics* (February 1992): 35-78; Janet Norwood, ed., *Widening Earnings Inequality: Why and Why Now* (Washington: The Urban Institute, 1994); David Segal, "High Tech Goes on a Hiring Spree," *Washington Post*, June 5, 1995, sec. Washington Business.

24. *Ibid.*

25. Quoted in Frank Swoboda, "How the Rules Have Changed," *Washington Post Magazine*, April 23, 1995.

26. The Urban Institute, "Does Work Pay for Welfare Recipients?," *The Urban Institute Policy and Research Report*, Winter/Spring 1995, pp. 7-8.

27. Rebecca Blank, "The Employment Strategy: Public Policies to Increase Work and Earnings," in Sheldon Danziger, Gary Sandefur and Daniel Weinberg, eds., *Confronting Poverty: Prescriptions for Change* (New York: Russell Sage Foundation, 1994), pp. 192-193; Bread for the World Institute, "Let's Get Real About Welfare," *Occasional Paper* No. 5 (Silver Spring, MD: Bread for the World Institute, 1995).

28. Louis Uchitelle, "'Good' Jobs in Hard Times," *New York Times*, October 3, 1993, sec. 3.

29. James Glassman, "Raising the Minimum Wage Isn't the Answer," *Washington Post*, April 4, 1995. David Card and Alan Krueger of Princeton found that after New Jersey increased its hourly minimum wage from $4.25 to $5.05, employment at fast-food restaurants in New Jersey *increased* by 12 percent relative to fast food employment in Pennsylvania (whose minimum wage remained unchanged). David Neumark of Michigan State University and William Wascher of the Federal Reserve Board found that employment at Burger King and Wendy's franchises in New Jersey *fell* by 5 percent relative to Pennsylvania. Analysts on both sides of the debate point to differences in sample sizes and data sources between the two studies. See also Richard Morin, "The Social Consequences of a Minimum Wage Hike," *Washington Post*, April 23, 1995, sec. Business, citing a study estimating that increasing the minimum wage by 20 percent would boost the number of working teens who are not in school by 5 percent.

30. Michael Keane, "This Safety Net Supports Work," *Christian Science Monitor*, May 1, 1995.

31. U.S. Department of Labor, *What's Working and What's Not* (Office of the Chief Economist, U.S. Department of Labor, January 1995).

32. *Ibid.*, p. 16.

33. *Ibid.*, p. 23.

34. U.S. General Accounting Office, *Welfare to Work*, GAO/HEHS-95-28, December 1994.

35. Lawrence Katz, "Active Labor Market Policies to Expand Employment and Opportunity," in *Reducing Unemployment: Current Issues and Policy Options*, (Kansas City: The Federal Reserve Bank, 1994), p. 278 and Table 2.

36. Jerry Jasinowski, "America's Manufacturing Revolution," *Vital Speeches*, March 15, 1995, p. 352.

37. Report on manufacturing in the Mid-West by Joe Smith, Cleveland Bureau, "Marketplace," *Public Radio International*, January 4, 1995; Colin Greer, "We Can Save Jobs," *Parade*, May 21, 1995, pp. 4-5.

38. Barbara Vobejda, "Relying on 'Immediate and Full-time Immersion,'" *Washington Post,* March 5, 1995.

39. Philip Harvey, "Paying for Full Employment: A Hard-Nosed Look at Finances," *Social Policy*, Spring 1995, p. 3.

40. Bread for the World Institute.

41. Roberta Spalter-Roth, Enrique Soto and Lily Zandniapour, *Micro-Enterprise and Women: The Viability of Self-Employment as a Strategy for Alleviating Poverty* (Washington: Institute for Women's Policy Research, 1994).

42. U.S. Department of Labor, Preface.

43. The proportion of all married women with children under six who worked rose from 19 percent in 1960 to 59 percent in 1990. Richard Morin, "Working Moms and Single Mothers," *Washington Post,* July 2, 1995.

44. Barbara Vobejda, "Inching into Employment," *Washington Post*, May 8, 1995.

45. David Roth, interviewed by Joe Smith, Cleveland Bureau, "Marketplace," *Public Radio International*, March 2, 1995.

46. Quoted in William Raspberry, "High Standards for Black Children," *Washington Post*, August 6, 1993.

Sponsors

Bread for the World Institute seeks to inform, educate, nurture and motivate concerned citizens for action on policies that affect hungry people. Based on policy analysis and consultation with poor people, it develops educational resources and activities, including its annual report on the state of world hunger, policy briefs and study guides, together with workshops, seminars, briefings and an anti-hunger leadership development program. Contributions to the Institute are tax-deductible. It works closely with Bread for the World, a Christian citizens' movement of 44,000 members who advocate specific policy changes to help overcome hunger in the United States and overseas.

> 1100 Wayne Avenue, Suite 1000
> Silver Spring, MD 20910
> Ph. (301) 608-2400
> Fx. (301) 608-2401
> E-mail: bread@igc.org

BROT für die Welt is an association of German Protestant churches that seeks to overcome poverty and hunger in developing countries, as an expression of their Christian faith and convictions, by funding programs of relief and development. Founded in 1959, BROT has funded more than 15,000 programs in over 100 nations in Africa, Latin America and Asia. The emphasis of the programs that BROT funds has shifted from relief to development and empowerment. BROT's programs of education in Germany are intended to lead to changes – in understanding and lifestyle at the personal level, and to policy changes at the national, European Community and international levels.

> Stafflenbergstrasse 76; Postfach 10 11 42
> D-70010 Stuttgart, Germany
> Ph. 011-49-7 11-2159-0
> Fx. 011-49-7 11-2159-368

Christian Children's Fund is the largest independent child-care agency in the world, providing assistance to more than half a million children and their families in 40 countries and the United States. An international, not-for-profit, nonsectarian agency, free of political associations, Christian Children's Fund provides education, medical care, food, clothing and shelter to children around the world, including programs in the United States. Services are provided based on need and without regard to sex, race, creed or religion. Christian Children's Fund recently began new programs in Central and Eastern Europe and southern Africa.

> 2821 Emerywood Parkway, PO Box 26484
> Richmond, VA 23261-6284
> Ph. (804) 756-2700
> Fx. (804) 756-2718

Covenant World Relief is the relief and development arm of The Evangelical Covenant Church. Dr. Timothy C. Ek is vice president of the Covenant and director of Covenant World Relief. The Evangelical Covenant Church has its national headquarters in Chicago, IL. The Covenant's historic commitment to being actively involved in Christ's mission to respond to the spiritual and physical needs of others was the basis for the formation of Covenant World Relief.

> 5101 North Francisco Avenue
> Chicago, IL 60625-3699
> Ph. (312) 784-3000
> Fx. (312) 684-4366

The **Evangelical Lutheran Church in America World Hunger Program** is a 21-year-old ministry that confronts hunger and poverty through emergency relief, long-term development, education, advocacy and stewardship of financial resources. Seventy-three percent of the program works internationally and 27 percent within the United States. Lutheran World Relief (New York City) and Lutheran World Federation (Geneva, Switzerland) are key partners in international relief and development. Twelve percent is used for domestic relief and development, 9 percent for education and advocacy work in the United States and 6 percent for fundraising and administration.

> 8765 West Higgins Road
> Chicago, IL 60631-4190
> Ph. (800) 638-3522
> Fx. (312) 380-2707

LCMS World Relief (The Lutheran Church – Missouri Synod) provides relief and development funding for domestic and international projects. Based under the Synod's Department of Human Care Ministries, LCMS World Relief provides domestic grants for Lutheran congregations and social ministry organizations as well as other groups with Lutheran involvement which are engaged in ministries of human care. Domestic support is also provided to Inter-Lutheran Disaster Response and Lutheran Immigration and Refugee Service. International relief and development assistance is channeled through the Synod's mission stations and partner churches as well as Lutheran World Relief.

> 1333 So. Kirkwood Road
> St. Louis, MO 63122-7295
> Ph. (800) 248-1930, ext. 1392
> Fx. (314) 965-0541

Lutheran World Relief (LWR), founded in 1945, acts on behalf of U.S. Lutherans in response to natural disasters, humanitarian crises and chronic poverty, in over 40 countries throughout Asia, Africa, Latin America and the Middle East. In partnership with local organizations, LWR supports over 150 community projects to improve food production, health care, environment and employment, with special emphasis on training and gender. LWR monitors legislation on foreign aid and development, and advocates for public policies which address the root causes of hunger and poverty. LWR values the God-given gifts that each person can bring to our common task to promote peace, justice and human dignity.

Lutheran World Relief	LWR/CWS Office on Development Policy
390 Park Avenue South	110 Maryland Avenue, N.E.
New York, NY 10016	Building Mailbox #45
Ph. (212) 532-6350	Washington, DC 20002-5694
800-LWR-LWR2	Ph. (202) 543-6336
Fx. (212) 213-6081	Fx. (202) 546-6232
E-mail: lwr@igc.apc.org	E-mail: cwslwr@igc.apc.org

Shield-Ayres Foundation

The **United Methodist Committee on Relief** (UMCOR) was formed in 1940 in response to the suffering of people during World War II. It was a "voice of conscience" expressing the concern of the church for the disrupted and devastated lives churned out by the war. UMCOR has expanded its ministry into more than 80 countries to minister with compassion to "persons in need, through programs and services which provide immediate relief and long-term attention to the root causes of their need. Focusing on refugee, hunger and disaster ministries, the work of UMCOR, a program department of the General Board of Global Ministries of the United Methodist Church, is carried out through direct services and a worldwide network of national and international church agencies that cooperate in the task of alleviating human suffering.

Headquarters	World Hunger/Poverty Office
475 Riverside Drive, Room 350	Suite 501
New York, NY 10115	100 Maryland Avenue, N.E.
Ph. (212) 870-3816	Washington, DC 20002
(800) 841-1235	Ph. (202) 546-0279
Fx. (212) 748-2641	Fx. (202) 546-0395

World Vision, founded in 1950, is an international Christian humanitarian aid organization carrying out relief and development activities in 94 countries, including the United States. The U.S. national support office is headquartered in Seattle, WA, and national support offices in 17 other countries raise funds for transforming the lives of the poor in Africa, Asia, Latin America and Eastern Europe. Meeting the health care, educational, vocational, and nutritional needs of children and their families is the focal point of programs leading to the long-term sustainable development of communities. Through 6,243 projects, worldwide, World Vision affirms the right of every child to education, good nutrition, health care and spiritual nurture. More than 1 million children are sponsored through World Vision donors from industrialized nations.

> P.O. Box 9716
> Federal Way, WA 98063-9716
> Ph. (206) 815-1000

Cosponsors

The **Academy for Educational Development** (AED), founded in 1961, is an independent, nonprofit service organization committed to addressing human development needs in the United States and throughout the world. Under contracts and grants the Academy operates programs in collaboration with policy leaders; nongovernmental and community-based organizations; governmental agencies; international multilateral and bilateral funders; and schools, colleges and universities. In partnership with its clients, the Academy seeks to meet today's social, economic and environmental challenges through education and human resource development; to apply state-of-the art education, training, research, technology, management, behavioral analysis and social marketing techniques to solve problems; and to improve knowledge and skills throughout the world as the most effective means for stimulating growth, reducing poverty, and promoting democratic and humanitarian ideals. AED is registered with the U.S. Agency for International Development as a private voluntary organization. The Academy is exempt from federal income taxes under Section 501 (c)(3) of the Internal Revenue Code. Contributions to the Academy are tax-deductible.

> 1875 Connecticut Avenue, N.W.
> Washington, DC 20009-1202
> Ph. (202) 884-8000
> Fx. (202) 884-8430
> Email: admindc@aed.org

CARE is one of the world's largest and most effective private relief and development organizations. Each year, CARE reaches more than 35 million people in over 60 nations in Africa, Asia and Latin America. The organization's work began in 1946, when CARE packages helped Europe recover from World War II. Today, CARE provides famine and disaster victims with emergency assistance, improves health care, helps subsistence farmers and small-business owners produce more goods, addresses population and environmental concerns, and helps to develop economies and societies in a sustainable manner. The scope of CARE's work is broad, but its vision focuses on a single concept – helping people help themselves.

> 151 Ellis Street
> Atlanta, GA 30303
> Ph. (404) 681-2552
> Fx. (404) 577-5977

Catholic Relief Services-USCC (CRS) is the overseas relief and development agency of the U.S. Catholic community. Founded in 1943, CRS provides over $300 million in development and relief assistance in 76 nations around the world. Working in partnership with the Catholic Church and other local institutions in each country, CRS works to alleviate poverty, hunger and suffering, and supports reconciliation and peace-making initiatives. Assistance is given solely on the basis of need. Even while responding to emergencies, CRS supports over 2,000 development projects designed to build local self-sufficiency. CRS works in conjunction with Caritas International and CIDSE, worldwide associations of Catholic relief and development agencies. Together, these groups build the capacity of local nonprofit organizations to provide long-term solutions.

In the United States, CRS seeks to educate and build awareness on issues of world poverty and hunger and serve as an advocate for public policy changes in the interest of the poor overseas.

> 209 West Fayette Street
> Baltimore, MD 21201-3443
> Ph. (410) 625-2220
> Fx. (410) 685-1635

Christian Reformed World Relief Committee (CRWRC) is the relief and development agency of the Christian Reformed Church in North America, with offices in Grand Rapids, MI and Burlington, Ontario, Canada. CRWRC was begun in 1962 to respond to the needs of Korean war victims, Cuban refugees, and victims of natural disasters in North America. Today, CRWRC focuses on community development in over 30 countries worldwide, including the United States and Canada. Through cooperative efforts with national Christian churches and organizations, CRWRC works with communities in need to create permanent, positive change in Christ's name.

> CRWRC U.S.   CRWRC CANADA
> 2850 Kalamazoo Avenue, S.E.   3475 Mainway, P.O. Box 5070
> Grand Rapids, MI 49560-0600   Burlington, ON L7R 3Y8
> Ph. (800) 55-CRWRC   Ph. (905) 336-2920
> Fx. (616) 246-0806   Fx. (905) 336-8344

Church World Service (CWS) is a global relief, development, and refugee assistance ministry of the 33 Protestant and Orthodox communities that work together through the National Council of Churches. Founded in 1946, CWS works in partnership with local church organizations in more than 70 countries worldwide, supporting sustainable self-help development of people which respects the environment, meets emergency needs, and addresses root causes of poverty and powerlessness. Within the United States, CWS resettles refugees, assists communities in responding to disasters, advocates for justice in U.S. policies which relate to global issues, provides educational resources, and offers opportunities for communities to join a people-to-people network of global and local caring through participation in a CROP WALK.

> 475 Riverside Drive, Suite 678
> New York, NY 10115-0050
> Ph. (212) 870-2257
> Fx. (212) 870-3523

EuronAid is a European association of nongovernmental organizations (NGOs) which facilitates dialogue with the Commission of the European Union. EuronAid cooperates with the Commission in programming and procuring food aid for the NGOs, then arranges and accounts for delivery to Third World NGOs for distribution. In recent years, triangular operations (purchases within Third World nations) have accounted for half of EuronAid's food aid, which meets mainly development purposes. EuronAid assimilates the experiences of NGOs involved in food aid and employs this knowledge in its dialogue with the Commission and the European Parliament to achieve improved management of food aid. EuronAid was created in 1980 by major European NGOs in cooperation with the Commission of the European Union. The association has at present 27 member agencies, and services an additional 60 European NGOs on a regular basis.

> PO Box 12
> NL-2501 CA Den Haag
> The Netherlands
> Ph. 31 70 330 57 57
> Fx. 31 70 362 17 39

Food for the Hungry International (FHI) is an organization of Christian motivation committed to working with poor people to overcome hunger and poverty through development and, where needed, appropriate relief. Founded in 1971, FHI is incorporated in Switzerland and works in over 20 countries of Asia, Africa and Latin America. As its name implies, FHI focuses on poverty needs that relate to food and nutrition. Its primary emphasis is on long-term development among the extremely poor, recognizing their dignity, creativity and ability to solve their own problems. The international staff numbers more than 1,200 persons. Autonomous Food for the Hungry partner entities in several different countries such as Food for the Hungry (USA) contribute resources.

> 7807 East Greenway Road, Suite 3
> Scottsdale, AZ 85260
> Ph: (602) 951-5090
> Fx: (602) 951-9035

International Orthodox Christian Charities (IOCC). As the official overseas humanitarian assistance organization of Orthodox Christians in the United States and Canada, the mission of IOCC is to: provide relief to victims of disasters; support efforts which create economic and social self-sufficiency among impoverished families and communities; assist the Orthodox Church worldwide to bring effective assistance to the poor, in their own countries; and help educate the public on the causes of poverty and on their duty to act for the elimination of global poverty. Assistance will be provided solely on the basis of need.

> 711 West 40th Street, Suite 306
> Baltimore, MD 21211
> Ph. (410) 243-9820
> Fx. (410) 243-9824

MAZON: A Jewish Response to Hunger has granted more than $10 million since 1986 to nonprofit organizations confronting hunger in the United States and abroad. MAZON (the Hebrew word for "food") awards grants principally to programs working to prevent and alleviate hunger in the United States. Grantees include emergency and direct food assistance programs, food banks, multi-service organizations, anti-hunger advocacy/education and research projects, and international hunger-relief and agricultural development programs in Israel and impoverished countries. Although responsive to organizations serving impoverished Jews, in keeping with the best of Jewish tradition, MAZON responds to all who are in need.

> 12401 Wilshire Boulevard, Suite 303
> Los Angeles, CA 90025-1015
> Ph. (310) 442-0020
> Fx. (310) 442-0030

Mennonite Central Committee (MCC), founded in 1920, is an agency of the Mennonite and Brethren in Christ Churches in North America, and seeks to demonstrate God's love through committed women and men who work among people suffering from poverty, conflict, oppression and natural disaster. MCC serves as a channel for interchange between churches and community groups where it works around the world and North American churches. MCC strives for peace, justice and dignity of all people by sharing experiences, resources and faith. MCC's priorities include disaster relief and refugee assistance, rural and agricultural development, job creation (SELFHELP Crafts), health and education.

> 21 South 12th Street
> Akron, PA 17501-0500
> Ph. (717) 859-1151
> Fx. (717) 859-2171

Save the Children Federation/U.S. (SC/U.S.) helps to make positive change in the lives of disadvantaged children in the United States and over 40 other countries. Focus places children at the center of activities and women as key decision makers and participants. Key principles are child centeredness, women focus, participation and empowerment, sustainability, scaling up and maximizing impact. Programs aim at community empowerment and institutional development, working with disadvantaged groups as they identify problems and solutions. Primary development sectors are: health/population/nutrition, education/early childhood development and economic opportunity development. SC/U.S. also manages major refugee programs and emergency response with a special emergency focus on child victims of conflict and displacement.

> 54 Wilton Road
> Westport, CT 06880
> Ph. (203) 221-4100
> Fx. (203) 227-5667

Second Harvest is the largest charitable hunger relief organization in the United States. Through a nationwide network of nearly 200 food banks, Second Harvest distributes surplus food and grocery products to nearly 50,000 charitable agencies. These food pantries, soup kitchens, homeless shelters and other feeding programs serve nearly 26 million people each year.

> 116 South Michigan Avenue, Suite 4
> Chicago, IL 60603-6001
> Ph. (312) 263-2303
> Fx. (312) 263-5626

Share Our Strength (SOS) is the nation's leading anti-hunger organization that mobilizes industries and individuals to contribute their talents to fight hunger.

Since its founding in 1984, SOS has distributed more than $26 million in grants to over 800 anti-hunger organizations in the United States, Canada and developing countries. SOS awards grants to organizations that distribute food (e.g., food banks), treat the consequences of hunger (e.g., growth and nutrition clinics) and build self-sufficiency among people in need (e.g., community development). SOS's direct service program, Operation Frontline, trains culinary professionals to teach nutrition and food budgeting skills to people at risk of hunger. SOS's fundraising efforts allow individuals to become involved with SOS at many levels. Those efforts include: Taste of the Nation, which mobilizes the food industry annually and involves 5,000 chefs and hundreds of volunteers in 100 cities throughout the United States and Canada; Writers Harvest; The National Reading, an annual event in which over 1,000 authors such as Gloria Naylor, Paul Auster, Rita Dove and others read from their work in over 300 locations nationwide; and Charge Against Hunger, a partnership with American Express that has raised over $10 million for anti-hunger programs in all 50 states. SOS features its own line of products as well as a series of books, which include original work donated by acclaimed authors, artists and chefs.

> 1511 K Street, N.W., Suite 940
> Washington, DC 20005
> Ph. (202) 393-2925
> Fx. (202) 347-5868

The Trull Foundation (and predecessor B.W. Trull Foundation) has been interested in educational, religious, cultural and social programs since 1948. Current priorities include concern for:

 1. The needs of the Palacios, TX area where the Foundation has its roots;

 2. Pre-adolescents, and opportunities to direct lives away from child abuse, neglect and hunger, towards an adolescence of good mental and physical growth; and

 3. Mexican-Americans in south Texas, to help them "catch up," hurdle a language barrier, a poverty barrier, and a system which has consistently kept them poor, uneducated and unrepresented.

> 404 Fourth St.
> Palacios, TX 77465
> Ph. (512) 972-5241

United Church Board for World Ministries (UCBWM) is the instrumentality of the United Church of Christ for the planning and conduct of its program of global missions, development and emergency relief. The UCBWM's fundamental mission commitment is to share life in partnership with global church partners and ecumenical bodies. Through service, advocacy and mission program, the UCBWM sends as well as receives persons in mission; is committed to the healing of God's creation; engages in dialogue, witness and common cause with people of other faiths; and seeks a prophetic vision of a just and peaceful world order so that all might have access to wholeness of life.

> 475 Riverside Drive, Fl. 16
> New York, NY 10115
> Ph. (212) 870-2637
> Fx. (212) 932-1236

United Church of Christ Hunger Action program coordinates and stimulates all UCC hunger and hunger-related ministries; increases awareness and understanding of world hunger and related issues; and promotes, interprets and administrates the Hunger Action Fund of the United Church of Christ. The Hunger Action Program is celebrating its 20th anniversary in 1995.

> 700 Prospect Avenue
> Cleveland, OH 44115
> Ph. (216) 736-3290
> Fx. (216) 736-3293

The **United Nations Children's Fund** (UNICEF) implements programs for children and women through 200 field offices in 141 developing countries. It works in partnership with national governments to support community-based activities in primary health care, nutrition, basic education, and water and sanitation and provision of services in emergencies. UNICEF is a semi-autonomous but integral part of the U.N. system, with its own governing body. Since its creation in 1946, it has affirmed the link between progress, peace and children's well-being. UNICEF was awarded the Nobel Peace Prize in 1965.

> UNICEF Division of Information
> 3 United Nations Plaza
> New York, NY 10017-4414
> Ph. (212) 326-7035
> Fx. (212) 888-7465

The **United Nations Development Programme** (UNDP) is the United Nations' largest provider of technical cooperation grants and the main coordinator of U.N. development assistance. It works with governments, U.N. agencies, organizations of civil society and individuals in 175 countries and territories to build national capacities for sustainable human development. Activities focus on poverty elimination, creation of jobs and sustainable livelihoods, advancement of women, and protection and regeneration of the environment. UNDP's central resources, totalling about US$1 billion a year, are derived from the voluntary contributions of governments. UNDP also administers several special purpose funds (U.N. Capital Development Fund, U.N. Development Fund for Women, U.N. Volunteers) and, with the World Bank and the U.N. Environment Programme, the $1.3 billion Global Environment Facility.

> 1 United Nations Plaza
> New York, NY 10017
> Ph. (212) 906-5000
> Fx. (212) 906-5001

Winrock International is a leader in sustainable agricultural, rural development and environmental programs that help people increase food production and stimulate economic growth, without threatening natural resources. Projects provide technical assistance, human resource development, policy and institutional improvement. Winrock works in the United States, Asia, Africa, the Middle East, Latin America, the Caribbean, Eastern Europe and the former Soviet Union. Projects are funded by grants, contracts and contributions from public and private sources. Operations are headquartered outside Little Rock, AR, on the mountain-top farm of the late Winthrop Rockefeller. Regional offices are located in Arlington, VA; Manila, the Philippines; and Abidjan, Côte d'Ivoire.

> Route 3, Box 376
> Morrilton, AR 72110-9537
> Ph. (501) 727-5435
> Fx. (501) 727-5242

World Hunger Committee is the official committee responsible for engaging the membership of the Reorganized Church of Jesus Christ of Latter Day Saints (**RLDS**) in a corporate response to world hunger. Since 1979, the World Hunger Committee, appointed by the RLDS First Presidency, has considered grant proposals submitted by such organizations as Outreach International, World Accord, Oxfam America and the Red Cross. Advocacy, education and direct relief are the committee's main areas of interest. The largest portion of the World Hunger funds is used for relief in disaster aid and self-help programs. Church groups in 12 states have also received World Hunger grants to help establish soup kitchens, food pantries and food banks. Because of the gracious response of RLDS church members, projects funded through the World Hunger Committee include: food aid for Somalia, Africa and Haiti; nutrition centers in Haiti, Honduras and the Dominican Republic; rice improvement projects in the Philippines; disaster aid for countries such as India, Bangladesh, Mexico and Haiti; farming projects in India, Nepal, Sri Lanka and Haiti; and the establishment of a food bank in Florida.

    P.O. Box 1059
    Independence, MO 64051-0559
    Ph. (816) 833-1000
    Fx. (816) 521-3097

World Relief is the relief and development arm of the National Association of Evangelicals in the United States. Since 1944, World Relief has provided both immediate and long-term assistance to people who suffer from poverty, disease, hunger and war. Working with groups in Asia, Latin America, Africa, the Middle East and the United States, World Relief supports programs focused on disaster relief, refugee assistance, income generation and health.

    P.O. Box WRC
    Wheaton, IL 60189
    Ph. (708) 665-0235
    Fx. (708) 653-8023

World SHARE provides resources to build and support self-sustaining community institutions in which all may participate, serve and lead with dignity. SHARE is committed to sustainable growth in all communities through the creating of and service to a network of locally based community organizations. It nurtures, trains and offers leadership development to organizations as they identify and address needs in their community. In the United States and Mexico, SHARE operates a self-supporting food and community development program in over 30 locations serving over 400,000 families each month. Participant contributions and service hours provide the resource base for the program. In Guatemala, World SHARE secures food commodities from the U.S. government. Portions are sold to support programs of NGO coordination, maternal/child health, infrastructure development, agroforestry and income generation.

    World SHARE
    6950 Friars Road
    San Diego, CA 92108-1137
    Ph. (619) 686-5818
    Fx. (619) 686-5815
    E-mail: mtruax@wshare.com

For uprooted people, psychological trauma
often lasts long beyond a crisis.

NOTES

NOTES

NOTES